T0271111

Innovative Federal Reserve Policies During the Great Financial Crisis

World Scientific–Now Publishers Series in Business

ISSN: 2251-3442

The World Scientific–Now Publishers Series in Business publishes advanced textbooks, research monographs, and edited volumes on a variety of topics in business studies including accounting, entrepreneurship, finance, management, marketing, operations, and strategy. The Series includes both applied and theoretical topics that present current research and represent the state-of-the-art work in their respective fields. Contributed by academic scholars from academic and research institutions worldwide, books published under this Series will be of interest to researchers, doctoral students, and technical professionals.

Published:

Forthcoming:

The complete list of titles in the series can be found at
https://www.worldscientific.com/series/ws-npsb

(Continued at the end of the book)

World Scientific – Now Publishers Series in Business: **Vol.15**

Innovative Federal Reserve Policies During the Great Financial Crisis

Editors

Douglas D Evanoff
Federal Reserve Bank of Chicago, USA

George G Kaufman
Loyola University Chicago, USA

A G Malliaris
Loyola University Chicago, USA

 World Scientific

Published by

World Scientific Publishing Co. Pte. Ltd.

5 Toh Tuck Link, Singapore 596224

USA office: 27 Warren Street, Suite 401-402, Hackensack, NJ 07601

UK office: 57 Shelton Street, Covent Garden, London WC2H 9HE

and

now publishers Inc.
PO Box 1024
Hanover, MA 02339
USA

Library of Congress Cataloging-in-Publication Data
Names: Evanoff, Douglas Darrell, 1951–   editor. | Kaufman, George G., editor. |
    Malliaris, A. G., editor.
Title: Innovative Federal Reserve policies during the great financial crisis / [edited by]
    Douglas D. Evanoff, (Federal Reserve Bank of Chicago), George G. Kaufman
    (Loyola University Chicago), A.G. Malliaris (Loyola University Chicago).
Description: New Jersey : World Scientific, [2018]. | Series: World scientific-now publishers
    series in business ; Volume 15
Identifiers: LCCN 2017060743 | ISBN 9789813236585 (hardcover)
Subjects: LCSH: Monetary policy--United States--History--21st century. |
    Board of Governors of the Federal Reserve System (U.S.)--History--21st century. |
    Global Financial Crisis, 2008-2009.
Classification: LCC HG540 .I55 2018 | DDC 339.5/30973090511--dc23
LC record available at https://lccn.loc.gov/2017060743

British Library Cataloguing-in-Publication Data
A catalogue record for this book is available from the British Library.

For any available supplementary material, please visit
https://www.worldscientific.com/worldscibooks/10.1142/10891#t=suppl

Desk Editor: Karimah Samsudin

Typeset by Stallion Press
Email: enquiries@stallionpress.com

Printed in Singapore

Preface and Acknowledgements

In mid-2007, the United States (and most industrial countries) experienced a major financial crisis. Near record numbers of commercial banks, thrift institutions, and insurance companies, among others, experienced losses that drove them into economic insolvency, and many were subsequently failed by their respective regulators. These included three of the five largest commercial banks.

The widespread impact of the failures and the speed with which the losses occurred caused the traditional tools of the Federal Reserve and monetary policy (changes in reserve requirement, the discount rates, and the dollar amount of the reserves held by banks) to not have the expansive impact that they had in combatting previous financial downturns and their accompanying economic recessions. As a result, innovative monetary (and regulatory) tools were utilized.

The 10 essays in this volume discuss the experiences of the Federal Reserve in the usage of its traditional tools, the impact these tools had, the development of additional tools to supplement or replace the traditional tools, and the preliminary outcomes. Most of these essays were originally papers presented at the annual meeting of the Western Economic Association in 2016, held in Portland, Oregon. They are brought together in this volume to provide a historical record of this innovative period of Federal Reserve policy.

The editors are grateful to the authors for their dedication to the development of this historical record, and to the following for their assistance in the production process: Lauren Duffy, Jennifer Hernandez, Anne Divita Kopaz, Susan Phillips, Sandy Schneider, and Yinyui Wang. To all, we are exceedingly appreciative.

About the Editors

Douglas D. Evanoff is Vice President and Senior Research Advisor for banking and financial institutions at the Federal Reserve Bank of Chicago. He serves as an advisor to the senior management of the Federal Reserve System on regulatory issues, and chairs the Federal Reserve Bank of Chicago's 'International Banking Conference.' His current research interests include financial regulation, consumer credit issues, mortgage markets, bank cost and merger analysis, antitrust analysis, payments system mechanisms, and credit accessibility. Prior to joining the Chicago Fed, Evanoff was a Lecturer in Finance at Southern Illinois University, and Assistant Professor at St. Cloud State University. He currently is an adjunct faculty member in the School of Business at DePaul University, and is Associate Editor of *the Journal of Economics and Business,* the *Journal of Applied Banking and Finance*, and the *Global Finance Journal.* He is also an institutional director on the board of the Midwest Finance Association. His research has been published in academic journals including the *American Economic Review; Journal of Financial Economics; Journal of Money, Credit and Banking; Journal of Financial Services Research;* and the *Journal of Banking and Finance*, among others. He has also published chapters in numerous books, articles in practitioner journals, and has edited a number of books addressing issues associated with financial institutions; most recently, *New Perspectives on Asset Price Bubbles* (Oxford University Press), *Dodd–Frank Wall Street Reform and Consumer Protection Act* (now publishers), and *Public Policy & Financial Economics* (World Scientific Publishing). He holds a Ph.D. in Economics from Southern Illinois University.

George G. Kaufman was the John F. Smith Professor of Economics and Finance at Loyola University Chicago, and a consultant to the Federal Reserve Bank of Chicago until his retirement in December 2016. He continues to coordinate the efforts of the *Center for Financial and Policy Studies* at Loyola University Chicago's Quinlan School of Business. From 1959 to 1970, he was at the Federal Reserve Bank of Chicago, and after teaching for 10 years at the University of Oregon, he returned as a consultant to the Bank in 1981. He has also been a Visiting Professor at Stanford University, the University of California, Berkeley, and the University of Southern California, as well as a Visiting Scholar at the Reserve Bank of New Zealand, the Federal Reserve Bank of San Francisco, and the Office of the Comptroller of the Currency. He has also served as the Deputy to the Assistant Secretary for economic policy at the US Department of the Treasury. He is Co-editor of the *Journal of Financial Stability*; a founding Co-editor of the *Journal of Financial Services Research*; past President of the Western Finance Association, Midwest Finance Association, and the North American Economics and Finance Association; President-elect of the Western Economic Association; past Director of the American Finance Association; and Co-chair of the Shadow Financial Regulatory Committee. Kaufman holds a Ph.D. in Economics from the University of Iowa.

A.G. (Tassos) Malliaris joined Loyola University Chicago in 1972, and is currently Professor of Economics and Finance, and holds the Walter F. Mullady Sr. Chair in Business Administration. He graduated from the Athens School of Economics and Business in 1965, and received his Ph.D. in Economics from the University of Oklahoma in 1971. From 1972 to 1978, he did post-graduate studies in mathematics and economics at The University of Chicago and earned a second Ph.D. in applied mathematics. He specializes in financial economics and has contributed in the area of derivatives markets, asset price bubbles and monetary policy. His book on *Stochastic Methods in Economics and Finance* was the first book to exposit the mathematics used in pricing options and other derivative instruments. This book was translated into Chinese in 2004. He was selected by the Loyola University Chicago Faculty Council as the Outstanding Faculty

Member for 2001, and by the Faculty of the School of Business as the Outstanding Researcher for the Year 1999 and a second time for Year 2008. He has served as past President of the North American Economics and Finance Association, the Athenian Policy Forum and the Multinational Finance Society.

About the Contributors
(in alphabetical order)

Martina Cecioni is an Economist in the Monetary Analysis Division in the Research Department of the Bank of Italy.

Robert A. Eisenbeis is Vice Chairman and Chief Monetary Economist at Cumberland Advisors.

Giuseppe Ferrero is in the Research Department at the Bank of Italy. From 2008–2009, he was at the Department of Economics of the University of Chicago as a visiting scholar.

Gillian Garcia is Senior Economist, retired, at the International Monetary Fund, and President of Gillian G.H. Garcia Associates.

Robin Greenwood is the George Gund Professor of Finance and Banking at Harvard Business School. At HBS he is the Faculty Director of the Behavioral Finance and Financial Stability project, and serves as Finance Unit Head.

Samuel Hanson is a Marvin Bower Associate Professor in the Finance Unit at Harvard Business School, and a Faculty Research Fellow at the National Bureau of Economic Research.

Robert L. Hetzel is a Senior Economist and Research Advisor in the Research Department of the Federal Reserve Bank of Richmond.

Edward J. Kane is a Professor of Finance at Boston College, and a Research Associate of the National Bureau of Economic Research.

Richard W. Nelson is the Principal of RWNelson Economics.

Harvey Rosenblum is Professor of Business and Financial Economics, Cox School of Business, Southern Methodist University, Dallas, Texas.

Eric Rosengren is the President and Chief Executive Officer of the Federal Reserve Bank of Boston.

Alessandro Secchi is an Economist in the Research Department of the Bank of Italy.

Jeremy Stein is the Moise Y. Safra Professor of Economics at Harvard University. From May 2012 to May 2014, he was a member of the Board of Governors of the Federal Reserve System.

Ellis Tallman is Executive Vice President and Director of Research at the Federal Reserve Bank of Cleveland.

Contents

Chapter One

Unconventional Monetary Policy in Theory and in Practice

Martina Cecioni, Giuseppe Ferrero, and Alessandro Secchi*

Bank of Italy

Abstract

In this chapter, after discussing the theoretical underpinnings of unconventional monetary policy measures, we review the existing empirical evidence on their effectiveness, focusing on those adopted by central banks, particularly the Federal Reserve. These measures operate in two ways — through the signaling channel and through the portfolio balance channel. In the former, the central bank uses communication to steer interest rates and to restore confidence in the financial markets; the latter hinges on the imperfect substitutability of assets and liabilities in the balance sheet of the private sector and postulates that the central bank's asset purchases and liquidity provision lower financial yields and improve funding conditions in some markets. Our review of the empirical literature suggests that the unconventional measures were effective and that their impact on the economy was sizeable. However, a large degree of uncertainty surrounds the precise quantification of these effects.

1. Introduction

In normal times, central banks implement monetary policy by steering official interest rates and explaining to the public how a particular

*Bank of Italy, Directorate General for Economics, Statistics and Research. This paper is an abridged version of an earlier study published by the Bank of Italy: Cecioni, Ferrero, and Secchi (2011). The reader is encouraged to see the original publication for additional details and for a comparison of the unconventional measures undertaken by the ECB in the same period. The authors would like to thank Paolo Del Giovane, Eugenio Gaiotti, Stefano Neri, and Luca Sessa for useful comments and suggestions. All remaining errors are our own. The views expressed in this paper do not necessarily reflect those of the Bank of Italy.

monetary stance in a given economic environment should contribute to achieving the final goals. To this purpose, central banks may decide to share with the public their views about the future evolution of some key macroeconomic variables or even their policy intentions.

Monetary policy decisions and announcements are first transmitted to the interbank market (the market for central bank reserves). When market conditions are quiet, central banks' monopolistic power in the provision of reserves allows them to steer interest rates in the interbank market accurately.

In such an environment, the provision of liquidity to the banking system is a mechanical exercise and liquidity management operations are designed exclusively to implement the desired level of short-term interest rates. In particular, the provision of liquidity does not contain any information about the monetary policy stance beyond that included in the official interest rate.[1] Moreover, during normal times, the central bank is only concerned about injecting the banking system with the appropriate amount of reserves while their distribution among depository institutions takes place through the interbank market.

The monetary impulse is then transmitted through different channels to all the other financial markets.[2] In particular, it also affects credit market conditions and long-term interest rates, which are key elements in the public's investment-consumption decisions through this conventional transmission mechanism.

However, implementing monetary policy is a much more complex exercise during a financial crisis, as the transmission mechanism can be severely impaired by disruptions in the financial markets. First, the increase in the volatility of the demand for reserves and the limited redistribution of liquidity among depository institutions may adversely affect the central bank's ability to control short-term interest rates in the interbank market. Second, disruptions in other segments of the financial market may hamper the transmission of the monetary impulse across the full spectrum of financial assets. Finally, when the effect of the crisis on the

---

[1]This independence between policy decisions and liquidity provision is called the "separation" or "decoupling" principle (Borio and Disyatat, 2010).

[2]Bernanke and Gertler (1995), Mishkin (1996), Blinder, Ehrmann, Fratzscher, de Haan, Jansen (2008) and Boivin, Kiley and Mishkin (2010).

real economy is large, the zero lower bound for interest rates may become a binding constraint for monetary policy decisions.[3] In these situations, central banks may need to resort to unconventional measures to regain control on the economy.

There is not a universally accepted definition of a non-standard monetary policy measure; indeed, the difference between a conventional and an unconventional tool might, in some cases, be quite tenuous.[4] We include in the set of unconventional measures any policy intervention that aims to rectify a malfunctioning of the monetary transmission mechanism or to provide further stimulus to the economy when the official interest rates reach the zero bound. We therefore classify as non-standard tools all the measures implemented during the global financial crisis that addressed liquidity shortages, including of depository institutions and of other important segments of the financial market, the direct purchase of private and public securities, and the adoption of particular forms of communication designed to restore a more normal functioning of the markets and influence expectations about future official interest rates.

During the global financial crisis, recourse to these measures varied across countries. This reflected the differences in the structure of the respective financial systems, in the severity of market disruptions, and the role of central banks' judgment. During unconventional times, this last factor contributes more because of the lack of both sound theory and empirical evidence on the effectiveness of non-standard measures (Trichet, 2010). To fill this gap, and to increase our understanding of the mechanisms through which unconventional monetary measures influence the economy, the profession intensified its research activities in this area.

In this chapter, we touch on measures adopted in the U.S. during the global financial crisis, we provide a review of the main theoretical underpinnings that support the use of unconventional measures, and we survey the evidence on their effectiveness. While these measures may have

---

[3] "The zero lower bound on nominal interest rates limits the ability of central banks to reduce short-term interest rates. As a result, when nominal interest rates are near zero, central banks are unable to use further reductions in short-term interest rates to provide additional stimulus to the economy and check unwelcome disinflation." (Chung *et al.*, 2012).

[4] While the adoption of a new monetary policy tool is certainly an unconventional measure, it is less clear whether more frequent and more intense use of a standard tool can be classified as a conventional or as an unconventional measure, especially when it is used for non-standard purposes.

prevented a collapse of the financial system and a deeper contraction of the real economy as a result of the global crisis, a clearer understanding of the contribution of each of them is a necessary step towards defining an "optimal unconventional tool-box" to deal with future crises.

The theoretical literature on the functioning of unconventional policy tools identifies two transmission channels.

The *signaling channel* enables the central bank to use communication to restore confidence in the markets and influence private expectations about future policy decisions. This channel may be particularly useful when official interest rates reach the zero lower bound and the central bank needs to provide further stimulus to the economy.

The purchase of both public and private securities and the provision of credit to financial and non-financial institutions affect the economy through the *portfolio-balance channel*, which operates when assets and liabilities in the balance sheets of the private sector are imperfectly substitutable. The central bank can exploit this channel when it wants to alleviate tensions in particular segments of the financial markets, when it seeks to reduce yields more widely, and when it decides to counteract the impact of financial frictions on funding conditions.

Our review of the theoretical and empirical evidence suggests that the unconventional measures have been effective in influencing financial and macroeconomic variables. However, considerable uncertainty surrounds the quantification of these effects.

The chapter is organized as follows. Section 2 analyses the theoretical support for the effectiveness of the unconventional measures adopted in the U.S. up to mid-2011. Section 3 surveys the empirical evidence, and Section 4 concludes.

2.   Unconventional Monetary Policy in Theory

In this section, we describe two channels through which the unconventional monetary policy is transmitted to the economy — the signaling and the portfolio-balance channel.

2.1. *The signaling channel*

The signaling channel is activated through central bank's communications informing the public about its intentions regarding the future evolution of short-term interest rates, or the implementation of other measures targeted at counteracting market dysfunctions. The efficacy of this channel relies on the credibility of the central bank and on the extent to which private expectations and confidence affect macroeconomic and financial market conditions.

Not all forms of communication that exploit the signaling channel should be seen as "unconventional" measures. Since the 1990s, it has become increasingly clear that managing expectations is a crucial task of monetary policy; therefore, communication aimed at sharing with the public central bank views about the macroeconomic outlook and, in some cases, about the future evolution of short-term interest rates has evolved into a standard tool of monetary policy.[5] Thus, communication should be considered an unconventional tool of monetary policy only when it is used by a central bank to convey information or pursue objectives that go beyond its standard practice.[6]

In the literature, the signaling channel has been highlighted as the mechanism to escape the zero lower bound on official interest rates. Krugman (1998) claims that when the zero lower bound binds, the central bank should follow an "irresponsibility principle", that is, convince the market that it will allow prices to raise so to increase inflationary expectations. Eggertsson and Woodford (2003) embed this result in the New Keynesian (NK) framework, concluding that not only is the signaling channel (or, as they call it, the management of expectations) crucial, but it is the only channel that is effective. In the NK model, long-term interest rates, on which firms' and households' consumption, investment, and borrowing decisions are based, depend entirely on financial market participants' expectations about the future path of short-term rates.

During the financial crisis, the Fed provided forward guidance about the likely path of the federal funds rate to promote economic recovery and

---

[5] An exhaustive analysis of the role of communication in monetary policy is provided by Blinder *et al.* (2008); Ferrero and Secchi (2009; 2010) analyze the effects and the desirability of communication of the future interest rate path in "normal" times.

[6] Note that according to this definition, certain types of communication can be conventional for some central banks and unconventional for others. This is certainly the case with the announcement of future policy intentions, which is an unconventional tool for most central banks but a conventional measure for central banks such as the Reserve Bank of New Zealand, the Norges Bank, and the Swedish Riksbank.

price stability. However, the central bank did not explicitly commit to the irresponsibility principle advocated by Krugman (1998), and announced that the future official interest rate path would depend on the evolution of the macroeconomic outlook.[7] Clarida (2012) argues that this type of commitment, if not properly qualified, may in practice be confused by the public with a policy of discretion ("policy rates are expected to be low because and so long as output and inflation are expected to be low") which, in the case of perfect information, is not expected to exert any influence on long-term interest rates. On the contrary, Walsh (2008) shows that when the central bank is endowed with superior information, the provision of forward guidance about future interest rates is welfare-improving, even when monetary policy is discretionary.

Time inconsistency may severely limit the effectiveness of the announcement of an interest rate path — a change in the size and composition of its balance sheet may help to overcome this obstacle. For instance, large purchases of long-term securities may strengthen the promise to keep short-term rates low for some time owing to the adverse effect that an increase in official interest rates would have on the health of the central bank's balance sheet (Bernanke, Reinhart and Sack, 2004). The central bank could also enforce its commitment about future official interest rates by entering into more explicit contingent contracts with market participants. Tinsley (1998), for example, suggests that by selling short-horizon bond put options, the credibility of the central bank's policy would be enforced by binding contractual arrangements with private sector agents, who will be compensated for any future deviations from the policy terms designated in the contingent contracts.

The practical relevance of these mechanisms is questioned by Rudebusch (2011), who estimates that, notwithstanding its large bond purchases, the Fed's losses due to an increase in short-term interest rates would be almost negligible. Moreover, these losses would only be realized on the share of the portfolio of long-term securities that is not held to maturity. These estimates and the fact that the central bank is not a

---

[7] "The [Federal Open Market] Committee's forward guidance has been framed not as an unconditional commitment to a specific federal funds rate path, but rather as an expectation that is explicitly contingent on economic conditions" (Yellen, 2011).

private institution with profitability as its main objective suggest that the effectiveness of such a device in preventing short-term rate increases by the central bank is arguable.

Communication aimed at reassuring markets on the central bank's active role during episodes of financial turbulence can also help to restore the functioning of the monetary transmission mechanism. For example, the announcement of the intention to intervene in illiquid markets provides a signal to market participants that the central bank stands ready to contrast undue volatility in asset prices and provide liquidity in case of necessity. By assuring markets about the central bank's role of lender of last resort and by providing an implicit guarantee of the intermediation role of the central bank, the announcement itself may influence market behavior even before any action is taken.[8] The information released, concerning the size, speed and, more in general, the terms of the intervention, is crucial for the effectiveness of the signaling channel. The central bank's optimal degree of transparency must trade off the credibility and effectiveness potentially gained with a clear and transparent plan against the risks of providing inappropriate incentives to the market participants and of higher volatility due to not meeting market expectations.

2.2. The portfolio-balance channel

The portfolio-balance channel is activated through central bank operations such as outright purchases of securities, asset swaps, and liquidity injections, which modify the size and composition of the balance sheet of both the central bank and the private sector. The central bank is the only economic player that can conduct this kind of intervention on a large scale since, in principle, it can expand its balance sheet indefinitely owing to its monopolistic power in the provision of monetary base.[9]

The central bank's outright purchases and swap operations aim to influence prices in some specific dysfunctional segments of the financial market or to affect yields more widely. The latter is the case, for example,

---

[8] However, it should be taken into consideration that such an announcement may increase moral hazard and therefore contribute to risk-taking behavior.

[9] The central bank is constrained in expanding its balance sheet only to the extent that this undermines its credibility.

when the conventional monetary policy instrument is constrained at the zero lower bound and, to provide further stimulus to the economy, the central bank decides to purchase government bonds to reduce the returns on a wide range of financial assets. The efficacy of this channel hinges on the imperfect substitutability among private sector's balance sheet items, which arises in the presence of economic frictions (e.g., asymmetric information, limited commitment, and limited participation), and on the impact that changes in the supply of private assets and liabilities have on individual decisions.[10]

Imperfect substitutability on the asset side of the private sector balance sheet has been proposed by the *preferred habitat theory*, first introduced by Modigliani and Sutch (1966) and recently included in a more formal model for the interest rate term structure by Vayanos and Vila (2009). According to the preferred habitat view, whenever there is a group of investors with preferences for specific maturities (typically long-term, as is the case of pension funds and life insurance companies), the net supply of securities at that maturity is a determinant of their yields. In this setup, changes in the net supply of assets of a given maturity by the central bank or government affect the yields of the assets. Moreover, when agents are heterogeneous, either because some of them are locked into their portfolio choices or because they have different degrees of risk-aversion (Ashcraft, Garleanu and Pedersen, 2011) or different impatience to consume (Curdia and Woodford, 2010), open market operations have distributional effects with potential influence on real activity and inflation.

The items on the liability side of the private sector balance sheet also become imperfect substitutes when the economic environment is characterized by the presence of *information asymmetries* or *limited commitment*. In this situation, external funds tend to be charged with an extra return (with respect to the opportunity cost of internally generated funds), which generally depends on the severity of the friction and on the quality of the borrower's assets. In some cases, external funds might even be rationed.[11] During a financial crisis, when the health of the balance sheet

---

[10]On the contrary, central bank/government purchases are ineffective when financial assets are perfectly substitutable and changes in the composition of government's portfolio do not involve distortionary changes in taxes (Wallace, 1981), (Eggertson and Woodford, 2003).

deteriorates and confidence collapses, the extra return charged on external funds might become quite large and lenders might be willing to provide funds only for very short periods of time.

To avoid a collapse of credit availability, the central bank can enhance its liquidity provision to depository institutions both to accommodate the increased demand for precautionary motive and to contrast the reduction in the circulation of reserves (Keister and McAndrews, 2009; Freixas, Martin and Skeie, 2011). To alleviate tensions associated with the liquidity mismatch between the asset and the liability side of private banks, it can also decide to provide liquidity for terms that are longer than normal. In this way, the central bank sustains the provision of credit to the economy and reduces term spreads.

However, a too prolonged recourse to these unconventional measures might create market distortions and significantly increase the central bank's financial risk.[12,13] Christiano and Ikeda (2011) provide one caveat associated with the use of unconventional measures, arguing that their effectiveness might depend on the specific set of financial frictions that affect economic behavior.[14]

3. Unconventional Monetary Policy in Practice

In this section, we review the empirical literature on the effectiveness of the unconventional measures adopted by the Fed. We classify the various studies according to whether they measure the impact of non-traditional tools (1) on financial variables or (2) on macroeconomic variables.

The first of these two groups, which is presented in the next sub-section, is further split into two sub-categories, depending on whether the

---

[11]There is a vast literature on the role of financial frictions in shaping economic dynamics. According to the credit channel theory the presence of financial frictions amplifies the effects of monetary policy on the real economy through the effects that policy decisions have on the health of the balance sheet of private agents and, in turn, on the external premium. For a review of this literature, see Bernanke and Gertler, 1995. More recent analyses include Cúrdia and Woodford, 2011; De Fiore and Tristani, 2009; Demirel, 2009; Gertler and Karadi, 2011; Gertler and Kiyotaki, 2010; and Gerali *et al.*, 2010.

[12]Gertler and Kiyotaki (2010) assume that unconventional monetary interventions entail some inefficiency cost.

[13]This risk is mitigated by the fact that central banks supply loans only against collateral.

[14]They argue that with moral hazard and hidden effort, the unconventional measures that have been used during the great financial crisis (equity injections and credit provision to financial intermediaries) might not be effective in restoring an appropriate provision of credit to firms and households.

measure analyzed was first implemented before or after the bankruptcy of Lehman Brothers. A synthetic description of the methodology and of the main results of the various studies is reported in the tables at the end of each sub-section (*see* Tables 1.1 and 1.2).[15] In the following sub-section, we review the evidence on the effects on macroeconomic variables with a summary description provided in Table 1.3.

3.1. *Effects of the unconventional measures on financial variables*

3.1.1. *Effects of the measures adopted by the Fed in the pre-Lehman phase*

The first phase of the crisis featured a significantly higher volatility of banks' liquidity demand, a heightened preference for long-term liquidity, and severe impairments in the redistribution of funds in the interbank market. During this period, the Fed aimed at preventing disorders in money markets, and implemented a series of measures to extend the availability of emergency and long-term funding to primary dealers, through which in normal times the reserves are channeled to the banking system, and depository institutions.

The empirical literature on the effectiveness of unconventional measures adopted by the Fed before the bankruptcy of Lehman has mainly focused on the *Term Auction Facility*, on the *Term Securities Lending Facility*, and on the *Reciprocal Currency Agreements*.[16]

There is no formal analysis of the other measures, namely the *Term Discount Window Program*, the *Single-Tranche Open Market Program* and the *Primary Dealers Credit Facility*. However, the heavy recourse to this group of facilities suggests that they were perceived by depository institutions and by primary dealers as effective in alleviating the significant funding tensions to which they were exposed during the crisis.[17]

---

[15] In the tables, we only include papers that use an econometric approach, while the studies based on more anecdotal approach are only commented in the text.

[16] *See* Table 1.1.

[17] Recourse to the Term Discount Window Facility and to the Primary Dealers Credit Facility reached a value close to $100 billion and $150 billion respectively after the bankruptcy of Lehman (Adrian, Burke and McAndrews, 2009). Auctions associated with the Single-Tranche Open Market Program were characterized by very high bid-to cover ratios (2.8 on average until August 2008).

Table 1.1: Measures Adopted by the Fed in the Pre-Lehman Phase: Effects on Financial Variables.

Paper	Program Evaluated	Methodology	Variable of Interest	Results	Notes
Taylor and Williams (2009)	TAF	Event study	Libor-OIS spread	No significant impact on the Libor-OIS spread	Dependent variable in levels; TAF dummy equal to one on announcement days
McAndrews, Sarkar and Wang (2017)	TAF	Event study	First-difference of the Libor-OIS spread	50 basis points reduction in the Libor-OIS spread; both announcement and implementation effective	Dependent variable in differences; TAF dummy equal to one on announcement and implementation days
Wu (2010)	TAF	Event study	Libor-OIS spread	50 basis points reduction in the Libor-OIS spread	Dependent variable in levels; TAF dummy equal to one after announcement day
Christensen, Lopez and Rudebusch (2009)	TAF	Multifactor arbitrage-free model for the term structure; counterfactual analysis	Libor rate	70 basis points reduction in the liquidity risk component of the three-month Libor	—

(Continued)

Table 1.1: *(Continued)*

Paper	Program Evaluated	Methodology	Variable of Interest	Results	Notes
Thornton (2011)	TAF	Event study	Ted spread	No effect on liquidity premium in the Libor market	—
Fleming, Hrung and Keane (2010)	TSLF	OLS regression	Levels of repo rates and spread between Treasury repos and repos based on other less liquid collateral	0.4 basis points reduction in Agency Debt-Treasury and Agency MBS-Treasury repo spreads for each extra billion of Treasury lent	—
Hrung and Seligman (2015)	TSLF	OLS regression	Spread between federal funds [both target and effective] and Treasury GC repos	1 basis points reduction in Spread between federal funds [both target and effective] and Treasury GC repos for each billion of Treasury lent	Interaction terms show that the impact of TSLF was larger during period of stress
Baba and Packer (2009)	RCA	Principal component analysis and EGARCH	Deviations from the covered interest parity in FX swap	30 basis points reduction in EUR/USD FX swap deviations	Sample period: August 2007–January 2009

Note: TAF = Term Auction Facility; TSFL = Term Securities Lending Facility; RCA = Reciprocal Currency Agreement.

The *Term Auction Facility* (TAF) was intended to fight back against dysfunctionalities in the interbank market by providing collateralized long-term liquidity to depository institutions. Taylor and Williams (2009) assess its effectiveness by measuring the impact on the Libor-OIS spread. Their analysis is based on three hypotheses. First, the Libor-OIS spread is affected by a liquidity and a credit risk, which are independent of each other. Second, the credit risk can be approximated with measurable variables (CDS on financial institutions, Libor-Tibor spread, Libor-Repo spread). Third, the TAF may only influence the liquidity risk. Building on these assumptions, they regress the Libor-OIS spread on different measures of credit risk and a dummy variable which is set to one on the days of announcement/implementation of the TAF. These regressions fail to find any significant impact of the TAF-dummies on the Libor-OIS spread and lead the authors to conclude against the effectiveness of this measure.

McAndrews, Sarkar and Wang (2017) and Wu (2010) suggest that the baseline specification used by Taylor and Williams (2009) to measure the impact of the TAF might be inappropriate, particularly if the effect of this facility on the Libor-OIS spread is permanent. They propose two alternative approaches. McAndrews *et al.* (2017) substitute the dependent variable with the first difference of the Libor-OIS spread. Wu (2010) sets the TAF-dummy equal to zero before the announcement of the program and to one thereafter.[18] Both analyses overturn the original result and find that the TAF reduced the three-month Libor-OIS spread by around 50 basis points. The analysis of McAndrews *et al.* (2017) provides two further pieces of evidence. First, both the announcements concerning the program and its actual implementation were effective in reducing liquidity risks. Moreover, it also turns out that both domestic and international TAF operations (currency swaps) provided a significant contribution in alleviating tensions in the interbank market.

Christensen, Lopez and Rudebusch (2014) analyze the effectiveness of the TAF using a six-factor arbitrage-free representation of the term structures of risk-free (Treasuries) and risky interest rates (financial bonds

---

[18]Wu (2010) also differs with respect to Taylor and Williams (2010) for a slightly different definition of banks' counterparty risk (first principal component of a large set of CDS on both commercial and investment banks) and for the hypothesis that bank's counterparty and liquidity risks might be correlated.

and Libor).[19] This approach allows the authors to disentangle the liquidity risk component implicit in Libor rates and to verify whether the TAF was effective in contrasting its increase. The counterfactual exercise that is reported in the paper suggests that the TAF lowered the liquidity risk component of three-month Libor rates by around 70 basis points over the period of December 2007 to mid-2008.

Thornton (2010) disputes this finding claiming that financial bonds and Libors are influenced by different credit risks. In particular, he argues that the narrowing of the Libor-financial bond spread observed after the implementation of this unconventional measure was not due to a reduction of liquidity premia in the interbank market, but instead, to an increase in the credit risk on financial bonds due to a more pessimistic view of the depth of the crisis.

Fleming, Hrung and Keane (2010) assess the effectiveness of the *Term Securities Lending Facility* (TSLF) focusing on the impact of the provision of Treasuries on the spread between Treasury repos and repos based on less liquid collateral. They regress repo rates and spreads on the amount of Treasuries made available through the TSLF program, taking into account the type of securities pledged as collateral and whether auctions were fully or undersubscribed. The results suggest that the TSLF was effective in contrasting tensions in the secured funding market and, in particular, in satisfying market participants' increased demand for Treasuries. According to one of the specifications presented in the paper, each extra billion of Treasuries provided through the TSLF reduced the "Agency Debt-Treasury" and the "Agency MBS-Treasury" repo spreads by around 0.4 basis points on average. This implies an overall contraction of the spread of around 80 basis points.[20] The empirical analysis also shows that the

---

[19]Three factors — constant, slope and curvature — are used to model the dynamics of "risk-free" Treasury rates. Two more factors are used to capture the counterparty risk implicit in financial bonds and the last factor is used to measure the liquidity risk component of the Libor. According to Christensen *et al.* (2014), liquidity premia affect Libor rates and financial bonds' yields in different ways because the holders of the latter class of assets have a higher tolerance than banks with regard to liquidity problems. Moreover, they also suggest that financial bond returns capture short-term credit risk more precisely than long-term bank CDS.

[20]This effect was mainly due to an increase in Treasury repo rates, evidence that confirms that the TSLF was effective in addressing the shortage of government bonds and in contrasting the emergence of settlement problems in the repo market.

effect of the TSLF on repo spreads was most noticeable in the case of fully subscribed operations, when the set of eligible collateral was broad and when the Treasury repo rate was far below the federal funds target rate.

Hrung and Seligman (2015) extend the analysis of Fleming *et al.* (2010) by taking into account that the availability of Treasuries was also affected by the Supplemental Financing Program (SFP), by changes in government issuance, by the TARP, and by the Fed's Open Market Operations (OMO). Their econometric analysis confirms that the impact of the TSLF on Treasury repo rates was significant (1 basis point for each billion of Treasuries made available to market participants) and that it was even larger during periods of intense market stress. Moreover, they also find that the TSLF was uniquely effective compared with other policies that influenced the availability of Treasuries and associate this evidence with the fact that TSLF operations were explicitly "directed" to dealers in the General Collateral repo market.

Baba and Packer (2009) study the impact of *Reciprocal Currency Agreements* on the foreign exchange (FX) swap market between the U.S. dollar and the euro, the Swiss franc and the pound sterling. They found that the program was effective in improving FX swap market dislocations, especially from mid-October 2008, when the Fed uncapped the amount of dollar liquidity provided. Goldberg *et al.* (2010), reporting formal research as well as more descriptive accounts from market participants, also conclude that dollar swap lines were effective in reducing dollar funding pressures.

3.1.2. *Effects of the measures adopted by the Fed in the post-Lehman phase*

After the bankruptcy of Lehman Brothers in September 2008, the financial crisis became more severe and spread to the shadow banking system. In the U.S., it quickly became clear that the provision of funds and high-quality securities to depository institutions and primary dealers would not be sufficient to avert a collapse of the financial system. The liquidity in critical non-bank markets evaporated and financial spreads reached unprecedented levels. To address these issues, the Fed enhanced the non-standard measures adopted before Lehman's bankruptcy and extended the provision of temporary liquidity to the most important part of the shadow banking system.

In this section, we describe the empirical evidence on the effectiveness of the *ABCP Money Market Fund Liquidity Facility*, of the *Commercial Paper Funding Facility*, of the *Term ABS Loan Facility* and of the purchase of Agency debt, Agency MBS and long-term government bonds.[21]

The objective of the *ABCP Money Market Fund Liquidity Facility* (AMLF) was to support the liquidity of high-quality asset-backed commercial paper (ABCP) and to break the vicious circle between money market share redemptions and ABCP fire sales. Duygan-Bump, Parkinson, Rosengren, Suarez and Willen (2010) analyze both these aspects and conclude in favor of the effectiveness of this unconventional measure. In particular, using a difference-in-difference approach they show that, following the introduction of the AMLF, the reduction in redemptions was greater for those money market funds that owned a larger proportion of AMLF-eligible assets. Similarly, by comparing the yields on AMLF-eligible ABCP with those of otherwise equivalent AMLF-ineligible commercial paper they also conclude that the AMLF reduced the liquidity risk component of the former by around 80 basis points.[22]

The *Commercial Paper Funding Facility* (CPFF) provided a temporary liquidity backstop to issuers of commercial paper and was intended, in particular, to limit investors' and borrowers' concerns about "roll-over risk." Anderson and Gascon (2009) and Adrian, Kimbrough and Marchioni (2011) observe that the heavy recourse to this facility and the fact that the implementation of the program has prompted a significant increase in term commercial paper issuance and a sharp reduction in commercial paper spreads tend to support its effectiveness.[23]

A statistical assessment of the effects of the CPFF is provided by Duca (2013). He employs a VECM methodology to study the determinants of the relative use of bank loans and of debt funded by commercial paper by US firms since the early 1960s. He finds that up until the adoption of the CPFF,

---

[21] *See* Table 1.2.

[22] This analysis is based on the impact of the AMLF on the spread between returns on AMLF-eligible ABCP with those of the unsecured commercial paper issued by the sponsor of the same ABCP program, which should be characterized by a similar credit risk.

[23] During the first quarter of implementation of the CPFF, the spread associated with A2/P2 commercial paper, which was not eligible for the CPFF, remained substantially stable at around 500 basis points while the spreads of CPFF-eligible securities shrank from more than 200 to around 50–100 basis points.

when corporate spreads rose, the use of commercial paper fell relative to bank loans, which could be funded with insured deposits. However, the fact that this link broke down after the implementation of the CPFF suggests that this measure may have prevented an even sharper fall in commercial paper.

With the *Term ABS Loan Facility* (TALF) the Fed provided investors with long-term loans for the purchase of newly issued high-quality ABS backed by consumer and small business loans and commercial mortgages. Agarwal *et al.* (2010) offer an extensive description of the ABS market and observe that the implementation of the program was quickly followed by a recovery in ABS issuance and a reduction in the spreads between AAA-rated ABS and interest rate swaps of the order of 200–300 basis points.

Campbell *et al.* (2011) provide a more formal assessment of the effectiveness of the TALF with an event study approach. Their analysis is based on two assumptions. First, the announcements concerning the program were unexpected. Second, they also postulate that, without the TALF, the spreads between eligible ABS and broader financial market returns would have remained unchanged. Under these two assumptions, they study the dynamics of these ABS spreads in periods around TALF announcements, using both market and security level data. The analysis based on market level data suggests that the program was effective. In particular, they find that the announcements led to a reduction in ABS and in CMBS spreads by, respectively, 10–60 and 50–150 basis points. The analysis based on security-level data fails to find specific effects on ABS returns associated with its acceptance or rejection in the program. The authors interpret this last evidence as suggesting that the TALF program has affected overall market conditions for high-rate ABS without providing advantages to specific securities.

A vast literature analyzed the effects of the *Large-Scale Asset Purchases of Agency debt* and *Agency MBS*. Stroebel and Taylor (2012) analyze the effect of the MBS purchases by the Treasury and the Fed with an event study methodology. In particular, they regress a measure of MBS spreads which controls for prepayment risk on different measures of credit-default risk of the underlying mortgages, on the percentage of outstanding MBS purchased at each point of the program, and on a series of dummies that are intended to capture the effects of the announcements of the program.

Even if the results are somehow conflicting, they tend to suggest that the announcements concerning purchases in the secondary market had some effect and contributed to reduce spreads by around 30–60 basis points. At the same time, they fail to find a relationship between the size of the purchases and the change in MBS spreads.[24]

The empirical pricing model adopted by Hancock and Passmore (2011) assumes that MBS yields are determined by long-term swap rates, a short-term spread between swaps and Treasuries, and a series of risk premia. The authors estimate this equation with pre-crisis data and use the estimated parameters to provide an out-of-sample assessment of the effects of the crisis on MBS yields. They are able to show that after the announcement of the MBS purchase program, the gap between actual yields on MBS and those predicted using parameters based on the pre-crisis sample (around 50 basis points) progressively shrank and, by the end of the first quarter of 2009, vanished completely. This evidence therefore suggests that the Fed's intervention improved the functioning of the MBS market.

Fuster and Willen (2010) apply an event study methodology on individual level mortgage data to assess the impact of the announcements concerning the purchase of Agency debt and MBS on the characteristics of newly issued mortgage loans and on the selection of the borrowers that apply for a mortgage. They find three main results. First, both the initial announcement and the subsequent changes to the program led to significant reductions in the interest rates paid by borrowers. These reductions, however, were heterogeneous across mortgage contracts. Second, the intervention of the Fed coincided with a significant increase in borrowing activity, mainly for refinancing purposes as opposed to purchases of new houses. Third, the MBS program generated a significant shift in borrowers' characteristics. In particular, refinancing activity became highly skewed towards borrowers with high credit scores. The authors conclude that the Agency debt and MBS purchase program had a large effect on mortgage prices and jump-started activity in the primary market. Moreover, they also observe that the almost immediate market response to the announcement of

---

[24] Since the Fed pre-announced both the size and the pace of the purchases, this evidence is not necessarily inconsistent with the hypothesis that the size might also matter since the markets are likely to front-load the effects.

the program suggests that the effectiveness of this measure is not subject to "long and variable lags," as is the case with other consumer-targeted policies such as tax cuts.

Moving to the empirical evidence on the effectiveness of large-scale asset purchases of Treasuries in lowering long-term interest rates. This issue was addressed in the literature even before the great financial crisis, with largely inconclusive results. Early studies found that open market operations had little impact on yields, supporting the view that the price of an asset does not depend on its relative supply. The most influential paper is that of Modigliani and Sutch (1967) on the effect of Operation Twist, the joint intervention in the government bond market by the Fed and the Treasury in 1961 aimed at reducing long-term interest rates while keeping short-term rates constant.[25] Their main finding is that the impact on term spreads is, at most, quite modest. On the contrary, more recent analyses, such as Bernanke, Reihnart and Sack (2004), provide more optimistic results regarding the effectiveness of debt management operations. The Fed's purchases of Treasuries during the great financial crisis spurred a series of new analyses. We classify these studies in two groups according to whether they adopt an event study approach or a more structural time series analysis. In the first group of studies, Gagnon *et al.* (2011) find that around the main announcements of QE1, 10-year Treasury interest rates recorded a cumulative drop of about 90 basis points. The same result is documented by Yellen (2011b), who analyses a slightly different set of events. Krishnamurthy and Vissing-Jorgensen (2011) provide results for both QE1 and QE2, showing that Treasury and Agency debt yields displayed a cumulative reduction of more than 100 basis points in QE1 and around 20 points in QE2. The large difference between the responses in these two episodes suggests that there may be some factors, such as market conditions, liquidity or market expectations, which are not properly taken into account by this kind of study. Swanson (2011) provides estimates of the effects of QE2 by studying Operation Twist, considering that the size of this program as a fraction of the Treasury debt is comparable to that of QE2. His results

---

[25] Operation Twist was a quantitative policy in which the Fed purchased longer-term government notes while maintaining its official rate constant and the Treasury reduced the issuance of longer-term notes in favor of short-term securities.

suggest that the cumulative effect on 10-year Treasury yields would be around 15 basis points.[26]

The second group of studies uses time series methods, which require selecting stronger assumptions on the data. If causal links are properly identified, those methods allow the researcher to perform policy experiments. Overall, these studies tend to find that the Fed's purchases have a significant effect on Treasury yields. In particular, a purchase of $400 billion of long-term securities sterilized with an equivalent issuance of short-term notes would reduce 10-year Treasury yields by between 14 and 67 basis points.[27]

The lowest value of this range is found by Hamilton and Wu (2012) using a model based on the "preferred habitat" theory as in Vayanos and Vila (2009). They show that their results hold even when the short-term rates are at the zero lower bound and the sterilization becomes irrelevant. Gagnon *et al.* (2011) find similar results adopting a model that explains 10-year term spread using business cycle indicators, measures of uncertainty about economic fundamentals, and the net public sector supply of Treasury bonds. Greenwood and Vayanos (2014) find a positive correlation between the maturity structure of U.S. government debt and the associated interest rate term structure. According to their analysis, a purchase of $400 billion of Treasury bonds would reduce long-term rates by around 40 basis points. The highest value of the range is found by D'Amico and King (2013), using data from a panel of yields at different maturities in the period in which QE1 was ongoing (March–October 2009).

The findings of both groups of studies must be interpreted with caution. Results from event studies are based on the hypothesis that announcements/actions are not anticipated, they are conditional on the specific market conditions on the day of the announcement, they usually rely on a small number of data points and, finally, they might be strongly affected by the choice of events that are included in the sample and by

---

[26]The fairness of this comparison is arguable as the ample difference between estimates of QE1 and QE2 in Krishnamurthy and Vissing-Jorgensen (2011) suggests that the size of the purchase program is not the only variable that is relevant to their effectiveness. In particular, financial strains and low liquidity at the time of the operations as well as the zero lower bound on the short-term interest rates are other important factors that could influence the effectiveness of purchase programs.

[27]This is the experiment proposed by Hamilton and Wu (2012).

the hypothesis on the responsiveness of financial markets to news, i.e., the window over which changes are computed. Furthermore, even though high-frequency event studies permit straightforward measurement of the correlation between changes in the supply of financial assets and variations in financial prices, a causal interpretation is correct only insofar as policy announcements or actions are not a response to market conditions on that day. This note of caution is even more relevant when the analysis is based on time series data with a monthly or even lower frequency — since the supply of government bonds is influenced by the interest rate structure, the identification of the link of causality from the former to the latter requires strong and perhaps arguable hypotheses.

Summing up, the evidence on the effectiveness of purchases of Treasury bonds in lowering long-term interest rates suggests that central banks have some power, although considerable uncertainty still surrounds the exact quantification of the impact.

The evidence on the ability of the Fed to use communication to control market expectations about future short-term and, in turn, long-term interest rates is scant. According to Yellen (2011a), the statements of the December 2008 and January 2009 FOMC meetings suggesting that short-term rates would remain low "for some time" favored a decline in market expectations about the one-year-ahead federal funds rate by about 90 basis points.

Courtois, Haltom, and Hatchondo (2011) explored the possibility that the effectiveness of forward guidance could be enhanced by asset purchases which transmit information about the likelihood of policy interest rates remaining low for a long time. They find some evidence in support of this hypothesis. However, they also observe that the exact magnitude of the effect cannot be accurately evaluated, as the announcement might also influence the risk premium implicit in financial assets from which market expectations are extracted.

3.2. Effects of the unconventional measures on macroeconomic variables

This section reviews the evidence on the effects on output, inflation, and other relevant macroeconomic variables of the unconventional monetary policy measures put in place by the Fed during the great financial crisis.

Table 1.2:   Measures Adopted by the Fed in the Post-Lehman Phase: Effects on the Financial Variables.

Paper	Program Evaluated	Methodology	Variable of Interest	Results	Notes
Duygan-Bump, Parkinson, Rosengren, Suarez and Willen (2010)	AMLF	Difference-in-difference estimation	Spread between returns on ABCP of a given issuer and the returns of the unsecured commercial paper issued by the sponsor of the same ABCP program	Reduction of about 80 basis points in the yields on ABCP	
Duca (2013)	CPFF	VEC model; linear regressions	Commercial paper–bank loan mix	Implementation of the CPFF coincided with a break in the relationship between the "commercial paper–bank loan mix" and the corporate–Treasury bond spread.	

Study	Policy	Method	Variable	Result	Notes
Campbell, Covitz, Nelson and Pence (2011)	TALF	Event study	Spreads of the ABS that were eligible for the TALF and spreads on broad market indices	Reduction of 10–60 basis points in spreads of highly rated ABS after announcement in March 2009	Results are conflicting across specifications and markets
Stroebel and Taylor (2012)	Purchases of Agency debt and Agency MBS	Event study	MBS spread	Reduction of 30–60 basis points in spreads on secondary markets after announcement of LSAP.	
Hancock and Passmore (2011)	Purchases of Agency debt and Agency MBS	Empirical pricing models [OLS regressions]	MBS yields, mortgage rates	Reduction of about 50 basis points in undue risk premia in MBS yields. The gap between actual MBS yields and "counterfactual" projections based on pre-crisis data disappears by Q1/2009	

(Continued)

Table 1.2: (*Continued*)

Paper	Program Evaluated	Methodology	Variable of Interest	Results	Notes
Fuster and Willen (2010)	Purchases of Agency debt and Agency MBS	Event study based on individual level mortgage application and origination	Effects on price and quantities of U.S. primary mortgage market	Boost in market activity [mainly refinancing]; significant reductions in mortgage rate for high-quality borrowers	
Gagnon *et al.* (2011)	LSAP Treasuries	Event study; changes in yields in the days of announcement	2-year and 10-year Treasury yields, 10-year agency debt yield, 10-year swap rate Baa corporate bond index yield	Change in 10-year Treasury yields: −91 basis points	Sample period: November 2008–November 2009
Yellen (2011b)	LSAP Treasuries	Event study; changes in yields on the days of announcement	10-year and 30-year yields on Treasuries, TIPS, MBS and corporate bond yields	Change in 10-year Treasury yields: −107 basis points	Sample period: November 2008–March 2009

Krishnamurthy and Vissing-Jorgensen (2011)	LSAP Treasuries	Event study; changes in yields on the days of announcement	Treasury yields at various maturities, agency debt, MBS corporate yields and TIPS	Change in 10-year Treasury yields: −100 basis points [QE1]; −30 basis points [QE2]	Sample period: November 2008–March 2009; August 2010–November 2010
Swanson (2011)	LSAP Treasuries	Event study	10-year Treasury yields	Change in 10-year Treasury yields: −16 basis points	Sample period: 1961–1962
Hamilton and Wu (2012)	LSAP Treasuries	Times series study	10-year Treasury yields	Following Fed purchase of $400 billion of long-term Treasury securities and equivalent sale of short-term Treasury notes 10 years Treasury yields drop by 14 basis points	Sample period: 1990–2007
Gagnon *et al.* (2011)	LSAP Treasuries	Times series study	Term premium on 10-year Treasury yields	Impact on 10-year Treasury yields following a 1% drop in the net supply of long-term government bonds over GDP: between −7 and −10 basis points.	Sample period: January 1985 – June 2008

(Continued)

Table 1.2: *(Continued)*

Paper	Program Evaluated	Methodology	Variable of Interest	Results	Notes
Greenwood and Vayanos (2014)	LSAP Treasuries	Times series study	Treasury spreads: 5-year over 1-yt and 20-yt over 1-yt	Following Fed purchase of $400 billion in long-term Treasury securities and equivalent sale of short-term notes 5 over 1-year spread [20 over 1-year spreads] drops by 39 [74 basis points]	Sample period: 1952–2006
D'Amico and King (2013)	LSAP Treasuries	Panel data study	10-year Treasury yields	Fed purchases $400 billion in long term Treasuries: −67 basis points	Sample period: March 2009–October 2009

Note: AMLF = ABCP Money Market Fund Liquidity Facility; TSFL = Term Securities Lending Facility; CPFF = Commercial Paper Funding Facility; TALF = Term ABS Loan Facility; LSAP Treasuries = Large-scale asset purchases of Treasuries.

Ideally, in order to gauge the effectiveness of unconventional measures, one would like to answer the question: "What would have happened to output and inflation had the unconventional monetary policy measures not been introduced?" Providing a convincing answer to such a question is difficult at best. For this reason, the literature has generally tried to answer the related but easier question: "What is the effect on output and inflation of a reduction in the long-term interest rates or credit spreads due to unconventional measures?"

Most of the studies that analyze the macroeconomic effects of the non-traditional measures adopt as a starting point of their analysis specific point estimates obtained from one of the papers presented in Section 3.1 or from narrative evidence. The channels through which the reduction in interest rates propagates to the real activity and prices are the usual ones — reduced borrowing costs that stimulate the investment and spending decisions; higher stock valuations that have positive wealth effects; and depreciation of the nominal exchange rate, which stimulates the export sector. So, in principle, the transmission mechanism is apparently not so different from the one of a more conventional reduction in short-term rates.

The studies on the macroeconomic effects follow two approaches: (1) the VAR analysis, which imposes little structure on the data, and (2) more structural models, such as medium-scale DSGE model or central banks' large-scale econometric models.[28] Baumeister and Benati (2010) estimate a structural time-varying VAR and identify a "pure spread shock," which increases the long-term rates without affecting the short-term ones. They find that this type of shock has important effects on real activity and prices in several industrialized countries. Using the estimates by Gagnon *et al.* (2011) of the effects of LSAP program on the term premia in the U.S., they analyze the dynamics of output and inflation had the reduction in the term spread not happened. They claim that central bank's purchases have prevented a large deflation and a strong collapse of output. According to their median estimates, GDP would have contracted by 10% in the first quarter of 2009 and inflation would have likely remained negative in most of 2009.

---

[28]*See* Table 1.3.

Another strand of literature studies the macroeconomic effects of unconventional measures using general equilibrium structural models. The main advantage of this approach is that a proper counterfactual can be constructed more easily without incurring the Lucas' critique. The drawback is that these models are more difficult to estimate. Del Negro *et al.* (2017) built a fully-fledged DSGE model, including financial frictions *à la* Kiyotaki and Moore (2008). Calibrating this model to match features of the U.S. economy, they find that the extraordinary monetary policy intervention of the Fed, that in the model is constructed as a swap of liquid for illiquid assets (the portfolio-balance channel), prevented a major collapse in output and the risk of persistent deflation. According to their model, this policy measure is especially effective when the economy reaches the zero lower bound.

Chung *et al.* (2012) measure the impact of the LSAP program using the FRB/US model, augmented to analyze portfolio-balance channel effects. The term premium in the model is assumed to be proportional to the discounted future expected Fed holdings of long-term securities as a ratio of nominal GDP. The model simulations have the advantage of considering not only the initial impact of the asset purchases but also the effects of the evolution of the program. They show that the LSAP program boosts output by almost 3% above the baseline in the second half of 2012, raises employment by about three million jobs, and keeps inflation about one percentage point higher than in the no-intervention scenario. According to the model, this would have corresponded to a reduction in the federal funds rate, relative to the baseline, of about 300 basis points relative since early-2009.

Fuhrer and Olivei (2011) assume that the reduction in long-term interest rates due to QE2 is quantifiable at around 20–30 basis points (as found in Gagnon *et al.*, 2011; and Hamilton and Wu, 2012) and estimate its effect on real GDP and unemployment. Combining information from a VAR, the Boston Fed, and the FRB/US models, they find that the implied increase in real GDP is around 60 to 90 basis points over two years, while the drop in the unemployment rate over the same period is slightly less than half a percentage point.

Summing up, the research on the macroeconomic effects of unconventional monetary policy suggests that the interventions of the Fed

Table 1.3: Effects of the Unconventional Measures on Macroeconomic Variables.

Paper	Country	Methodology	Description of the Exercise	Macroeconomic Effect		
				Output	Inflation	Other
Baumeister and Benati (2010)	U.S.	Structural time-varying VAR	Identification of a "pure spread" shock (i.e., a shock that affects the long-term rate leaving the short-term rate unchanged). Simulation of the effects of the reduction in the spread estimated by Gagnon *et al.* (2011) on some macroeconomic variables.	GDP would have contracted by 10% in Q1/2009.		
Del Negro, Eggertsson, Ferrero and Kiyotaki (2017)	U.S.	Calibrated DSGE model	Large-scale DSGE model with financial frictions. Assessment of the macroeconomic effects of a swap of liquid for illiquid assets by the central bank with and without the zero lower bound.	Output about 5 pp lower (in deviation from the baseline) after the shock.	Inflation about 5 pp lower (in deviation from the baseline) after the shock.	

(*Continued*)

Table 1.3: (*Continued*)

Paper	Country	Methodology	Description of the exercise	Macroeconomic effect		
				Output	Inflation	Other
Chung et al. (2012)	U.S.	FRB/US model	Simulation of the macroeconomic effects of central bank asset purchases in the large-scale macro-econometric model used at the Federal Reserve Board augmented with a term premium that depends on the net supply of assets.	Real GDP is boosted by almost 3% above the baseline in the second half of 2012.	Inflation is 1 pp higher in 2012.	Overall increase in employment by about three million jobs.
Fuhrer and Olivei (2011)	U.S.	VAR, Boston Fed and FRB/US models	Study of the effects of purchases of $600 billion of long-term Treasuries	Real GDP should rise by 60–90 basis points two years after the announcement.		Unemployment rate should decline by 30–45 base points over the two years.

were crucial in avoiding a collapse in output and the threat of deflation. Although we share this general conclusion, in our view, the magnitude of the stimulus is subject to a large uncertainty, both on the upside and on the downside, for four reasons.

First, most results are based on estimates of the impact of the unconventional measures on long-term interest rates that are still uncertain. Second, in most cases, they are based on the assumption that the global crisis had no effect on the relationship between macroeconomic variables when this need not be the case, as uncertainty, the deleveraging process and loss of confidence could severely impair the normal functioning of the economy. Third, studies of the macroeconomic effects of unconventional measures that focus exclusively on their impact transmitted through financial prices (such as market spreads) may underestimate the overall effectiveness of the interventions in presence of credit rationing; they do not capture the possible benefits in terms of greater availability of credit and liquidity in the economy. Finally, most of the models used do not feature a fully-fledged financial system, which is necessary to make a sound inference about the effects of the unconventional measures.

4. Conclusions

The Fed implemented a series of unconventional monetary measures aimed at avoiding a meltdown of the financial system and mitigating the effects of the turmoil on the real economy and on prices.

A deeper understanding of the relative role of the different unconventional measures in preventing disruptions and in restoring normal conditions in financial markets is a crucial ingredient for the selection of the instruments that should be included in the central banks' crisis toolbox. In this respect, the analysis of the theoretical underpinnings of the functioning of these measures and of the empirical evidence on the effectiveness of each of the specific unconventional measures can be of great help.

The literature suggests that unconventional interventions may affect economic variables through two channels of transmission — the signaling channel and the portfolio-balance channel. The first is activated through communication, and allows the central bank to restore confidence in the financial markets and to influence private expectations about future policy decisions and, in turn, long-term interest rates. The second operates when assets and liabilities in the balance sheets of the private sector are imperfectly substitutable. In such a situation, the central bank might resort to asset purchases and liquidity injections to influence the prices of a wide set of securities, and to mitigate the impact of financial frictions on funding conditions.

The review of the existing empirical literature on the unconventional measures put in place by the Fed since August 2007, and up to mid-2011, leads to the following considerations.

First, as far as it concerns the effects on financial market conditions, the available evidence suggests that most of the unconventional measures adopted by the Fed have been effective — in some cases, the estimated effects are sizeable. The adoption of the TSLF was helpful in counteracting the limited availability of Treasuries, and coincided with a decline in the spread between Treasury repos and Agency MBS repos of around 80 basis points. A similar effect was exerted by the AMLF on the yields on asset-backed commercial paper; an even larger impact on ABS yields (around 200–300 basis points) is associated with the implementation of the TALF. With regards to the effects of purchases of long-term Treasury bonds in the first round of quantitative easing, the estimates, based on time series models, suggest that long-term interest rates decreased by about 30–150 basis points.

Second, the degree of uncertainty that surrounds these results is large. For example, the measurement of the effectiveness of the TAF in reducing the Libor-OIS spread ranges from zero to around 70 basis points, depending on the econometric approach and on the specific variables adopted in the analysis. A similar range is observable in the measurement of the effects of the purchases of Treasuries on long-term interest rates (from 10 to more than 100 basis points). These differences are due to a large degree of heterogeneity in the selection of the variables used in the analysis and in the identification techniques. Further research is needed to better understand: (i) the determinants of the various risk premia that affect the returns on financial assets (e.g., counterparty, liquidity, term, etc.); (ii) how they are intertwined in normal times and during periods of financial stress; and (iii) how they can be influenced by unconventional measures of monetary policy. The availability of more sound theoretical underpinnings would help in the selection of the proxies for the risk premia and in the design of the appropriate econometric methodology. The classification of the transmission channels of unconventional measures, as illustrated in the first part of the chapter, is a step in this direction, but further analysis is necessary.

Third, the available evidence on the macroeconomic effects suggests that the interventions of the Fed were crucial in avoiding a larger collapse in output, persistent deflation, and in sustaining credit growth. Still, the magnitude of the stimulus is uncertain for four reasons. First, most macroeconomic results are inferred from uncertain estimates of the impact of the unconventional measures on long-term interest rates. Second, they are based on the assumption that the crisis had no effect on the relationship between macroeconomic variables. Third, the existing studies may underestimate the effectiveness of the interventions because they do not fully capture the role of the unconventional measures in contrasting forms of credit rationing. Finally, the models used in the analyses generally lack a fully-fledged description of the financial system.

To sum up, the available evidence suggests that the Fed interventions were effective; they avoided a financial meltdown in the presence of an impaired monetary transmission mechanism and a binding zero lower bound for interest rates. However, a definite assessment of the overall benefits and costs of unconventional measures is not yet possible. A fundamental issue that is not addressed in this chapter, but is crucial to a comprehensive evaluation of the whole policy experiment, is the costs that central banks may incur to reverse their unconventional policies. It remains an issue to measure and minimize the distortions associated with prolonged use of non-market-based liquidity provision mechanisms; in the longer term, the withdrawal of those operations that have permanent effects on the central banks' balance sheets may pose some challenges.

References

Adrian, T, K Kimbrough and D Marchioni (2011). The Federal Reserve's Commercial Paper Funding Facility. *Economic Policy Review*, Federal Reserve Bank of New York, issue May, pp. 25–39.

Adrian, T, C Burke and J McAndrews (2009). The Federal Reserve's Primary Dealer Credit Facility. *Current Issues in Economics and Finance*, Federal Reserve Bank of New York, 15 (4).

Agarwal, S, J Barrett, C Cun and M De Nardi (2010). The Asset-Backed Securities Markets, the Crisis, and TALF. *Economic Perspectives*, Federal Reserve Bank of Chicago.

Anderson, R and C Gascon (2009). The Commercial Paper Market, the Fed, and the 2007–2009 Financial Crisis. *Review*, Federal Reserve Bank of St. Louis, 1 (6), pp. 589–612.

Ashcraft, A, N Gârleanu and LH Pedersen (2011). Two Monetary Tools: Interest Rates and Haircuts. *NBER Macroeconomics Annual 2010*, 25, pp. 143–180.

Baumeister, C and L Benati (2013). Unconventional Monetary Policy and the Great Recession. *International Journal of Central Banking*, 9 (2), pp. 165–212, June.

Bernanke, B and M Gertler, M (1989). Agency Costs, Net Worth, and Business Fluctuations. *American Economic Review*, 79 (1), pp. 14–31.

Bernanke, B and M Gertler (1995). Inside the Black Box: The Credit Channel of Monetary Policy Transmission. *Journal of Economic Perspectives*, 9 (4), pp. 27–48.

Bernanke, B, V Reinhart and B Sack (2004). Monetary Policy Alternatives at the Zero Bound: An Empirical Assessment. *Brookings Papers on Economic Activity*, 2, pp. 1–100.

Blinder, A, M Ehrmann, J de Haan and DJ Jansen (2008). Central Bank Communication and Monetary Policy: A Survey of the Evidence. *Journal of Economic Literature*, 46 (4), pp. 910–945.

Boivin, J, M Kiley and F Mishkin (2010). How Has the Monetary Transmission Mechanism Evolved Over Time? 2010, *Handbook of Monetary Economics* (1st ed.), Friedman, BM and M Woodford (eds.), Elsevier, Vol. iii, No. 3–08.

Campbell, S, D Covitz, W Nelson and K Pence (2011). Securitization Markets and Central Banking: An Evaluation of the Term Asset-Backed Securities Loan Facility. *Journal of Monetary Economics*, 58 (5), pp. 518–531.

Cecioni, M, G Ferrero and A Secchi (2011). Unconventional Monetary Policy in Theory and in Practice. *Banca D'Italia Occasional Papers*, No. 102: September.

Christensen, J, J Lopez and G Rudebusch (2014). Do Central Bank Liquidity Facilities Affect Interbank Lending Rates? *Journal of Business & Economic Statistics*, Taylor & Francis Journals, 32 (1), pp. 136–151, January.

Christiano, L and K Ikeda (2011). Government Policy, Credit Markets and Economic Activity. *NBER Working Paper*, No. 17142, June.

Chung, H, JP Laforte, D Reifschneider and JC Williams (2012). Have We Underestimated the Likelihood and Severity of Zero Lower Bound Events? *Journal of Money, Credit and Banking*, 44 (s1), pp. 47–82.

Clarida, R (2012). What Has — And Has Not — Been Learned About Monetary Policy in a Low Inflation Environment? A Review of the 2000s. *Journal of Money, Credit and Banking*, 44 (s1), pp. 123–140.

Courtois-Haltom, R and JC Hatchondo (2011). How might the Fed's large-scale asset purchases lower long-term interest rates? *Economic Brief*, Federal Reserve Bank of Richmond, January.

Cúrdia, V and M Woodford (2010). Conventional and Unconventional Monetary Policy. *Review*, Federal Reserve Bank of St. Louis, pp. 229–264, May.

D'Amico, S and T King (2013). Flow and Stock Effects of Large-Scale Treasury Purchases: Evidence on the Importance of Local Supply. *Journal of Financial Economics*, 108 (2), pp. 425–448.

De Fiore, F and O Tristani (2009). Optimal Monetary Policy in a Model of the Credit Channel. *Economic Journal*, Royal Economic Society, 123 (571), pp. 906–931.

Del Negro, M, G Eggertsson, A Ferrero and N Kiyotaki (2017). The Great Escape? A Quantitative Evaluation of the Fed's Liquidity Facilities. *American Economic Review*, 107 (3), pp. 824–857.

Demirel, UD (2009). Optimal monetary policy in a financially fragile economy. *The B.E. Journal of Macroeconomics*, Berkeley Electronic Press, 9 (1).

Duca, J (2013). Did the Commercial Paper Funding Facility Prevent a Great Depression Style Money Market Meltdown? *Journal of Financial Stability*, 9 (4), pp. 747–758.

Duygan-Bump, B, P Parkinson, E Rosengren, G Suarez and P Willen (2010). How Effective Were the Federal Reserve Emergency Liquidity Facilities? Evidence from the Asset-Backed Commercial Paper Money Market Mutual Fund Liquidity Facility. *Journal of Finance*, 68 (2), pp. 715–737, 04.

Eggertsson, G and M Woodford (2003). The Zero Bound on Interest Rates and Optimal Monetary Policy. *Brookings Papers on Economic Activity*, 34 (1), pp. 139–235.

Ferrero, G and A Secchi (2009). The Announcement of Monetary Policy Intentions. *Banca d'Italia Temi di discussione*, No. 720.

Ferrero, G and A Secchi (2010). Central Banks' Macroeconomic Projections and Learning. *Banca d'Italia Temi di discussione*, No. 782.

Fleming, M, W Hrung and F Keane (2010). Repo Market Effects of the Term Securities Lending Facility. *American Economic Review*, 100 (2), pp. 591–596.

Freixas, X, A Martin and D Skeie (2011). Bank Liquidity, Interbank Markets, and Monetary Policy. *Review of Financial Studies*, 24 (8), pp. 2,656–2,692.

Fuster, A and P Willen (2010). $1.25 Trillion is Still Real Money: Some Facts About the Effects of the Federal Reserve's Mortgage Market Investments. *Federal Reserve Bank of Boston Public Policy Discussion Papers*, No. 10–4, November.

Gagnon, J, M Raskin, J Remache and B Sack (2011). Large-scale asset purchases by the Federal Reserve: Did they work? *Economic Policy Review*, Federal Reserve Bank of New York, issue May, pp. 41–59.

Gerali, A, S Neri, L Sessa and FM Signoretti (2010). Credit and Banking in a DSGE Model of the Euro Area. *Journal of Money, Credit and Banking*, 42 (s1), pp. 107–141.

Gertler, M and P Karadi (2011). A Model of Unconventional Monetary Policy. *Journal of Monetary Economics*, 58 (1), pp. 17–34, January.

Gertler, M and N Kiyotaki (2010). Financial Intermediation and Credit Policy in Business Cycle Analysis. In, 2010, *Handbook of Monetary Economics* (1st edn.), Friedman, BM and M Woodford (eds.), Elsevier, iii, p. 3.

Greenwood, R and D Vayanos (2014). Bond Supply and Excess Bond Returns. *Review of Financial Studies*, 27 (3), pp. 663–713.

Hamilton, J and C Wu (2012). The Effectiveness of Alternative Monetary Policy Tools in a Zero Lower Bound Environment. *Journal of Money, Credit and Banking*, 44 (2), pp. 3–46.

Hancock, D and W Passmore (2011). Did the Federal Reserve's MBS Purchase Program Lower Mortgage Rates? *Journal of Monetary Economics*, 58 (5), pp. 498–514.

Hrung, W and J Seligman (2015). Responses to the Financial Crisis, Treasury Debt, and the Impact on Short-Term Money Markets. *International Journal of Central Banking*, 11 (1), pp. 151–190, January.

Krishnamurthy, A and A Vissing-Jorgensen (2011). The Effects of Quantitative Easing on Interest Rates. *Brooking Papers on Economic Activity*, 42 (2), pp. 215–287.

Krugman, P (1998). It's Baaack: Japan's Slump and the Return of the Liquidity Trap. *Brookings Papers on Economic Activity*, 29 (2), pp. 137–206.

McAndrews, J, A Sarkar and Z Wang (2017). The Effect of the Term Auction Facility on the London Interbank Offered Rate. *Journal of Banking & Finance*, 83 (4), pp. 135–152.

Mishkin, F (1996). The Channels of Monetary Transmission: Lessons for Monetary Policy. *NBER Working Paper Series*, No. 5464, February.

Modigliani, F and R Sutch (1966). Innovations in Interest-Rate Policy. *American Economic Review*, 56 (1/2), pp. 178–197, March.

Modigliani, F and R Sutch (1967). Debt Management and the Term Structure of Interest Rates: An Empirical Analysis of Recent Experience. *Journal of Political Economy*, 75 (4), pp. 569–589.

Rudebusch, G (2011). The Fed's Interest Rate Risk. *Economic Letter*, Federal Reserve Bank of San Francisco, April.

Stroebel, J and J Taylor (2012). Estimated Impact of the Federal Reserve's Mortgage-Backed Securities Purchase Program. *International Journal of Central Banking*, 8 (2), pp. 1–42, June.

Swanson, E (2011). Let's Twist Again: A High-Frequency Event-Study Analysis of Operation Twist and Its Implications for QE2. *Brookings Papers on Economic Activity*, 42 (1), pp. 151–207.

Taylor, J and J Williams (2009). A Black Swan in the Money Market. *American Economic Journal: Macroeconomics*, 1 (1), pp. 58–83.

Thornton, D (2011). The Effectiveness of Unconventional Monetary Policy: The Term Auction Facility. *Review*, Federal Reserve Bank of St. Louis, pp. 439–454, November.

Tinsley, P (1998). Short Rate Expectations, Term Premiums, and Central Bank Use of Derivatives to Reduce Policy Uncertainty. *Board of Governors of the Federal Reserve System Finance and Economics Discussion Series*, No. 1999-14.

Trichet, JC (2010). Reflections on the Nature of Monetary Policy Non-Standard Measures and Finance Theory. Opening address at the ECB Central Banking Conference, Frankfurt, November.

Vayanos, D and J Vila (2009). A Preferred-Habitat Model of the Term Structure of Interest Rates. *NBER Working Paper Series*, No. 15487, November.

Wallace, N (1981). A Modigliani-Miller Theorem for Open-Market Operations. *American Economic Review*, 71 (3), pp. 267–274, June.

Walsh, C (2008). Announcements and the Role of Policy Guidance. *Review*, Federal Reserve Bank of St. Louis, 90 (4), pp. 421–442.

Wu, T (2008). On the Effectiveness of the Federal Reserve's New Liquidity Facilities. *Federal Reserve Bank of Dallas Working Paper*, No. 0808, May.

Yellen, J (2011a). Unconventional Monetary Policy and Central Bank Communications. Speech at The University of Chicago Booth School of Business U.S. Monetary Policy Forum, New York, February.

Yellen, J (2011b). The Federal Reserve's Asset Purchase Program. Speech at the Brimmer Policy Forum, Allied Social Science Associations Annual Meeting, Denver, Colorado, January.

Chapter Two

Monetary Policy with a Large Balance Sheet: Lessons from the Financial History of the United States

Ellis W. Tallman*

Federal Reserve Bank of Cleveland

Abstract

This paper examines how monetary policy implementation with a large balance sheet relies upon interest on excess reserves. The paper then examines the Federal Reserve System balance sheet from its inception in 1914 until the end of 2015. Noting periods when it either increased rapidly or was large relative to activity measures, we focus on the onset of the U.S. participation in World War One (WWI), the Great Depression, and the World War Two (WWII) experience. The rapid reduction in the Fed balance sheet following WWI was associated with a sharp real contraction, whereas the more gradual decline that followed WWII was associated with better real outcomes. The current Federal Reserve balance sheet will likely contract by between $1 trillion to $1.75 trillion to "normalize," and can contract gradually by allowing securities to mature without reinvestment. The large balance sheet might compromise policymaking if it persists indefinitely. Effective monetary policy could be threatened if, through a misunderstanding, interest on excess reserves was made unavailable. In a scenario analysis, the paper shows how Federal Reserve interest rate control would be compromised and force a sharp contraction of Federal Reserve credit, a speed more rapid than the unfavorable WWI credit contraction.

*The author is executive vice president and director of research at the Federal Reserve Bank of Cleveland. The views expressed are the author's and not necessarily those of the Federal Reserve Bank of Cleveland or the Federal Reserve System. Any remaining errors are the authors' responsibility.

1. Introduction

This chapter investigates how a large balance sheet for the Federal Reserve System affects the implementation of monetary policy. Several notable papers explain in detail the operational aspects of monetary policy as it was practiced before 2007, and compare that policy implementation structure with the one presently in place.[1] In this paper, I only summarize the findings in those papers to provide a brief description of the operational procedures for implementing monetary policy going forward. This chapter instead concentrates on conceptual questions such as what are perceived to be the costs and benefits associated with a large balance sheet — to both the economy and the central bank; and whether there is an "optimal" balance sheet size relative to some economic aggregate.

To gain perspective on the relative size of the Fed balance sheet, I investigate historical episodes in which the Federal Reserve System balance sheet increased rapidly or was large relative to nominal aggregate measures of financial quantities or economic activity. Two of the most distinct episodes of balance sheet expansion were WWI and WWII, and in each case, the U.S. Treasury in effect determined Federal Reserve monetary policy during and immediately following the wars. Separating Federal Reserve monetary policy from wartime Treasury policy to finance them was a negotiation — a slow and arduous process, but also a necessary one in order to preserve central bank and monetary policy independence.

The financial crisis of 2008–2009 posed a challenge of a character distinct from these historical episodes. The policies implemented to combat the financial crisis pushed interest rates close to zero. In addition, Fed policymakers used the Federal Reserve balance sheet as an explicit policy tool. However, it was an instance of fortuitous timing — or luck — that the Congress had passed legislation that gave the Federal Reserve System the ability to pay interest on reserves, and allowed the Fed to accelerate its implementation so that it was available in Fall 2008. Balance sheet policy could only be separated from interest rate policy after the payment of interest on reserves was available to the Federal Reserve System. This policy tool is a crucial one in the array of tools available to the Fed — it allows

---

[1] See, for example, Keister, Martin, and McAndrews (2008), Amstad and Martin (2011), and Ihrig, Meade and Weinbach (2015).

the Fed to implement interest rate policy without necessarily affecting the composition or size of the Federal Reserve System balance sheet.

Central banks worldwide presently face implementing monetary policy with large balance sheets — the functional legacy of "unconventional" policies meant to combat the crisis as well as to stimulate economic growth. The interest receipts that accumulate at central banks from the large asset holdings on their balance sheets draw attention to central bank income statements and perceived earnings. Real economic growth in developed economies has been sluggish during the aftermath of the financial crisis, and fiscal policies have been restrained in most of those economies. Some observers may perceive the accumulation of central bank interest receipts as a source of funding for fiscal initiatives, but the (mis) perception of fiscal relief arises from a misinterpretation of central bank accounting and an explicit oversight of the implied future interest receipts from central bank assets that would be lost if those central bank assets were sold to raise funds for fiscal initiatives. That misunderstanding of accounting may pose risks to central banks as independent institutions because any expenditure that is perceived to reduce the net transfer from central bank to the fiscal authority could be (mistakenly) considered as a rival to the funding of a desired fiscal activity. In the stylized example of this paper, it will become clear that payment of interest on reserves is a necessary tool of monetary policy and, in essence, has become a "cost of doing business" for the Federal Reserve System.

In part, the conclusions from this chapter highlight that central bank communication policy should work diligently to explain as clearly and distinctly as possible the content of their balance sheets and the structure of their assets and liabilities. With regard to the disposition of related interest receipts, central banks can provide an unequivocal explanation of the key expenses on the expenditure side of the income statement; the core of this explanation is well-expressed within the text of a number of expositions provided in expert witness testimony to Congress (as discussed later in this chapter). In effect, the gist of these presentations should accompany transparent accounting for the interest accumulated from central bank assets. With repeated explanation of these conceptual "big picture" issues, central bank independence can be insulated partially from threats arising from common misunderstandings of central bank accounting — like "fiscal relief."

2.   Operating Frameworks for Monetary Policy — Fed

2.1.   *Pre-2008 framework*

Before the payment of interest on reserves, the Federal Reserve System implemented monetary policy by targeting the interest rate in the market for federal funds, that is, the interest rate on loans (between banks) of bank balances held on deposit with the Federal Reserve Banks. In order to facilitate this operating structure, the Federal Reserve System provided a supply of the monetary base, which, on the liability side (the portion held by banks and the general public), consisted mainly of bank reserves [R] and Federal Reserve notes [C], such that the supply of aggregate reserves was "scarce." In effect, the Fed policies relied on providing a supply of reserves close to the volume of reserves demanded by the banking system. The relative scarcity of reserves led to them having a positive price, and scarcity of reserves meant that, in the aggregate, there were relatively few excess reserves, if any. Still, controlling the interest rate was a challenge because the Fed effectively controls the base [R+C]; the public and banks determine the relative quantities of each component demanded.

The Federal Reserve System expended the necessary resources to monitor and estimate the demand for reserves on a daily basis, in order to keep the supply of reserves consistent with the interest rate target (the "price" of reserves) determined by the Federal Open Market Committee (FOMC). Monetary policy implementation required the markets desk and the Board of Governors to make estimates of daily reserve demand. In those circumstances requiring a daily adjustment to bank reserve supply, relatively small changes in the supply of reserves would help achieve the target interest rate. Advances in banking and information system technology did not eliminate technical and operational challenges associated with the implementation of this framework. In this framework, banks did not receive interest on reserves, and it was therefore in the interest of banks to minimize their reserve balances.

The distribution of reserves among banks would not necessarily line up with the reserve needs of banks; as such, banks would generate a volume of trading in the federal funds market to allow the reallocation of reserves.

On occasion, unanticipated changes in reserve demand as well as shocks to specific bank balance sheets, in a reserve supply scheme that produced "structural deficiency" in bank reserves, could generate reserve demand that the supply of reserves was not capable of satisfying immediately. In those circumstances, there could be substantive fluctuations in the federal funds rate. Further, in cases when banks were unable to get sufficient reserves to fulfill daily payment obligations, the Fed would be forced to extend daylight overdrafts to banks, sometimes in large dollar volumes. This situation would put the Federal Reserve System at risk of a credit loss if that bank failed. These are just two of the potential costs of implementing this kind of monetary policy that hinges on a scarce supply of bank reserves.

The graphic in Figure 2.1 depicts a simple analysis of the determination of the federal funds rate in the pre-2007 Federal Reserve System monetary policy framework.[2] The blue curve in the graph is the stylized demand curve for aggregate reserve balances at the Fed. The vertical line represents the inelastic supply of reserves, which was estimated to be about $15 billion in Ihrig *et al.* (2015). The intersection of the supply and demand curves for reserve balances determines the federal funds rate, assumed to be equal

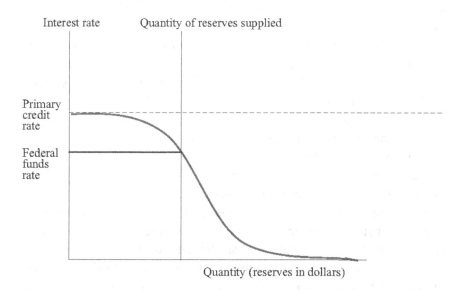

Fig. 2.1. The Determination of Short-Term Interest Rates (pre-2008).

---

[2] The graphical analysis is taken from Amstad and Martin (2011) and Ihrig *et al.* (2015).

to the target federal funds rate. Above the federal funds rate is a dashed line that represents the primary credit rate, the interest rate at which the Fed lends reserves to banks overnight. Conceptually, lending through the primary credit function is a liquidity provision mechanism offered at a "penalty" rate above the federal funds rate. These funds ensure that banks have an opportunity to borrow if they are struck with unanticipated reserve liquidity shortages.

As seen in Figure 2.1, if the supply of reserves (vertical line) moves far to the right, the equilibrium federal funds rate becomes zero in this operational framework. Under these circumstances, the "large-scale asset purchases" implemented by the Federal Reserve System would have pushed the federal funds to zero much sooner than was observed. As demonstrated below, the Federal Reserve payment of interest on reserves allowed the effective separation of interest rate policy from balance sheet-related actions.

3.   Policy Framework Presently (*circa* 2016)

Ihrig *et al.* (2015) provide an accessible and comprehensive treatment of the current monetary policy framework for the Federal Reserve System in the presence of a large balance sheet. When the paper was written, it was unclear how effectively the policy framework would work after the initial "lift-off" of the Federal Reserve System interest rate on reserves (and excess reserves). After liftoff on December 15, 2015, the federal funds rate was raised by 25 basis points as the FOMC decided, thus providing evidence that the present operating framework works as anticipated.

Figure 2.2 provides a simplified analysis of the monetary policy framework when the payment of interest on reserves allows the separation of interest rate policy from balance sheet actions. The key policy interest rate is the rate paid by the Fed to member banks on their deposits (reserves at the Fed, both required and reserves in excess of required reserves). It is set above the "target" federal funds rate because, for institutional reasons, the government-sponsored enterprises — Fannie Mae, Freddie Mac, and the Federal Home Loan Banks — have reserves that they are willing to lend at rates below the interest rate on excess reserves that the Fed pays to member banks. That is because these enterprises cannot receive interest from the Fed, but they can receive interest from the banks to which they lend reserves in the federal funds market. The interest on excess reserves

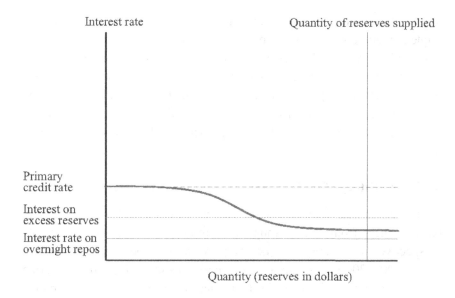

Fig. 2.2. The Determination of Short-Term Interest Rates (post-2008).

is a "leaky floor" interest rate in this setup as a result of this institutional complication. Below the federal funds rate target is the interest rate on overnight reverse repurchase (ONRRP) agreements between the Fed and its counterparties. The reverse repo is a transaction in which the Fed offers its securities as collateral in exchange for balances overnight, and sets that rate explicitly below the interest rate on reserves. The Fed can pay interest on excess reserve directly to banks that hold reserves with the Federal Reserve System, and can also pay a slightly lower rate of interest on reserves borrowed in (reverse) repurchase agreements (RRP) with banks and other intermediaries in search of an exchange of reserves for high-quality collateral assets.

In this framework, the Federal Reserve System can implement an increase in interest rates in the following way — the Fed can raise the interest rate on excess reserves (IOER) and make offering rates for reverse repurchase agreements below IOER thereby providing a gap or spread between those rates. The federal funds rate target will fluctuate around the midpoint of the spread as the market adjusts to the interest rate change.

Empirical observation indicates that both operational policies can determine and achieve a federal funds rate target. Going forward, the large balance sheet of the Federal Reserve System will not hinder the implementation of monetary policy because the target interest rate is effectively controlled by the interest rate on excess reserves and Federal Reserve actions regarding the size and composition of the assets on the balance sheet are separate and distinct. Further, the existence of a large Federal Reserve balance sheet (relative to macroeconomic aggregates) has historical precedents, although the large balance sheet arose for different reasons.

4. Brief History of Federal Reserve Balance Sheet Size

This discussion summarizes the evolution of the Federal Reserve System balance sheet from 1917 through the present from a general aggregate perspective.[3] Comparable to the sharp increase in the Fed balance sheet during 2008–2009, there are several experiences in the U.S. history during which the Federal Reserve System balance sheet was either growing rapidly relative to the growth rate of relevant nominal aggregate quantities or the balance sheet level was large relative to the level of those same nominal aggregates. The effects of both WWI and WWII on the Federal Reserve System balance sheet were immense as well as distinct from any other periods.[4] From a governance standpoint, the primacy of financing the wars placed the Treasury in an influential position relative to the Fed, and Fed policies designed to support the Treasury had important and long-lasting effects on the operations of the Federal Reserve System. In each case, the effects of war financing on the size of the Fed balance sheet were reversed, and in the case of WWI, relatively quickly. Perhaps for that reason, the ramifications of the reversal for the financial markets appear to have been far more serious after WWI, and I discuss briefly some of the perceived shortcomings from that first instance.

---

[3] This section provides a brief and narrow historical perspective on the Federal Reserve System balance sheet. For further detail on the history of the balance sheet and of the income derived from the SOMA portfolio, see two articles posted on Liberty Street Economics (Bukhari *et al.*, 2013; and Bukhari *et al.*, 2013). The sample begins at 1917 because, prior to 1917, the Federal Reserve System was small and increased its balance sheet rapidly. As such, the initial three years distorts inferences from Figure 2.5.

[4] The Federal Reserve balance sheet increased notably during the Great Depression, and more so after the devaluation of the dollar in 1934, when gold inflows into the U.S. led to an accumulation of gold assets at the Federal Reserve System. In Figure 2.5 (see below), the growth rate of the balance sheet in 1935 was nearly 27 percent, a rate not surpassed until 2008.

These two wartime experiences offer two lessons: (1) the size of the Federal Reserve System balance sheet can contract and has contracted following rapid increases in size; and (2) the U.S. Treasury played a central role in both the increase and the decrease in the balance sheet. In the WWI case, the Secretary of the Treasury was the Chairman of the Federal Reserve Board, *ex officio*. The Federal Reserve System during the war aimed its policies to support the Treasury's efforts to finance the war. Among the leading policies was the credit support offered by the Fed to its member banks on the purchase of Treasury securities.[5] The Federal Reserve used discount policy to stimulate the placement of Liberty Bonds by effectively subsidizing bond purchases by member banks (as well as non-members through correspondent relationships with members). That is, the Fed lent to banks through the discount window at rediscount rates below the rate earned on Treasury securities (lending at lower interest rates than the Treasury debt was yielding). In essence, the Fed was lending to allow banks a clear profit on the purchase of the Treasury debt (whether bonds or "certificates of indebtedness" that were the precursors to Treasury bills). However, the Fed did not accumulate Treasury securities on its balance sheet, and there was an explicit aversion to Treasury debt accumulation on the Fed balance sheet.[6]

Federal Reserve policies to finance the Treasury during WWII were more structured than those in WWI, and there was less of an aversion for the Federal Reserve System to accumulate a large stock of Treasury debt.[7] In fact, the Treasury arranged with the Fed to target the interest rate on long-term Treasury bonds, so the Fed balance sheet grew and, as a result of implementing that policy, increased sharply Treasury debt as a proportion of Fed assets. Further, the contraction of the balance sheet following the end of the war was delayed and more gradual than the one observed following WWI. In contrast to the contraction in discount window loans following WWI, it was Treasury debt and security holdings that were the main asset

---

[5]To promote the sale of Treasury debt, the Fed allowed member banks to provide their correspondent, non-member banks to borrow indirectly through the Fed's discount window function and pay interest at the preferential discount rates on loans using Treasury debt as collateral.

[6]See Wicker (1966) and Meltzer (2003).

[7]Among a number of explanations for the change in perspective regarding Treasury debt on the Fed balance sheet, the accumulation of huge gold-backed assets following the dollar depreciation in 1934, thereby limiting the threat that the Fed would lack backing for its liabilities and the severity of the war threat seem most pertinent.

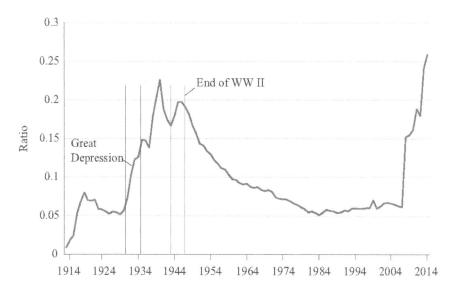

Fig. 2.3.   Federal Reserve System Total Assets Relative to Nominal GDP.

class that contracted in the Federal Reserve System balance sheet in 1949. The Treasury used the proceeds of the Victory loan and subsequent budget surpluses to buy debt from banks and the Federal Reserve System.

Figure 2.3 displays the ratio of Federal Reserve aggregate assets relative to nominal GDP from 1914 to 2015.[8] The most prominent periods for comparison are in WWII, and the recent accumulation since 2008. From 1937 to 1940, the asset that increased in the Federal Reserve balance sheet was mainly gold, and those gold inflows have been largely attributed to European capital flight along with European-based purchases of war material in the period just prior to and during the outbreak of war. Upon the U.S. entry into the war beginning in 1941, the level of the Federal Reserve assets to nominal GDP remained at about 0.2, although the composition of the assets changed dramatically. In 1940, over 85 percent of the assets on the

---

[8]For the graphics, the data are end of year figures for the balance sheet data. The level of the balance sheet is taken relative to nominal GDP (annual average basis, National Income and Product Accounts supplemented with estimates from "Measuring Wealth" for data prior to 1929), and relative to the M2 monetary aggregate (end of period stock). Taking balance sheet data relative to these aggregates helps detect previous periods during which the balance sheet was nearly as large as today relative to appropriate measures of economic activity or banking sector size.

Fed balance sheet was gold. Given the requirement to support the Treasury to finance the war, the Federal Reserve System assets shifted dramatically so that by 1945, more than 50 percent of System assets were Treasury debt, and gold's percentage of assets fell to just over 40 percent.

Three less obvious periods of balance sheet increase are worth mentioning. The Fed balance sheet ratio spikes upward from 1914 to 1916 as the Federal Reserve System is just getting started, and again from 1917 to 1919, the ratio rises sharply as the Federal Reserve credit policies — namely, providing a preferential discount rate for Treasury collateral — supports member bank discount window borrowing for the purchase of Treasury debt issues. In both cases, the increase in the nominal assets of the Federal Reserve System was substantial and the positive nominal GDP growth rates during the periods were moderating factors in the increase in the ratio. For example, in 1917, the nominal size of the Fed balance sheet nearly doubles from the previous year and nominal growth of GDP of around 25 percent moderates that change in the ratio. In contrast, during the Great Depression, the ratio of Federal Reserve total assets to nominal GDP rises substantially, but that is largely due to the 30 percent contraction in nominal GDP from 1929 to 1933.

Immediately following WWI, the nominal Federal Reserve balance sheet contracted as did the economy. From 1919 to 1921, the Federal Reserve balance sheet contracted by over 20 percent, and the major component of the contraction on the asset side of the balance sheet was in borrowing by member banks. Over the same period, nominal GDP contracted by just over six percent; however, the 1920–1921 contraction is often referred to as a depression. The economic impact of credit contraction in the U.S. economy during this period is a fertile area for economic research and has gained some prominence in public debate.[9] Federal Reserve interest rate policy required cooperation of the Treasury, because the Secretary of the Treasury held the position of Chairman of the Federal Reserve Board, and the adjustment of the discount rate was the main operational tool for monetary policy.

Figure 2.4 presents the ratio of Federal Reserve total assets to nominal M2. Similar points to Figure 2.3, the balance sheet size relative to M2 during

---

[9]See Grant (2014).

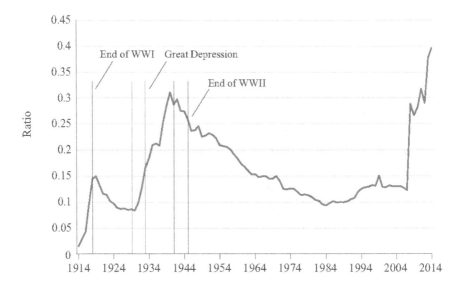

Fig. 2.4.   Federal Reserve System Assets Relative to M2.

WWII was comparable to that observed in 2012. The run-up in the ratio from 1937 to 1940 reflects the same gold inflows from Europe, and the relative increase in Federal Reserve total assets relative to M2 during the Great Depression reflects the fact that M2 contracted by over 40 percent from 1929 to 1933. The graph is particularly useful in highlighting the increase in the ratio of Fed total assets to M2 following the U.S. entry into WWI, as well as the subsequent reduction in the ratio in the years that immediately followed the war. The key factor is that nominal M2 held fairly steady in the aftermath of WWI, whereas the Federal Reserve balance sheet contracted sharply. Although Federal Reserve System credit tightening actions are often cited as the source of the economic contraction of 1920–1921, it is notable that M2 did not contract as it did during the Great Depression.

Figure 2.5 displays the growth rate of the total (nominal) assets for the Federal Reserve balance sheet. The main point to draw from the graph is the sharp contractions in the size of the balance sheet following WWI and also following WWII. The two other nominal contractions, in 2000 and in 1930, are notable. For the periods immediately following the end of the wars, the balance sheet contractions arise mainly from a conscious effort to reduce the size of the balance sheet, and not from other motivations. In

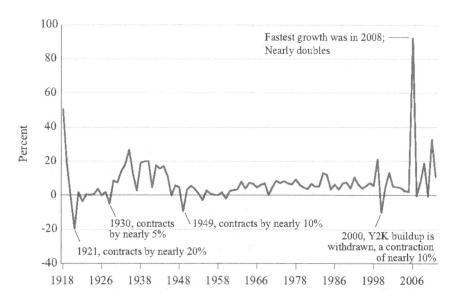

Fig. 2.5.   Growth Rate of Nominal Federal Reserve Balance Sheet.

1921, Federal Reserve System discount rate actions led to member bank actions to change their borrowing behavior (reducing it dramatically) so that the balance sheet of the Fed contracted by nearly 20 percent. Member bank borrowing declined from approximately $2.7 billion in 1920 to $1.1 billion in 1921, whereas the total balance sheet fell from $6.3 billion to $5.2 billion. From the liability side, the majority of the contraction was a net reduction in Federal Reserve notes outstanding, and bank reserves declined much less. A number of economic historians have studied this period in order to uncover the reasoning for the policy and whether the policymakers recognized the damaging effects of such a sharp reduction in credit made available to banks.[10] The absence of a banking crisis during this economic contraction is a notable feature, and research on that specific issue may offer insight about what specific characteristics of the economy or financial markets led to the stark contrast with the condition of the banking system

---

[10] During this period, there was a gold reserve requirement for Federal Reserve System liabilities, which allegedly was nearly binding and was perceived to have influenced policy maker decisions. Meltzer (2003: 254, footnote 54) suggests that the gold reserve was less of a threat and that discount rate policy was driven by other goals. Wicker (1966) offers a similar view.

during the Great Depression.[11] Overall, however, the rapid contraction in the balance sheet was not considered a successful policy.

In reference to governance and monetary policy, the negotiation of the Treasury–Fed Accord in 1951 was essential for reinstating the independence of Federal Reserve monetary policy.[12] Note that six years passed following the end of WWII before the accord was struck. In contrast, the implementation of monetary policy "independence" in the aftermath of WWI took hold after only one year (November 1919), when the Federal Reserve Banks increased the discount rate and started an upward path for interest rates that continued for another seven months. The Treasury was acquiescent to the increase in the discount rates only after federal revenues exceeded expenditures, but there is an extensive literature that investigates the negotiations between, for the most part, Benjamin Strong (Governor of the Federal Reserve Bank of New York) and the Federal Reserve Board (mainly, the Secretary of the Treasury at the time, Carter Glass). Reducing Treasury influence over monetary policy in the aftermath of each war was a challenging and yet necessary goal to preserve central bank independence.

5. Costs and Benefits of a Large Fed Balance Sheet

It is a challenging task to estimate tangible quantities for the costs and benefits of a large Federal Reserve balance sheet with respect to the overall economy.[13] Relatedly, divergent views are particularly useful for investigating the costs and benefits of interest on reserves, and interest on reserves is intimately related to the ability of the Fed to maintain a large balance sheet in the present operating framework. Without the payment of interest on reserves, as mentioned above, the Fed would likely be unable to maintain an interest rate control at the short-term end of the financial

---

[11] The contraction in the Federal Reserve balance sheet in 1930 is often perceived as evidence of a policy error by the Federal Reserve System. Without judging that speculation, I find it notable that the key source of the contraction in the Federal Reserve balance sheet on the asset side was a sharp decline in member bank borrowing. In 2000, the balance sheet contraction reflected the removal of additional liquidity that was provided in 1999 in anticipation of potential issues arising from the Y2K event. The additional liquidity was provided by tri-party repurchase agreements and the removal of that liquidity came about from reducing that volume.

[12] See, for example, Humpage (2014).

[13] For costs and benefits to the operational efficiency of the Fed, I cite evidence from the literature below.

market without selling a substantial portion of its asset portfolio. Here, I will only outline several for each side of the ledger, and leave the calculation of specific amounts for further study. Suffice to say that the evaluation of the net benefit or net cost without calculation is ambiguous; it remains an important element to the debate over the desired durability of the present monetary policy framework that enables the maintenance of a large balance sheet by the Federal Reserve System.

A key element to the accumulation of the large balance sheet was the payment of interest on reserves, which allowed the Fed to separate balance sheet operations from interest rate policy. During the fall of 2008, the payment of interest on reserves allowed the Fed to participate directly in a variety of markets, increase the size of bank reserve balances (and its own balance sheet), and maintain a separate interest rate policy. Without interest on reserves, the infusion of additional bank reserves would have been limited, or else interest rates would reach the zero lower bound. If there has been a measurable benefit from "large-scale asset purchases" in the crisis or afterward, then that benefit in itself is a benefit of the large balance sheet. Further, the 25-basis point increase in the target federal funds rate in December 2015 would not have been possible without a massive reduction in the Federal Reserve System balance sheet, a point that will be raised again below.

The benefits of a large balance sheet include: (1) a more efficient payments system, (2) smoother adjustment of reserve supply to increased reserve demand arising from "liquidity coverage ratio" regulations, and (3) an operational apparatus within the Federal Reserve System to initiate alternative liquidity injections (or withdrawals) into various financial markets directly.

As outlined above, the pre-2007 Federal Reserve operating policy implemented a framework that included a "structural deficiency" in reserves, in order to create a reserve scarcity for the banking system. In the absence of interest on reserves, banks have the incentive to minimize the opportunity costs of holding reserves, and any bank holding excess reserves would lend them to those banks that are short of reserves through the federal funds market. The scarcity of reserves led to occasions in which banks were short of reserves and had daylight overdrafts with the Federal Reserve Banks, which leaves the Fed in a position of holding payments risk.

Further, bank economizing on reserve balances tended to delay payment settlement until later in the day, contributing to less efficient payments. Among the benefits of a large balance sheet, Keister (2016) (citing Bech, Martin, and McAndrews, 2012) emphasizes that there has been a notable decline in daylight overdrafts, a notable increase in payments earlier in the day, and an overall increase in the efficiency of the payments system.

Through the Dodd–Frank Act, banks now face liquidity coverage ratio regulations that have increased the demand for reserve balances, which qualify as assets that satisfy this requirement. The ample supply of reserves made the transition to adapt to the new regulation smoother than would have been the case in the "scarce reserves" framework. That said, the financial crisis would likely have resulted in a general increase in reserve demand, even without the structural change in the operational structure of the Fed as banks would shift toward a balance sheet with lower risk exposure.

The large balance sheet of the Fed has led to the development of new tools, such as overnight reverse repurchase agreements, and with these instruments, the Fed has the capability of affecting liquidity conditions in a variety of markets and with a wide array of counterparties. During episodes of financial crises, the provision of liquidity through a variety of markets and across various counterparties appears associated with success in combatting the crises. Over time, it will be important to monitor the volume and importance of these new activities as the Fed develops its new operating framework for the longer term.

Among the costs of a large Federal Reserve balance sheet, there are: (1) a perceived inefficiency arising from a large, inactive stock of bank reserves, (2) constraint on Fed remittances to the Treasury if rising short-term interest rates raise expenditures faster than portfolio turnover increases Fed asset earnings, (3) misunderstanding the disbursement of Fed earnings and remittances to the Treasury, and (4) pressure to employ asset purchases to support specific markets. For the latter risk/cost, there are ample examples of such pressure throughout the history of the Federal Reserve System.[14]

In recent testimony to the House Financial Services Committee, academic economists and financial market participants provided conflicting opinions and contrary arguments (both pros and cons) on the payment

---

[14]See Chandler (1958).

of interest on reserves by the Federal Reserve Banks to their member banks. Robert Eisenbeis of Cumberland Advisors and Todd Keister of Rutgers University offered arguments in support of interest on reserves. George Selgin of the Cato Institute and John Taylor of Stanford University presented the view that, as implemented by the Federal Reserve System in 2008, interest on reserves — specifically, interest on excess reserves — was not a productive tool for implementing monetary policy. In the testimonies and their responses to questions, the comments had direct bearing on the issues that surround the costs and benefits to a large balance sheet for the Federal Reserve System.

George Selgin expressed concern for what he perceived as the contractionary effect of interest on (excess) reserves. Selgin argues that interest on excess reserves promotes "idle balances" and hinders bank lending. Hence, interest on reserves was contractionary and hindered economic recovery. Selgin's concern for the deleterious effects of LSAPs and the large Federal Reserve balance sheet is in the following text:

> Such a large increase in the Fed's role in the allocation of scarce savings is much to be regretted, as it almost certainly means that those savings are not being devoted to their most productive or welfare-enhancing uses. At best, central banks are inefficient financial intermediaries, not the least because efficient intermediation forms no part of their official responsibilities.

> — Selgin, Testimony to House Financial Services Committee, p. 13

Rather than confront Selgin's issue directly, I suggest that we wait until data sets are large enough to address his assertions directly with empirical evidence.

Robert Eisenbeis offers a differing view of interest on reserves in his testimony. He highlights how Federal Reserve asset purchases added reserves to the banking system, and draws a different conclusion from Selgin with respect to their activity. Simply put, banks individually can rearrange their assets to reduce their holdings of reserves, but the banking system has no alternative to holding the supply of reserves aside from exchanging them for currency. Only the Fed can create the reserves and only Fed actions can reduce the size of its balance sheet, that is, the sum of reserves and currency [R+C]. He points out that nearly 40 percent of excess reserves are held by affiliates and subsidiaries of foreign banks, few of which extensively intermediate deposits within the U.S. The potential for banks to expand their loan portfolios exists, but there are likely other issues (like, perhaps capital requirements and regulatory restrictions) that limit bank lending more than the 50 basis points paid on reserve balances by the Federal Reserve System.

5.1. Misperceptions of Federal Reserve balances

Remittance amounts paid to the Treasury have been large since the Fed has accumulated a large balance sheet during the past several years. However, if Federal Reserve monetary policy goals require that the short-term interest rate increase, then it is possible that interest payments to banks for their reserve holdings could approach the interest receipts from the Federal Reserve System holdings of Treasury and other interest-bearing assets. Generally, the problem that arises from this situation is one of accounting and explanation. However, it is the misperception of this issue — accounting for the "interest on Federal Reserve notes" that is transferred to the Treasury by the Federal Reserve System — that can lead to problems for the central bank. In a testimony by Robert Eisenbeis and Todd Keister, the accounting and conceptual framework for thinking about the remittances and the payment of interest on reserves becomes clear.

In his prepared statement along with testimony to the House Financial Services Committee, Eisenbeis provided (correctly) the following analysis:

> [t]he Fed can't make a profit. Rather, it issues one form of government debt for another. It receives interest payments from the government, takes out its operating costs, and returns the remainder to the Treasury. On balance, there is always a net payment from the Treasury to the Fed, and it is inappropriate to consider remittances as income for budget purposes, as is the present practice.

> — Dr. Robert A. Eisenbeis, Vice Chairman, Cumberland Advisors

In his written text, Eisenbeis described interest on excess reserves paid to banks by the Federal Reserve Banks as comparable to interest paid by banks to depositors because, like depositors, banks have an opportunity cost to holding reserves at the Fed. Further, when the Fed buys assets like in the LSAPs, banks must hold the reserves created by the Fed to purchase the asset. Payment of interest on reserves keeps banks from being penalized for holding them.

If interest rates on excess reserves rise as suggested above, the payments to banks holding those reserves rise, thereby increasing Federal Reserve expenses and also reducing the remittance amount that would be paid to the Treasury. Someone could misinterpret the accounting, and infer that the payment of interest on reserves could be redirected to the Treasury without ramifications. Then, that person might advocate ending the payment of interest on reserves because it would then reduce payments to banks and, one might think, increase the remittances to the Treasury as a result. However, this argument is flawed, as explained by Keister. Keister argues that if interest on reserves was eliminated, then the Fed would either lose control of the interest rate for setting monetary policy, or the Fed would have to reduce the supply of reserves to shrink the excess reserve supply and cause a scarcity of bank reserves in order to produce a positive interest rate for the federal funds rate. In essence, elimination of interest on reserves would force the Fed to return to the pre-2007 monetary policy operational framework.[15]

To shrink the supply of reserves and its balance sheet, the Fed would have to sell a large amount of its interest-bearing assets. The ramifications from this sale of assets should be examined so that the effect on the Fed's income statement is clear. If the Fed were to reduce its balance sheet and sell Treasury assets to private market participants, then the Treasury would pay interest directly to the private holders of the Treasury debt that the Fed was forced to sell. As a result, the Fed would not accumulate interest receipts from those assets, and the remittance that the Fed would pay to Treasury would be smaller by the amount of interest paid to the private holders of those assets.

To make the discussion above more concrete, I provide a simple stylized example with numbers in Table 2.1. Let us assume that the Fed holds $4 trillion in interest bearing assets that yield on average three percent, so that the annual gross interest receipts are $120 billion. Let us assume that operating expenses for the Federal Reserve System are $7 billion. This does not yet account for interest paid to depository institutions for reserve balances. Assume that interest is paid on $2.5 trillion in reserves (approximately). When interest on reserves is 0.5 percent, the interest

---

[15]The analysis that follows assumes that lacking the ability to pay interest on excess reserves would also prevent large-scale reverse repurchase agreements. If, in fact, large-scale repurchase agreements were available, the reduction in the Federal Reserve balance sheet would be limited, but the perceived remittance benefit to the Treasury would also be reduced. That circumstance is ignored here as an intermediate outcome.

Table 2.1:   Interest Receipts of Federal Reserve System with a Large Balance Sheet.

Example 1: IOER is set at 0.5 percent

1. Federal Reserve System holds $4 trillion in assets
2. Average maturity of the assets is 8 years
3. Average yield on assets is 3 percent
4. Banks hold $2.5 trillion in reserves
5. The only payment to member banks from the Federal Reserve System is IOER
6. IOER is set at **0.5 percent**

Revenues

Interest receipts to the Federal Reserve System from its asset portfolio are:
$4 trillion × 0.03 = $120 billion

Expenses

IOER expense: $2.5 trillion × 0.005 = $12.5 billion

Operating expenses	$7 billion
IOER expenses	$12.5 billion
Total expenses	$19.5 billion
Revenues of	$120 billion
less expenses of	$19.5 billion
Yields	$100.5 billion

Federal Reserve System remits to Treasury $100.5 billion

Example 2: IOER is set at 4.0 percent

1. Federal Reserve System holds $4 trillion in assets
2. Average maturity of the assets is 8 years
3. Average yield on assets is 3 percent
4. Banks hold $2.5 trillion in reserves
5. The only payment to member banks from the Federal Reserve System is IOER
6. IOER is set at **4.0 percent**

Revenues

Interest receipts to the Federal Reserve System from its asset portfolio are:
$4 trillion × 0.03 = $120 billion

(Continued)

Table 2.1:   (*Continued*)

Expenses

IOER expense: $ 2.5 trillion × 0.04 = $100 billion	
Operating expenses	$7 billion
IOER expenses	$100 billion
Total expenses	$107 billion
Revenues of	$120 billion
less expenses of	$107 billion
Yields	$13 billion
Federal Reserve System remits to Treasury $13 billion	

Example 3: No interest on excess reserves

1. Federal Reserve System holds $1.75 trillion in assets, having sold $2.25 trillion
2. Average maturity of the assets remains 8 years
3. Average yield on assets falls to 2 percent
4. There are no IOER payments to member banks from the Federal Reserve System
5. Fed sale of assets at 4 percent market interest rate implies 6.7 percent loss on asset sales

Revenues

Interest receipts to the Federal Reserve System from its asset portfolio are:
$1.75 trillion × 0.02 = $35 billion

Expenses

Operating expenses	$7 billion
Capital loss	$15 billion
Total expenses	$22 billion
Revenues of	$35 billion
less expenses of	$22 billion
Yields	$13 billion
Federal Reserve System remits to Treasury $13 billion	

payments to banks add to Federal Reserve expenses by $12.5 billion. Subtracting the two totals for Federal Reserve expenses [$12.5 billion + $7 billion] = $19.5 billion from the $120 billion of earnings leaves just over $100 billion to be transferred to the Treasury. This simple example is not so different from the actuals for the year 2015.

The challenge arises when the interest rate on reserves rises. If the quantities remain the same and the average yield on the $4 trillion in assets remains three percent, then the gross annual receipts remain $120 billion. However, if interest on reserves rises to four percent, and that interest rate applies to reserves of $2.5 billion, then interest payments to banks accounts for $100 billion in Fed expenses. If Federal Reserve operating expenses remain about the same at $7 billion, then the remittance to the Treasury falls to $13 billion from the $100 billion when the interest rate paid on excess reserves was 0.5 percent.

The optics of this example sets up a formidable situation for the misinformed critic — it looks like the Fed, when it raises the interest rate on reserves, is simply paying out more of its interest receipts to banks. The statement is accurate and also not all that meaningful. As described generally in the Keister example, I can illustrate the weakness in the viewpoint. Upon observing the decline in remittances to the Treasury when interest on reserves rose to four percent, suppose that interest on reserves was revoked in order to increase the transfer to the Treasury at the end of the year. As described earlier, the ability to pay interest on excess reserves allows the Fed to implement interest rate policy separately from balance sheet policy, and if the payment of interest on reserves was eliminated, then the large balance sheet of the Fed would have to be used to achieve an interest rate target in a way akin to the pre-2007 reserve scarcity framework. In that setting, the Fed would have to reduce the size of its balance sheet rapidly in order to increase short-term interest rates.

For clarity of this example, let us just assume that the Federal Reserve System sells off more than half of its asset portfolio — $2.25 trillion — in order to recalibrate short-term interest rates to be around four percent. The interest paid on these Treasury assets now goes to private investors and will no longer be transferred from the Fed to the Treasury. Let us also assume that the maturity of the Treasury securities sold by the Fed averages around eight years. Further, if market interest rates on longer-term assets increased to four percent, the same as the short rates, the Fed would be forced take a capital loss on the sale of its assets, which again for clarity of the example I assume is taken out of current earnings. To calibrate the example, I calculate the loss on a bond maturing in eight years with a three percent coupon yield when the interest rate rises from three to four percent. The loss is 6.7 percent and multiplied by the $2.25 trillion in Treasury debt sold, the capital loss expense to the Fed is approximately $15 billion. Now, instead of $4 trillion in assets, the Fed portfolio has $1.75 trillion in assets. It would not be a surprise if the average interest rate on the portfolio fell to two percent, depending on which assets were sold. Then, the interest earnings of the Fed would have fallen to $35 billion, out of which $7 billion in operating expenses along with capital loss expenses of $15 billion will be taken. The net transfer to the Treasury in this scenario is $13 billion, the same as would be made above. Clearly, the numbers fall out so neatly because this is a rigged example, but it is also feasible.

One can imagine a more unsettling market response upon the sale of $2.25 trillion in Treasury assets. The disruptive effects on the financial markets and the potential costs to the Fed and the economy could be much greater than the costs implied by the stylized example. However, that scenario would be distracting from the core mechanics of the accounting example. The point is the same — interest on (excess) reserves is an important monetary policy instrument. Without that tool, the only way for the Federal Reserve System to implement an interest rate policy would be through a rapid liquidation of Federal Reserve balance sheet assets. That situation would be undesirable because of the potential for large capital losses to the Federal Reserve System and that abstracts from the potential for destabilizing effects on financial markets of the large-scale sales of Treasury debt in order to regain influence over short-term interest rates.

6. Conclusions and a Speculation

From an operational standpoint, the implementation of large-scale asset purchases (LSAPs) as a tool for monetary policy intervention hinged on the ability of the Federal Reserve System to pay interest on reserves (and especially, excess reserves), so that interest rate policy could be effectively separated from a policy aimed at affecting the size (and composition) of the Federal Reserve System balance sheet. Presently, as a byproduct of LSAPs, the Federal Reserve System holds a large balance sheet and therefore relies on its ability to pay interest on reserves in order to influence short-term interest rates and financial markets distinctly from adjustments to its asset portfolio. The efficacy of interest on reserves for implementing monetary policy is not overtly controversial among monetary and financial market economists. However, it is less well understood in the public and media, and therefore can become a contestable issue in political circles.

The stark accounting example presented in this chapter illustrates the implication of an accounting misperception and abstracts from any estimation of the potential costs arising from financial instability that might be associated with large-scale liquidation of the Federal Reserve balance sheet. Interest on excess reserves is an important feature of the monetary policy operational framework for the Federal Reserve System as well as for financial stability policy. To defuse controversy, it is important to explain effectively how the new monetary policy operating framework relies on that instrument to maintain control of the short-term interest rate. With a large Federal Reserve balance sheet and, more specifically, a supply of bank reserves that is over 50 percent of Federal Reserve System total liabilities, the payment of interest on reserves may pose "optics" risks in the medium-term future.

The perspective of history illustrates that the Federal Reserve balance sheet has been large in the past, and has contracted and returned to a more normal size afterward, so that the large balance sheet presently may also contract in the future. However, as indicated by the experience of WWI, a rapid contraction of the balance sheet can adversely affect the real economy. A clear illustration of the economics that underlies the payment of interest on reserves should diffuse the misinformed idea that eliminating interest on excess reserves will generate net new additional funds to the Treasury. The chapter shows that funds made available by the sale of Fed assets are then offset by future shortfalls in interest receipts.

References

Amstad, M and A Martin (2011). Monetary policy implementation: Common goals but different practices. *Current Issues in Economics and Finance*, Federal Reserve Bank of New York, 17(7).

Bech, ML and E Klee (2011). The mechanics of a graceful exit: Interest on reserves and segmentation in the federal funds market. *Journal of Monetary Economics,* 58(5), pp. 415–536.

Bernanke, BS (2009). *Federal Reserve policies to ease credit and their implications for the Fed's balance sheet* [Speech]. National Press Club Luncheon, Washington D.C., 18 February.

Carpenter, S and S Demiralp (2012). Money, reserves, and the transmission of monetary policy: does the money multiplier exist? *Journal of Macroeconomics*, 34(1), pp. 59–75.

Eisenbeis, RA (2016). Statement to the House Subcommittee on Monetary and Trade Policy of the Committee on Financial Services. 17 May.

Friedman, M and A Schwartz (1963). A Monetary History of the United States, 1867–1960. In *National Bureau of Economic Research Studies in Business Cycles* (Vol. 12), Princeton, NJ: Princeton University Press.

Hackley, H (1973). *Lending Functions of the Federal Reserve Banks — A History.* Washington, D.C.: Board of Governors of the Federal Reserve System.

Hawtrey, RG (1922). The Federal Reserve System of the United States, *Journal of the Royal Statistical Society*, 85 (2), pp. 224–269.

Humpage, OF (2014). Cooperation, Conflict, and the Emergence of a Modern Federal Reserve. *Economic Commentary*, Federal Reserve Bank of Cleveland, April.

Goldenweiser, EA (1925). *Federal Reserve System in Operation.* New York: McGraw–Hill.

Grant, J (2014). *The Forgotten Depression: 1921: The Crash That Cured Itself.* New York: Simon and Schuster.

Ihrig, JE, EE Meade and GC Weinbach (2015). Rewriting Monetary Policy 101: What's the Fed's preferred post-Crisis approach to raising interest rates? *Journal of Economic Perspectives*, 29 (4), pp. 177–198.

Keister, T (2016). *Interest on Reserves.* Testimony before the House Subcommittee on Monetary and Trade Policy, Committee on Financial Services, 17 May.

Keister, T and GC McAndrews (2009). Why Are Banks Holding So Many Excess Reserves? *Staff Report*, Federal Reserve Bank of New York, No. 380.

Keister, T, A Martin, and GC McAndrews (2008). Divorcing Money from Monetary Policy, *Economic Policy Review*, Federal Reserve Bank of New York, pp. 41–56.

Martin, A, J McAndrews and D Skeie (2011). Bank Lending in Times of Large Bank Reserves. *Staff Report*, Federal Reserve Bank of New York, No. 497.

McLeay, M, A Radia and R Thomas (2014). *Money Creation in the Modern Economy, Quarterly Bulletin*, Bank of England, pp. 1–14.

Meryam B, A Cambron, M Del Negro and J Remache (2013). A History of SOMA Income, *Liberty Street Economics*, Federal Reserve Bank of New York, August.

Meryam B, A Cambron, M Fleming, J McCarthy and J Remache (2012). The SOMA Portfolio through Time, *Liberty Street Economics*, Federal Reserve Bank of New York, August.

Meltzer, AH (2003). *A History of the Federal Reserve, Vol. 1.* Chicago: University of Chicago Press.

Potter, S (2013). *Recent Developments in Monetary Policy Implementation.* Money Marketeers of New York University, 2 December.

Potter, S (2014). *Interest Rate Control During Normalization.* SIFMA Conference on Securities Financing Transactions, New York City, 7 October.

Reed, HL (1922). *Federal Reserve Policy: 1921–1930.* Boston: Houghton–Mifflin.

Reed, HL (1930). *The Development of Federal Reserve Policy.* New York: McGraw–Hill.

Selgin, G (2016). Testimony before the U.S. House of Representatives Committee on Financial Services, Monetary Policy, and Trade Subcommittee Hearing on Interest on Reserves and the Fed's Balance Sheet. 17 May.

Sims, C (2013). Paper money. *American Economic Review*, 103(2), pp. 563–584.

Stella, P (2015). *Exiting Well.* Stellar Consulting, LLC, 23 March.

Toma, M (1989). The policy effectiveness of Open Market operations in the 1920s. *Explorations in Economic History,* 26(1), pp. 99–116.

Wicker, ER (1966). *Federal Reserve Monetary Policy 1917–1933.* New York: Random House.

Wicker, ER (1966). A reconsideration of Federal Reserve monetary policy during the 1920–1921 depression. *Journal of Economic History,* 26(2), pp. 223–238.

Chapter Three

The Federal Reserve's Balance Sheet as a Financial-Stability Tool

Robin Greenwood*

Harvard Business School and The National Bureau of Economic Research

Samuel G. Hanson*

Harvard Business School and The National Bureau of Economic Research

Jeremy C. Stein*

Harvard University and The National Bureau of Economic Research

1. Introduction

In this chapter, we argue that the Federal Reserve should use its balance sheet to help reduce a key threat to financial stability: the tendency for private-sector financial intermediaries to engage in excessive amounts of maturity transformation — i.e., to finance risky assets using dangerously large volumes of runnable short-term liabilities. Specifically, we make the case that the Fed can complement its regulatory efforts on the financial-stability front by maintaining a relatively large balance sheet, even when policy rates have moved well away from the zero lower bound (ZLB). In so doing, it can help ensure that there is an ample supply of government-provided safe short-term claims — e.g., interest-bearing reserves and reverse repurchase agreements. By expanding the overall supply of safe

*This article was originally presented in August 2016 at the Federal Reserve Bank of Kansas City's Economic Policy Symposium, Jackson Hole, WY. It is published with permission from the Federal Reserve Bank of Kansas City. The authors thank Matteo Maggiori, Adi Sunderam and Matt Rutherford for helpful conversations, and Randall Kroszner for his discussion. An Internet Appendix is available at http://www.people.hbs.edu/rgreenwood/JH2016_IA.pdf.

short-term claims, the Fed can weaken the market-based incentives for private-sector intermediaries to issue too many of their own short-term liabilities. And, crucially, we argue that the Fed can crowd out private-sector maturity transformation in this way *without compromising the ability of conventional monetary policy to focus on its traditional dual mandate of promoting maximum employment and stable prices.*

To put our work in context, recall that in recent years, there has been a vigorous debate about whether monetary policy should be used to lean against threats to financial stability, especially when doing so might compromise the central bank's ability to hit its targets for employment and inflation. On one side of the fence, a number of prominent observers have invoked what amounts to a separation principle: monetary policy should stick to its traditional knitting, because it is not possible to satisfactorily solve for multiple goals with a single instrument. According to this view, threats to financial stability should be addressed via enhanced regulation alone. Put differently, the costs of allowing current employment and inflation to deviate from their respective targets are likely to be unacceptably large, compared to any future economic benefits that might accrue from using monetary policy to lean against financial-market imbalances.[1]

On the other side, some have argued that existing regulatory tools are imperfect in both their effectiveness and scope of coverage. And these imperfections may loom particularly large when the configuration of market interest rates and spreads creates strong incentives for financial intermediaries to either "reach for yield" on the asset side of their balance sheets or to fund on an overly short-term basis on the liability side. According to this logic, an advantage of monetary policy is that it "gets in all the cracks," in the sense of acting directly on the market rates and spreads that confront all actors in the financial system, irrespective of the regulatory regime they operate under. Nevertheless, advocates of this viewpoint do not deny that it is less than ideal to have more goals than instruments. Rather, they simply argue that falling short on one particular goal — e.g., current employment relative to target — may be a price that

---

[1] See Bernanke (2002, 2015a), Yellen (2014) and Svensson (2015, 2016a, 2016b) for articulations of this view.

is sometimes worth paying to do better on another goal, namely financial stability, and, by extension, future employment.[2]

Interestingly, while this debate has been going on, the monetary policy toolkit has become more multi-dimensional, as central banks have dramatically expanded their balance sheets in an effort to circumvent the limitations associated with the zero lower bound (ZLB). However, the regulatory and financial-stability implications of larger central-bank balance sheets have not received much attention. Instead, the focus has been on whether, given the ZLB constraint, central bank asset purchases can be an effective substitute for conventional monetary stimulus.

The main message of this chapter is that the added dimensionality that a large central-bank balance sheet affords may be quite valuable away from the ZLB, but no longer for the purpose of providing traditional monetary-policy accommodation. Rather, by influencing the relative yields on safe claims at the front end of the yield curve, a plentiful supply of central-bank liabilities — e.g., interest-bearing reserves or overnight reverse repurchase agreements (RRP) — *can reduce the economic incentives for private-sector intermediaries to engage in excessive amounts of maturity transformation.* Because this incentive effect operates through market-determined prices, it applies to both regulated and unregulated financial intermediaries. Thus, the impact of a large central-bank balance sheet can be said to get in all the cracks of the financial system, much like conventional monetary policy. However, given the extra degree of freedom associated with an additional tool, a central bank that uses its balance sheet in this way would remain free to set the *level* of the short-term policy rate according to the usual macroeconomic stabilization criteria, and would not have to sacrifice meeting its targets for current inflation and employment in order to make further progress on the financial-stability front.

The first step in our argument is to note that much of the time — and particularly away from the ZLB — the very front end of the yield curve tends to be steeply upward-sloping. For example, over the period of 1983 to 2009, the yield on one-week Treasury bills averaged 72 basis points less than the yield on six-month T-bills. A natural interpretation of

---

[2] See, e.g., Borio and Drehmann (2009), Stein (2013, 2014), Adrian and Liang (2016) and Juselius *et al.* (2016).

this phenomenon is that the shortest-maturity safe claims have many of the same properties as traditional money and that certain investors, such as money-market funds, are willing to pay a substantial premium for these moneylike attributes.[3] Moreover, in a world where the Treasury's issuance of the shortest-maturity bills is insufficient to fully satiate this demand for moneylike claims, the resulting money premiums at the front end of the curve create a strong incentive for private-sector intermediaries to fill the void and replicate something like one-week bills, for example, by funding themselves with overnight repurchase agreements or short-maturity asset-backed commercial paper.

This observation suggests a potential crowding-out motive for government debt maturity. In previous work, we and others have documented that when the supply of T-bills increases, this front-end money premium declines in magnitude, and private-sector issuance of short-term paper declines.[4] In other words, when the government creates more in the way of short-term safe claims, it reduces the incentive for the private sector to step in and manufacture such claims. Given the systemic-risk externalities associated with private-sector maturity transformation, we argue that it is desirable for the government to be an aggressive supplier of safe short-term claims, thereby encouraging private firms to lengthen the maturity structure of their own funding. We flesh out this line of reasoning and present some of the relevant empirical evidence in Section 2.

However, even if one accepts the premise that an increased supply of short-term government liabilities would have a beneficial impact on financial stability through this crowding-out channel, it does not follow that the central bank needs to be the institution that provides these claims. The job could instead be handled by the finance ministry. In other words, rather than advocating for the Fed to provide, say, an extra $3 trillion in reserves or RRP to the market so as to discourage private-sector issuance of short-term debt, it would seem that one could equally well recommend that the Treasury Department shorten its debt maturity profile to supply $3 trillion more of short-term bills and $3 trillion less of longer-term bonds.

---

[3] See Gorton (2016), Gorton and Metrick (2012) and Stein (2012).
[4] See Greenwood, Hanson and Stein (2015); Sunderam (2015); Krishnamurthy and Vissing-Jorgensen (2015); and Carlson, Duygan-Bump, Natalucci, Nelson, Ochoa, Stein and Van den Heuvel (2016).

In Section 3, we take on this Fed-versus-Treasury question, and identify the following trade-off. On the one hand, it would appear that the Fed has a comparative advantage in providing very short-term government liabilities, because as the sole provider of the final means of payment, it does not face the same kind of "auction risk" that the Treasury does. Concretely, if the Treasury had to roll over $3 trillion of one-week bills every week at auction, it might be concerned about the possibility that there would be insufficient demand on a given date and that the auction might fail, leaving it unable to pay off the maturing bills and forcing it to default on its obligations. By contrast, while interest-bearing reserves are, in many ways, economically similar to overnight Treasury bills, the Fed does not have to re-auction them in order to pay off investors, and there is no corresponding notion of default. Again, this is because these central bank reserves are already the final means of payment.

Against this advantage of the Fed, there is a potential political-economy disadvantage. When the Fed maintains a larger balance sheet, it effectively takes over a part of the traditional debt management role from the Treasury, along with the associated fiscal risk. For example, if the Fed holds an extra $3 trillion of long-term Treasuries in order to be able to issue $3 trillion of interest-bearing reserves and RRP, it faces correspondingly more variation in its profits — and hence in its remittances to the Treasury — due to variations in the general level of interest rates. Now, from a consolidated government balance sheet perspective, one might argue that it does not matter whether it is the Fed or the Treasury that bears this interest-rate risk: the ultimate taxpayer exposure is the same either way. However, to the extent that the decision of how much of this risk to take is viewed by Congress and the public at large as being in the proper domain of fiscal policy, a Fed that is protective of its political independence might prefer not to be the agency that chooses the government's overall debt-maturity stance, especially when — unlike in the quantitative-easing (QE) era — doing so is not as obviously motivated by an attempt to deliver on its traditional monetary-policy mandate.

While we believe that this political-economy consideration should be taken seriously, we argue that it can be managed to a significant extent. This is because, for the purpose of crowding out private maturity transformation and in sharp contrast to QE, what mostly matters is *the size of the liability side of the Fed's balance sheet, not the total duration of the bonds it holds on the asset side.* As we quantify in detail below, the Fed may be able to accomplish much the same thing from a financial stability perspective by backing its moneylike liabilities with bonds that have an average maturity of somewhere between two to six years, as opposed to the current value of approximately 8.6 years.

In other words, one can envision an outcome in which the Treasury still does almost all of the economically meaningful debt management decision-making with respect to the overall duration of the government debt, and the Fed is only responsible for the "last mile" with relatively little consequence for the consolidated government's exposure to interest-rate risk. Thus, while we argue that the Fed should maintain a relatively large balance sheet measured in nominal dollars going forward, we do not believe that it needs to maintain its large current net interest-rate exposure. Indeed, our calculations suggest that, once the need for QE-style monetary accommodation wanes, the Fed can significantly reduce its current interest-rate exposure while continuing to supply a similar quantity of moneylike claims. Such a strategy should help to ease any political-economy concerns about the Fed overstepping its fiscal boundaries.

In Section 4, we turn to a series of more detailed implementation issues. The first of these concerns the appropriate mix of the Fed's liabilities in terms of reserves versus RRP. In its communications to date, the Fed has expressed reservations about the RRP program, saying that it "will use an overnight RRP facility only to the extent necessary and will phase it out when it is no longer needed to help control the federal funds rate."[5] We argue that, from the perspective of our crowding-out paradigm, these reservations are misplaced. An advantage of the RRP program is that it creates a set of safe claims that are available to a wide range of investors, including, for example, money-market funds. By contrast, only regulated depository institutions are eligible to earn interest on reserves. If the ultimate goal is to offer a form of short-term government debt that competes effectively as a substitute for short-term private-sector claims, the wider eligibility

---

[5]Federal Reserve Open Market Committee statement on "Policy Normalization Principles and Plans," September 17, 2014, available at http://www.federalreserve.gov/newsevents/press/monetary/20140917c.htm.

associated with the RRP program is a significant advantage. To be clear, the logic of our crowding-out argument in Sections 2 and 3 suggests that the ideal policy would be for the Fed to directly issue short-term securities — i.e., "Fed bills" — that can be held by all investors. Our proposal to significantly expand the RRP program can thus be seen as a second-best approximation to this ideal, but one that can be comfortably achieved in the current institutional framework.

As a practical matter, this logic implies that it is desirable to reduce the wedge, which currently stands at 25 basis points, between the interest that the Fed pays on reserves (IOR) and the interest it pays on overnight RRP. Doing so would encourage a Fed liability mix more heavily tilted toward RRP and one that more efficiently crowds out private-sector creation of moneylike claims. Indeed, in the spirit of Milton Friedman, a natural frictionless benchmark would be one in which the Fed effectively sells its liabilities to the highest bidder, which would amount to allowing these rates to be driven to equality in equilibrium.[6] While various real-world frictions may ultimately weigh against going all the way to this IOR-equals-RRP limit, it seems to us like a more natural starting point for discussion, as opposed to the current policy, which begins with a strong and not-clearly-articulated presumption against the RRP program.[7]

Section 4 also considers the interaction of the liability side of the Fed's balance sheet with two of the most important regulatory innovations in recent years, namely the supplementary leverage ratio (SLR) and the liquidity coverage ratio (LCR). For example, we note that the SLR has had the effect of taxing a relatively benign form of private-sector money creation that occurs when dealer banks offer their customers the ability to repo finance their inventories of long-term Treasuries. To the extent that the Fed steps in and takes over this specific money-creation role by doing more RRP against its own holdings of Treasury bonds, it can be said to be

---

[6]Friedman (1969) argued that the government should expand the monetary base until the opportunity cost of holding money was equal to the social cost of creating additional money.

[7]In this regard, we are following Gagnon and Sack (2014), who argue in favor of this RRP-equals-IOR limit and a permanent expansion of the Fed's balance sheet, emphasizing that these changes would enhance monetary control, create an efficient level playing field between banks and nonbank financial institutions and save money for taxpayers. Bernanke (2015b) also points out that an expanded Fed balance sheet would enhance monetary transmission and alleviate the shortage of safe assets.

helpfully compensating for the distortion created by the SLR. We view this as another variation on our core theme, which is that the Fed's balance sheet can, if thoughtfully deployed, serve as a valuable complement to its efforts on the regulatory front.

Finally, in Section 5, we ask whether the crowding-out motive that we emphasize applies with greater force in some interest-rate environments than in others. We conjecture that it may become all the more urgent for the Fed to use its balance sheet to lean against private-sector money creation when short rates move away from the ZLB. This is because, when short rates are very low, investors seeking a safe place to put their cash are likely to be content with insured bank deposits, which represent a relatively stable source of funding for the financial system. However, as short-term market rates rise, the rates on certain bank deposit products (transactions accounts, savings accounts) tend to lag behind, and we provide evidence that funds flow out of these products and into money-market funds, which in turn invest in more runnable types of claims such as wholesale bank CDs, asset-backed commercial paper, and repo.[8] In other words, rising short-term rates tend to be associated with a change in the composition of financial-sector liabilities, away from sticky insured bank deposits and toward more flighty forms of what might be called shadow-bank money. Thus, as rates rise, it arguably becomes all the more important to have a policy tool that can mitigate the risks associated with such shadow-bank money creation.

2. The Crowding-Out Role of Short-Term Government Liabilities

In this section, we review the basic crowding-out argument from Greenwood, Hanson and Stein (2015), hereafter GHS. We then summarize some of the supporting empirical evidence. In the internet Appendix, we sketch a simplified version of the GHS model.

2.1. *The logic of crowding out private-sector maturity transformation*

GHS begins with the observation that there is a *special demand for financial claims that are safe, short term and liquid* — i.e., claims that

---

[8]Our argument in Section 5 is based on ongoing research Hanson is carrying out with Juliane Begenau and Adi Sunderam, both of Harvard Business School.

share many of the core attributes of traditional money. As a result, these moneylike financial claims, including Treasury bills and highly-rated short-term private debt, typically command a meaningful money premium in equilibrium — i.e., they offer rates of interest that appear to be too low from a textbook risk-return perspective.

Chart 3.1 plots the evolution of moneylike claims in the U.S. economy as a percentage of gross domestic product (GDP) from 1951–2015, broken down by different instruments in Panel A and by different end-users in the nonfinancial sector in Panel B. In Chart 3.1, we estimate the net supply of moneylike claims to nonfinancial end users. Note that because financial intermediaries themselves hold many moneylike claims, this net supply is far lower than the gross supply of these claims.[9] Chart 3.1 shows that total moneylike claims began at 42 percent of GDP in 1951, declined steadily until 1978 when they bottomed at 22 percent of GDP, and have risen back to 42 percent of GDP in 2015.

What are these moneylike claims? The claims in Chart 3.1 include T-bills, checking deposits, money market fund shares, as well as other short-term private debt (open market paper, repurchase agreements, and foreign deposits).[10] The U.S. Treasury can create moneylike claims by issuing short-term T-bills. Alternatively, the Federal Reserve can do so by issuing reserves or reverse repurchase agreements to finance purchases of longer-term Treasury bonds, which are also safe but do not command the same money premium due to their longer maturity. Private financial intermediaries can also issue moneylike claims. This function is performed by traditional insured depository institutions that offer government-insured checking deposits, as well as by more lightly regulated shadow banks that create uninsured moneylike claims — money market fund shares, open market paper and repurchase agreements — backed by assets that are sometimes risky, long term, or illiquid.

Turning to the composition of moneylike claims, Panel A shows that government-backed moneylike claims — checking deposits and T-bills — have declined in relative importance compared to money fund shares and

---

[9]See Gallin (2013) for a discussion of the difference between gross and net financial intermediation flows as well as a rigorous approach to estimating the latter based on the Financial Accounts of the United States.

[10]Chart 3.1 does not include savings deposits, which are typically longer term and less liquid than moneylike claims.

Chart 3.1.   Moneylike Claims.

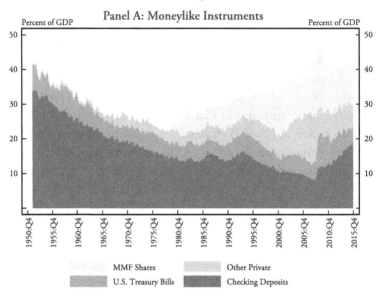

Panel A: Moneylike Instruments

Percent of GDP

MMF Shares   Other Private

U.S. Treasury Bills   Checking Deposits

Panel B: Nonfinancial Holders of Moneylike Claims

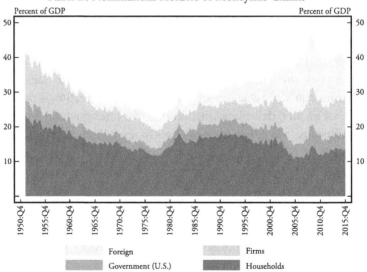

Foreign   Firms

Government (U.S.)   Households

←——

(caption continued) This chart plots moneylike claims — i.e., short-term, safe, liquid claims—held by end-users in the nonfinancial sector as a percentage of U.S. GDP on a quarterly basis from 1951 to 2015. Panel A shows holdings by instrument. Panel B shows holdings by holder type. All series are based on the Financial Accounts of the United States. Moneylike claims consist of checkable deposits and currency, U.S. Treasury bills, money market fund shares, other uninsured short-term safe assets held directly by the nonfinancial sector (open market paper, repurchase agreements and foreign deposits). Savings deposits are not included. The nonfinancial sector consists of households, nonfinancial businesses, the U.S. federal, state, and local government, and the rest of the world. Holdings of T-bills are estimated by taking the product of each sector's total holdings of U.S. Treasuries and the fraction of marketable Treasuries that are bills from Table L.210.

other short-term private debt. Specifically, checking deposits and T-bills accounted for over 99 percent of all moneylike claims in 1951. This fraction fell somewhat during the late 1970s and then fell rapidly from 1995 to 2007, reaching just 31 percent in the second quarter of 2007 on the eve of the financial crisis. Since the crisis, these government-backed moneylike claims have accounted for a growing fraction of the total, rising to 58 percent in 2015.

Where does the demand for these claims come from? Panel B shows household ownership of moneylike claims has been fairly stable over the past 65 years, averaging 16 percent of GDP. However, corporate holdings of such claims have increased substantially since the early 1990s, rising from five percent of GDP in the fourth quarter of 1990 to 10 percent in fourth quarter of 2015.[11] Consistent with Bernanke's (2005) discussion of a global savings glut, foreign holdings of U.S.-produced moneylike claims have also risen sharply since the early 2000s.[12]

How much moneylike short-term debt should the Treasury and Federal Reserve issue to the public? GHS points out that while issuing more short-term debt may help satiate the public's demand for these securities (and also lower the government's overall cost of financing), doing so exposes the government to the risk that it will have to refinance maturing debt at higher interest rates in the future. Because large shocks to the interest bill can force the government to either raise taxes or cut back on desirable expenditures,

----

[11] See Bates, Kahle and Stulz (2009) for an analysis of the evolution of corporate cash holdings.
[12] See also Caballero, Farhi and Gourinchas (2008), and Caballero and Farhi (2016) on the macroeconomic implications of the demand for safe assets.

fiscal prudence — the desire to smooth tax rates and expenditures over time — suggests it is unwise for the government to be overly reliant on short-term debt. Greenwood, Hanson, Rudolph and Summers (2015) point out that the same fiscal risk logic applies to the Federal Reserve, since buying long-term Treasury bonds and mortgage-backed securities financed with interest-bearing reserves or RRP introduces volatility into the remittances that the Fed ultimately returns to Treasury.

Thus, if the government were the only actor in the economy that could issue moneylike claims, the optimal maturity of government debt would be pinned down by a simple trade-off that balances the direct monetary benefits of issuing shorter-term debt against the greater fiscal risk that doing so entails. This logic suggests that concerns about refinancing risk should become more important as the total debt burden goes up, and the government therefore should opt for a longer debt maturity as the debt-to-GDP ratio rises. As can be seen in Chart 3.2, this prediction is consistent with U.S. government debt management policy during the post-war era. The chart plots the weighted average maturity of outstanding U.S. government debt against the debt-to-GDP ratio using monthly data from 1952 to 2015. The two series are strongly positively correlated — the correlation coefficient is 0.61. Indeed, as debt levels have increased sharply since the 2008 financial crisis, Treasury officials have cited refinancing risk as a material consideration driving their recent decision to term out the maturity of the debt.[13]

However, the government's choice of how much moneylike paper to issue is complicated by the fact that the private sector can also issue short-term moneylike claims. Financial intermediaries find short-term debt attractive for the same reason as the government: because of the money premium, it is cheaper than longer-term funding. But, private money creation comes with its own set of risks. In particular, private financial intermediaries that rely heavily on short-term financing may be forced to liquidate assets in the event of an adverse shock. As a result, short-term financing may amplify the transmission of financial distress

---

[13] According to the minutes from the November 2009 Treasury Borrowing Advisory Committee (TBAC) meeting, the TBAC recommended "lengthening the average maturity of debt from 53 months to 74–90 months" based on the "potential for inflation, higher interest rates, and rollover risk." See https://www.treasury.gov/press-center/press-releases/ Pages/tg348.aspx.

Chart 3.2.   Government Lengthens Debt Maturity as Debt/GDP Rises.

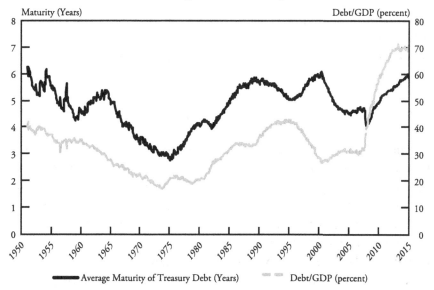

Maturity (Years)   Debt/GDP (percent)

■■■■■ Average Maturity of Treasury Debt (Years)   ▀▀ ▀▀   Debt/GDP (percent)

Note: The chart plots the weighted average maturity of Treasury debt versus the debt-to-GDP ratio. The average maturity of Treasury debt is based on authors' calculations using the CRSP government debt database.

across institutions, as one intermediary's fire sales cause price declines that threaten the solvency of others and, potentially, the stability of the broader financial system. These threats — which stem from the financing choices of private financial intermediaries — are not taken fully into account when individual intermediaries choose how to fund themselves. Thus, there is an externality associated with capital structure choice that leads to a socially excessive level of private short-term funding (Stein, 2012).

One response to this externality is to try to limit intermediaries' use of short-term debt with regulation. The recently-introduced liquidity coverage ratio (LCR) and net stable funding ratio (NFSR) rules, for example, are attempts to reign in excessive maturity transformation. However, such regulations may only be partially effective, because they do not apply to shadow banks, leading activity to migrate to unregulated intermediaries. Moreover, any form of regulation may have its own deadweight costs, for example, by discouraging certain desirable activities along with the undesirable ones.

Given the imperfections of regulation, GHS argues that a useful complement to a purely regulatory approach is for the government to issue more short-term debt than it otherwise would in a world with no externalities in private-sector money creation. The idea is that, by issuing additional short-term debt itself, the government can depress the moneylike yield premium on short-term debt, thereby reducing its attractiveness as a form of financing for private-sector intermediaries. A key assumption underlying this argument is that short-term government debt and short-term private debt are partial substitutes for each other.

In summary, GHS presents two reasons for the government to supply the economy with an ample amount of short-term debt. The first is that it is cheap to do so, reflecting the monetary benefits accruing to the holders of short-term government claims; the financing savings realized are effectively a generalized form of seignorage. The second is the crowding-out argument developed above. Importantly, the logic of crowding out implies that the appeal of providing short-term government claims is greater in settings where either: (1) regulation imposes greater unintended costs on the economy; or (2) private-sector money creation can more readily migrate from the regulated traditional banking sector to the less-regulated shadow banking sector. We believe that the latter qualification applies particularly well to the institutional environment in the U.S. and other advanced economies. And as we argue in Section 5, it may become all the more relevant once interest rates begin to rise meaningfully above the ZLB.

2.2. *Empirical support for the crowding-out argument*

Our crowding-out argument rests on three related assumptions. First, there is a special demand for moneylike claims. Second, the demand for moneylike claims is downward sloping, so the government can influence the premium on moneylike claims by adjusting the supply of T-bills, or in the Fed's case, the supply of reserves or RRP. Third, short-term government debt and short-term private debt are partial substitutes, so changes in the money premium caused by shifts in government supply also influence the amount of private maturity transformation. GHS presents detailed evidence in support of these claims; we summarize and update the relevant evidence here.

2.2.1. *The money premium on short-term treasuries*

A simple way to illustrate the premium commanded by the shortest-term Treasury bills is shown in Panel A of Chart 3.3, which plots the average spread between the 26-week bill and bills of various other maturities over the sample period of 1983 to 2009. On average, the one-week T-bill offers a yield that is 72 basis points less than that of a 26-week bill.

A limitation of looking at raw T-bill yields is that we may conflate the fact that the term structure is upward sloping simply because investors expect rates to rise, with the specific money premium that we seek to capture here.[14] In an effort to control for the general shape of the term structure, Panel A of Chart 3.3 also shows the average spread from 1983 to 2009 between actual T-bill yields and fitted T-bill yields. The fitted yields are based on the flexible model of the Treasury yield curve from Gürkaynak, Sack and Wright (2007). Gürkaynak *et al.* estimate Svensson's (1995) six-parameter model of the yield curve using notes and bonds with remaining maturities greater than three months. The n-week "z-spread", $z_t^{(n)} = y_t^{(n)} - \hat{y}_t^{(n)}$, captures the extent to which n-week T-bills have yields that differ from what one would expect based on a flexible extrapolation of the rest of the yield curve, i.e., that portion from three months on out.

As can be seen in the chart, the z-spreads for short-term bills are economically large. Four-week bills have yields that are roughly 40 basis points *below* their fitted values. And, for one-week bills, the average z-spread is about 60 basis points. Our interpretation of these z-spreads is that they reflect a moneylike premium on short-term T-bills, above and beyond any safety and liquidity premiums embedded in longer-term Treasury yields.[15]

A second way to cleanly capture the premium associated with short-term T-bills — and to net out the effects associated with the expectations

---

[14]In practice, it seems unlikely that expectations of rising interest rates could explain the sizable 72 basis point average spread between one-week and 26-week bills. For instance, from their introduction in late 1988 until 2009, the average spread between six-month fed funds futures and the current effective fed funds rate was only eight basis points.

[15]Krishnamurthy and Vissing-Jorgensen (2012) argue that all Treasuries, including long-term Treasuries, embed a safety and liquidity premium that reduces their yields relative to a textbook risk-versus-return view. They estimate that this premium on long-term Treasuries averaged 73 basis points from 1926 to 2008. However, the money premiums in Chart 3.3 reflect a further premium on short-term Treasuries above and beyond that on long-term Treasuries.

Chart 3.3.   The Money Premium on Short-Term Treasury Bills.

Panel A: Yield Spreads on Short-Term Treasury Bills

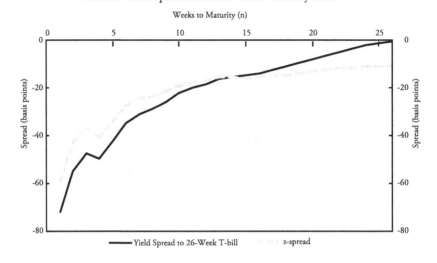

Panel B: Excess Returns over One-Week Treasury Bills

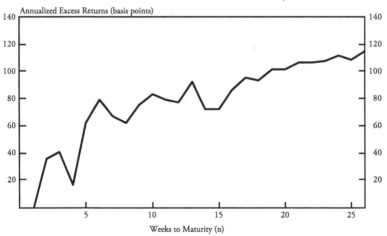

Note: Panel A plots the average spread, over the period of 1983 to 2009, between T-bill yields of maturities from one to 26 weeks and the yield on the 26-week bill. It also plots the z-spread, defined as the difference between T-bill yields and fitted yields, where fitted yields are based on the flexible extrapolation of the Treasury yield curve from Gürkaynak, Sack, and Wright (2007). Panel B shows average excess returns of n-week T-bills over the one-week bill return over the same time period. Panel A follows Greenwood, Hanson and Stein (2015); Panel B follows Carlson, Duygan-Bump, Natalucci, Nelson, Ochoa, Stein and Van den Heuvel (2016).

hypothesis — is shown in Panel B, where we plot the realized annualized returns of holding a T-bill with n weeks to maturity in excess of the one-week bill rate, computed over the same 1983 to 2009 period. These results follow Carlson *et al.* (2016), with the logic being that if a money premium exists, then it should be more profitable to buy bills with longer maturities and hold them, as opposed to rolling over a series of one-week bills. Panel B of Chart 3.3 confirms that this is indeed the case.

2.2.2. The response of the money premium to shifts in treasury bill supply

The plots in Chart 3.3 refer to the *average level* of the money premium. But in the time series, the value of this premium depends on the supply of T-bills, consistent with a downward-sloping demand curve for short-term moneylike claims. Chart 3.4 shows that z-spreads are less negative — i.e., the shortest-maturity T-bills have relatively higher yields — when the supply of T-bills is larger. Specifically, each quarter from 1983 to 2009, we plot the average z-spread for four-week bills alongside the ratio of T-bills

Chart 3.4. The Money Premium on T-Bills and the Supply of T-Bills, 1983 to 2009.

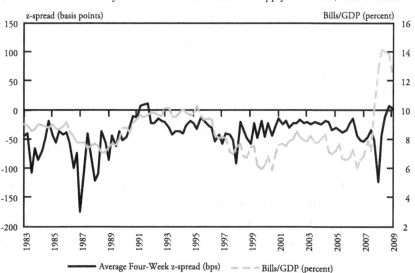

Note: The chart plots the four-week z-spread against the ratio of T-bills to GDP. The z-spread is the difference between T-bill yields and fitted yields, where fitted yields are based on the flexible extrapolation of the Treasury yield curve from Gürkaynak, Sack and Wright (2007).

to GDP. As can be seen, there is a positive relationship between the two series in levels ($R^2 = 0.19$); when there are more of the safest short-term securities, the convenience premium on these securities declines.

Table 3.1 shows this more formally. We estimate weekly regressions of the n-week z-spread on *BILLS/GDP* for $n = 2, 4$ and 10:

$$z_t^{(n)} = a^{(n)} + b^{(n)} \cdot (BILLS/GDP)_t + c^{(n)} \cdot t + \varepsilon_t^{(n)}. \tag{1a}$$

To compute *BILLS/GDP* each week, we use detailed data on the size and timing of Treasury auctions. We include a linear time trend as a control to remove any common trends in the data. Table 3.1 shows that z-spreads respond positively to the supply of T-bills. For instance, the coefficient of 5.8 ($t = 2.3$) in column (1) of Panel A means a 1-percentage-point increase in the ratio of bills to GDP (roughly half of a standard deviation) leads to an increase of 5.8 basis points in the two-week z-spread. As in Chart 3.2, Table 3.1 shows that the effect is strongest for very short-term bills: the coefficient on the two-week spread is more than twice that for the 10-week spread.

We next estimate Equation (1a) in changes to focus on the high-frequency variation in the data. Specifically, we regress four-week changes in the *n*-week z-spread on four-week changes in *BILLS/GDP* for $n = 2, 4$ and 10:

$$\Delta_4 z_t^{(n)} = a^{(n)} + b^{(n)} \cdot \Delta_4 (BILLS/GDP)_t + \varepsilon_t^{(n)}. \tag{1b}$$

Columns (4) to (6) of Panel A show that, when estimated in changes, the slope coefficients $b^{(n)}$ are generally larger than the estimates from the levels regressions in columns (1) to (3). However, the estimates are not significant for the full 1983–2009 period.[16]

Because bill yields and bill supply are simultaneously determined in equilibrium, this evidence is subject to an obvious endogeneity concern. Specifically, the government might respond to a rise in the demand for short-term moneylike assets by tilting its issuance toward bills. Indeed, Chart 3.4 shows that *BILLS/GDP* jumps in the fall of 2008 just as z-spreads plummet — the telltale sign of an endogenous supply response to positive

---

[16]Consistent with the idea that there is a special demand for short-term safe assets as opposed to simply all safe assets irrespective of their maturity, GHS shows that z-spreads respond strongly to fluctuations in T-bill supply but not to fluctuations in nonbill Treasury supply.

Table 3.1: The Money Premium on T-Bills and the Supply of T-Bills, 1983 to 2009.

	Levels			Four-week Changes		
	Two-week z (1)	Four-week z (2)	10-week z (3)	Two-week z (4)	Four-week z (5)	10-week z (6)
Panel A: 1983 to 2009 (N = 1,408)						
$b^{(n)}$	5.78	4.17	1.96	15.75	7.59	0.65
[t]	[2.30]	[1.74]	[1.19]	[1.55]	[1.20]	[0.22]
$c^{(n)}$	28.06	33.62	−13.13			
[t]	[3.36]	[3.66]	[−2.20]			
R^2	0.05	0.08	0.06	0.01	0.00	0.00
Panel B: 1983 to 2007 (N = 1,303)						
$b^{(n)}$	16.73	13.80	6.21	34.89	20.29	7.41
[t]	[7.73]	[7.17]	[6.59]	[6.35]	[5.04]	[3.67]
$c^{(n)}$	60.22	61.52	2.62			
[t]	[7.49]	[7.58]	[0.61]			
R^2	0.11	0.17	0.15	0.03	0.02	0.02

Note: The table reports weekly regressions of z-spreads on the supply on T-bills scaled by GDP. The n-week z-spread $z_t^{(n)} = y_t^{(n)} - \hat{y}_t^{(n)}$ is the difference between the actual yield on an n-week T-bill and the n-week fitted yield, based on the fitted Treasury yield curve in Gürkaynak, Sack and Wright (2007). We estimate this specification in both levels and four-week differences:

$$z_t^{(n)} = a^{(n)} + b^{(n)} \cdot (BILLS/GDP)_t + c^{(n)} \cdot t + \varepsilon_t^{(n)} \text{ and } \Delta_4 z_t^{(n)}$$
$$= a^{(n)} + b^{(n)} \cdot \Delta_4 (BILLS/GDP)_t + \varepsilon_t^{(n)}.$$

To compute the ratio of T-bills to GDP at the end of each week, we use data on the size and timing of Treasury auctions from http://www.treasurydirect.gov/. The units of the dependent variable are basis points and the units of the independent variables are percentage points. T-statistics are shown in brackets. For the levels regressions in columns (1) to (3), we compute standard errors assuming that the residuals follow an AR(1) process. For the changes regressions in columns (4) to (6), we compute Newey-West (1987) standard errors, allowing for serial correlation up to eight weeks. Additional related results are shown in Table 3.1 of Greenwood, Hanson and Stein (2015).

demand shock. If T-bill supply responds to money demand shocks, this would tend to bias our OLS estimates downward. To address this concern, we focus on the 1983 to 2007 period in Panel B of Table 3.1, thereby omitting the financial crisis and focusing on a period when the demand for moneylike financial claims was arguably more stable. As expected, the coefficients are roughly twice as large and are more precisely estimated when we omit 2008 to 2009. For instance, the estimated response of two-week z-spreads to a 1-percentage-point increase in *BILLS/GDP* rises from 5.8 basis points in Panel A to 16.7 basis points in Panel B.

Admittedly, simply dropping the outlying 2008 and 2009 observations is *ad hoc*. To better address this endogeneity concern, GHS adopts an instrumental-variables strategy designed to exploit plausibly exogenous variation in T-bill supply. Specifically, we rely on the fact that much of the high-frequency variation in the supply of T-bills is associated with seasonal fluctuations in tax receipts: the Treasury tends to expand the supply of short-term bills ahead of statutory tax deadlines (e.g., April 15) to meet its ongoing cash needs, and these borrowings are then repaid rapidly following the deadlines. Thus, in the first stage, we regress $\Delta_4 (BILLS/GDP)$ on a set of week-of-year dummies; in the second stage, we regress changes in z-spreads on fitted values from the first stage. Consistent with the idea that the demand for moneylike claims was fairly stable outside of the 2008 to 2009 episode, these IV estimates are similar to the OLS estimates for 1983 to 2007, but are much larger than the OLS estimates for the 1983 to 2009 sample.

2.2.3. *The response of private-sector issuance to shifts in treasury bill supply*

Next, we provide direct empirical support for the idea that an increase in the supply of short-term government debt crowds out the issuance of short-term financial paper. Specifically, in Table 3.2, we regress the ratio of unsecured financial commercial paper to GDP — arguably the most direct form of private money creation that we can measure at high frequencies — on the ratio of T-bills to GDP. Other than the different dependent variable, the specifications mirror those in Table 3.1. That is, we estimate:

$$(FINCP/GDP)_t = a + b \cdot (BILLS/GDP)_t + c \cdot t + u_t, \qquad (2a)$$

and

$$\Delta_k (FINCP/GDP)_t = a + b \cdot \Delta_k (BILLS/GDP)_t + \Delta_k u_t, \qquad (2b)$$

for changes computed at a variety of different horizons k. We obtain weekly data on outstanding commercial paper from 2001 to 2009, monthly data from 1992 to 2009, and quarterly data from 1952 to 2009. Panel A reports results for samples ending in 2009, and Panel B reports results for samples ending in 2007.

Table 3.2 shows that financial commercial paper issuance falls when the supply of T-bills rises. The estimated coefficients on *BILLS/GDP* and Δ_k (*BILLS/GDP*) in Table 3.2 are almost always negative and statistically significant, with means of −0.13 in Panel A and −0.24 in Panel B. The interpretation is that, on average, for every dollar increase in T-bills, financial commercial paper falls between 14 cents and 24 cents.

Many of the coefficients in Table 3.2 are identified using high-frequency variation in T-bill supply. While this variation provides a useful source of identification in Table 3.1, we would not necessarily expect private issuance to respond as quickly as yields to changes in T-bill supply. Consistent with the notion of gradual adjustment on the part of private intermediaries, the magnitude of the crowding-out coefficient on T-bills in Equation (2b) typically rises as we consider differences at longer horizons. And the coefficients from the levels-on-levels regressions tend to be larger than those on from the differences-on-differences regressions.

Complementary evidence comes from Sunderam (2015), who shows that asset-backed commercial paper (ABCP) issuance is elevated when liquidity premiums on T-bills are high and that increases in T-bill supply depress liquidity premiums and ABCP issuance. Similarly, Carlson *et al.* (2016) document that increased T-bill issuance crowds out financial commercial paper, nonfinancial commercial paper, ABCP and time deposits. Using vector autoregressions, they find that the supply of private moneylike claims typically responds within two to three months to shocks to the supply of T-bills. Krishnamurthy and Vissing-Jorgensen (2015) take a somewhat related approach that exploits low-frequency variation in government debt supply. Specifically, using annual data from 1875 to 2014, they show that increases in the ratio of U.S. government debt to GDP are associated with reductions in the net short-term debt of the financial sector. However, they focus on changes in all forms of government debt, not just T-bills, so their results are less directly applicable to thinking about optimal debt maturity.

3. Fed versus Treasury as the Primary Supplier of Short-Term Claims

Thus far, we have argued that by expanding the supply of safe short-term claims, the government can discourage private-sector maturity

Table 3.2: Financial Commercial Paper and the Supply of Short-Term Treasuries.

	Weekly (2001+)		Monthly (1992+)				Quartely (1952+)	
		Four-week		One-mo	Three-mo	12-mo		Four-qtr
	Levels	Changes	Levels	Changes	Changes	Changes	Levels	Changes
	(1)	(2)	(3)	(4)	(5)	(6)	(7)	(8)
Panel A: Samples ending in 2009								
b	−0.174	−0.139	−0.165	−0.060	−0.115	−0.210	−0.116	−0.087
[t]	[−2.79]	[−3.21]	[−2.20]	[−1.39]	[−6.43]	[−5.34]	[−0.14]	[−3.22]
c	0.197		−0.018				0.051	
[t]	[0.35]		[−3.12]				[1.84]	
N	469	465	214	213	211	202	232	228
SEs	AR1	NW 8	AR1	NW 0	NW 6	NW 24	AR1	NW 8
R^2	0.42	0.14	0.56	0.03	0.12	0.45	0.74	0.11
Panel B: Samples ending in 2007								
b	−0.592	−0.082	−0.528	−0.043	−0.081	−0.527	0.017	−0.073
[t]	[−7.18]	[−2.28]	[−6.07]	[−1.24]	[−1.56]	[−8.32]	[0.13]	[−1.98]
c	−0.549	−0.032					0.055	
[t]	[−2.51]	[−6.90]					[2.03]	
N	364	360	190	189	187	178	224	220
SEs	AR1	NW 8	AR1	NW 0	NW 6	NW 24	AR1	NW 8
R^2	0.70	0.04	0.72	0.01	0.02	0.54	0.78	0.06

Note: The table reports regressions of financial commercial paper supply on the supply on T-bills scaled by GDP: $(FINCP/GDP)_t = a + b \cdot (BILLS/GDP)_t + c \cdot t + u_t$ and $\Delta_k(FINCP/GDP)_t = a + b \cdot \Delta_k(BILLS/GDP)_t + \Delta_k u_t$.

Weekly data on outstanding unsecured financial commercial paper are available from the Federal Reserve starting in 2001, monthly data are available from the Federal Reserve starting in 1992, and quarterly data are available from Table 209 of the Financial Accounts of the United States starting in 1952. (To maintain comparability with the recent weekly and monthly data, we use open market paper issued by "financial businesses" less open market paper issued by "ABS issuers" in Table 209.) Data on T-bills outstanding are constructed using data on Treasury auctions and from the Monthly Statement of the Public Debt. We include marketable Treasury certificates (interest-bearing issues with original maturities less than one year) that the Treasury issued until 1967 in our T-bills measure. T-statistics are shown in brackets. For the levels regressions, we compute standard errors assuming that the residuals follow an AR(1) process. For the changes regressions, we compute Newey-West (1987) standard errors. For each specification, the table lists the number of lags used in computing Newey-West standard errors. Panel A shows results for samples ending in 2009; Panel B shows results for samples ending in 2007. Additional related results are in Table 3.2 of Greenwood, Hanson and Stein (2015).

transformation, thereby complementing its efforts on the regulatory front. However, this line of reasoning does not establish a unique role for the Federal Reserve. After all, any desired supply increase could, in principle, be implemented simply by having the Treasury issue more short-term bills, thereby shortening the average maturity of the government debt. Indeed, Congress has historically delegated the choice of debt maturity to the Treasury and not to the Fed. Also, many would argue that this arrangement is appropriate given the inherently fiscal nature of these debt management choices: the maturity of the government's debt determines taxpayers' exposure to interest-rate risk. So why should the Fed, as opposed to the Treasury, take the lead in expanding the supply of short-term safe claims?

3.1. The Fed's comparative advantage: Supplier of final means of payment

To answer this question, it is useful to begin by looking at the Treasury's issuance behavior at the very front end of the yield curve. As of year-end 2015, the weighted average maturity of the outstanding public debt was 5.7 years. Just 11 percent of the outstanding debt was in the form of T-bills, and only 3.6 percent of the debt (just 2.6 percent of GDP) was in bills maturing in less than 30 days — precisely those bills that our analysis of yield differentials in the previous section suggested are in the greatest demand by investors looking for money like debt instruments.

It is interesting to contrast the Treasury's issuance behavior at the front end of the curve with that of private financial intermediaries. Chart 3.5 compares the maturity distribution of T-bills with that of privately issued commercial paper as of year-end 2015. We plot the cumulative percentage of each instrument outstanding by weeks to maturity. The chart makes clear that the private sector is much more aggressive than the Treasury in providing the shortest maturity claims. Moreover, by focusing just on commercial paper — and omitting other private money-market instruments such as repurchase agreements, which are usually structured as overnight loans — the figure significantly understates the differential between Treasury and private-sector intermediaries. Considering the financial stability risks associated with very short-term private funding, we find this divergence to be particularly striking.

Chart 3.5.   Comparing the Maturity Distribution of T-Bills with that of Commercial Paper.

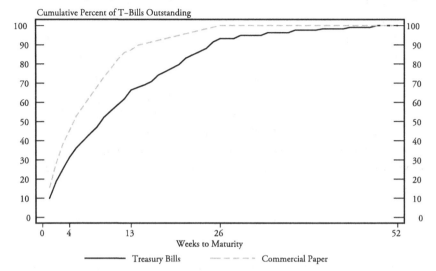

Note: The chart compares the maturity distribution of T-bills with that of commercial paper as of year-end 2015, and is based on data from CRSP and the Federal Reserve (https://www.federalreserve.gov/releases/cp/yrend.htm). The maturity breakdown for commercial paper is for all commercial paper and includes unsecured nonfinancial paper, unsecured financial paper and asset-backed commercial paper.

What explains the Treasury's apparent reluctance to more fully satiate the market's demand for short-term bills, thereby leaving a large void for the private sector to fill? In public testimony, Treasury officials tend to speak of a trade-off between the lower costs associated with financing at the short end of the yield curve versus the increased "refunding risk" that such an approach necessarily entails.[17] Evidently, this refunding risk limits the Treasury's willingness to finance itself using short-term T-bills as a general matter and (as we noted earlier) does so even more when the aggregate debt burden goes up, since refunding risk looms larger in absolute dollar terms at those times.

For our purposes, it is crucial to distinguish between two different types of refunding risk. The first, which we label "duration risk," captures the idea

---

[17] See Gensler (1998) and Ramanathan (2008). In congressional testimony, Gensler argued that "Treasury finances across the yield curve" because "a balanced maturity structure mitigates refunding risks."

that the shorter the average maturity of the debt, the more the government's interest expense — and hence required future tax rates — will increase if the general level of interest rates rises. To the extent that the deadweight losses from taxation are a convex function of tax rates, the Treasury should limit its duration risk exposure in order to limit the variability of tax rates over time. This is the form of fiscal risk that we discussed in the previous section when reviewing the GHS model and that has been explored in a large literature on optimal government debt maturity.[18]

A second distinct type of refunding risk might be called "auction risk." The idea here is that as debt maturity becomes more skewed toward shorter-term bills, the Treasury has to conduct larger and more frequent T-bill auctions, and such auctions are, independent of the general level of interest rates, a source of potential concern in their own right. For example, with larger and more frequent T-bill auctions, the probability of an auction failure — e.g., a situation where the Treasury does not receive enough bids to auction the desired quantity of bills at any reasonable price — might be expected to rise. While such a failure might be promptly cured by rounding up more participants and re-running the auction later in the day, the failure itself might be both politically damaging and hurt investor confidence, thereby raising the Treasury's future borrowing costs. Auction risk as we have defined it has received far less attention in the academic literature on government debt maturity, but it figures prominently in practitioner thinking.[19]

With this distinction in place, we can make a couple of observations. First, as noted by Greenwood *et al.* (2015), if the only source of refunding risk for the Treasury was due to duration risk, nothing could be gained by having the Fed issue short-term liabilities instead of the Treasury, as the net impact on the consolidated government balance sheet would

---

[18] See, for example, Barro (1979), Bohn (1990), and Aiyagari, Marcet, Sargent and Seppala (2002).

[19] See Friedman (1964), Cecchetti (1988) and Garbade (2012). Garbade (2004) argues that, prior to the emergence of regular auctions in the early 1970s, the U.S. Treasury paid a significant premium to avoid the potential for an undersubscribed offering. In recent years, the Treasury Borrowing Advisory Committee has cited "reduced rollover risk" as a benefit of issuing longer-term debt (https://www.treasury.gov/resource-center/data-chart-center/quarterly-refunding/Documents/dc-2006-q1.pdf). Other G-7 governments emphasize the importance of auction risk. For instance, the Bank of Canada notes that "execution risk is still the most important risk regardless of market conditions." Indeed, the United Kingdom Treasury suffered high-profile auction failures in 2002 and 2009.

be the same either way. For instance, if the Federal Reserve decided to finance an additional $1 trillion in long-term Treasuries with interest-bearing reserves, the Fed's income — and hence its remittances to the Treasury — would bear the same exposure to rising rates as the Treasury would if it were it to replace $1 trillion in long-term bonds with short-term T-bills. Thus, a desire to help the Treasury manage its duration risk exposure obviously cannot be a coherent rationale for the Fed to maintain a larger balance sheet.

Second, if duration risk were the only problem, then a "barbell" debt management strategy of issuing mostly short-term and long-term debt — while largely avoiding intermediate maturities — might allow the Treasury acting on its own to provide more of the most highly valued short-term claims without meaningfully increasing the government's overall duration risk. Consider the following example. As of December 31, 2015, the average maturity of the $1.5 trillion of T-bills was 83 days, with only $474 billion having a remaining maturity of 30 days or less. Now suppose the Treasury eliminated the $488 billion of bills with maturities greater than 100 days and replaced them with more sought-after 30-day bills. In the simple case where interest-rate movements across the yield curve are governed by a single-factor model, the Treasury could fully offset the duration-exposure impact of this swap by simultaneously replacing $15 billion of 10-year bonds with 30-year bonds.[20] The fact that the Treasury has not made more use of this barbell approach suggests that duration exposure may not be the only factor constraining its issuance of the shortest-maturity T-bills and that auction risk may also play an important role.

A further clue pointing in the same direction is the Treasury's 2014 decision to begin issuing floating-rate notes (FRNs). Treasury FRNs have a contractual maturity of two years but pay a variable interest rate tied to the realized auction yield on 13-week bills. As shown in Chart 3.6, FRNs have

---

[20] Swapping $488 billion of bills with an average maturity of 169 days for 30-day bills achieves a net reduction in maturity of 139 days. At the time of writing, the duration of an on-the-run 30-year Treasury bond was 21.5, and the duration of a 10-year bond was 9.1. To offset the reduction in the maturity of bills, the Treasury could swap $488 × (139 ÷ 365) ÷ (21.5 − 9.1) = $15 billion of 10-year bonds for 30-year bonds. This calculation is only suggestive, because if there is more than one factor governing yield-curve movements, the offset is no longer perfect, although some of the appeal of the barbell approach remains. See Greenwood, Hanson and Stein (2015) for a formal analysis.

Chart 3.6. Yields on Treasury Floating Rate Notes.

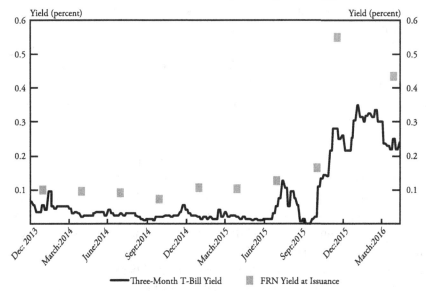

Note: The chart compares the yield at issuance on Treasury Floating Rate Notes (FRNs) with the yield on three-month Treasury bills. The Treasury first began issuing FRNs in January 2014. FRN issues are marked with squares on the chart.
Source: Federal Reserve and Bloomberg.

been issued at nontrivial yield spread to the 13-week bill rate, with FRN investors receiving an average of 11 basis points above the 13-week bill rate. This raises the question of why FRNs are appealing to the Treasury. From a duration-risk perspective, FRNs are identical to 13-week bills, only more expensive. So why not just sell more 13-week bills and pocket the savings? A natural answer is that because FRNs have a longer contractual maturity, they do not have to be rolled over as often and hence contribute less to auction risk. Indeed, a key stated rationale for introducing FRNs was to "reduce Treasury's roll-over burden."[21] Thus, we interpret the existence of expensive FRNs as strong evidence that when the Treasury says it is concerned with "refunding risk," part of what it has in mind is auction risk, rather than pure duration risk.

---

[21] See the minutes from the January 31, 2012, meeting of the Treasury Borrowing Advisory Committee available at https://www.treasury.gov/ press-center/press-releases/Pages/tg1404.aspx.

If this is indeed the case, then there is a meaningful distinction between short-term claims produced by the Fed and the Treasury. And because the Fed is the sole provider of the final legal means of payment, the Fed arguably has an important comparative advantage over the Treasury in supplying such claims. To see this point, think about what happens if the Treasury has a large quantity of maturing T-bills coming due that it needs to roll over at an upcoming auction. It is obligated to pay the holders of these maturing bills in legal tender — i.e., with Fed-created reserves. If for some reason the upcoming bill auction were to fail, the Treasury would be in default on its existing obligation, with all the attendant consequences of such a highly visible default. By contrast, there is no analogous notion of the Fed being at risk of default: a holder of reserves is only ever entitled to ask for either the same reserves, or for currency, which the Fed can also elastically provide. So interest-bearing reserves, while similar to overnight T-bills in terms of their duration risk exposure, effectively do not have to be rolled over and hence involve no auction risk. In this sense, central bank reserves are closer in spirit to infinite-maturity floating rate notes than to overnight Treasury bills.

Relatedly, the Fed can afford to be indifferent to the quantity taken up in its overnight RRP auctions, because if there is less RRP outstanding, the quantity of reserves seamlessly expands to fill the gap.[22] Indeed, the take-up in RRP auctions routinely spikes around quarter-ends due to window-dressing demand from money market funds. For instance, RRP take-up jumped from $162 billion on December 24, 2015, to $475 billion on December 31, before falling back to $117 billion on January 7, 2016. However, because these swings in outstanding RRP are perfectly offset by changes in the quantity of bank reserves, the size of the Fed's balance sheet remains fixed and does not need to expand around quarter-ends.

Chart 3.7 provides some further perspective on the magnitude of the Fed's comparative advantage over the Treasury as a supplier of very short-term claims. We plot selected Fed liabilities alongside the quantity of

---

[22]This observation may help to explain a key difference between T-bill auctions and RRP auctions. In a T-bill auction, the Treasury seeks to sell a fixed quantity of bills, presumably because it has to come up with enough in the way of proceeds to pay off maturing debt. In an RRP auction, the Fed sets a rate and lets the quantity adjust however it may; the Fed does not have to care in any funding-needs sense if the resulting quantity is small or even zero.

Chart 3.7.   Government Supply of Money and Moneylike Claims.

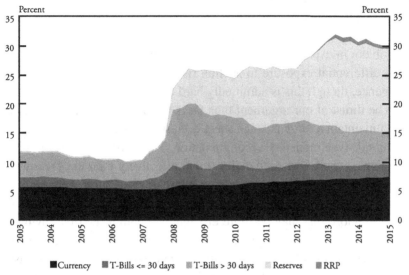

■Currency   ■T-Bills <= 30 days   ■T-Bills > 30 days   Reserves   ■RRP

Note: This chart plots the government supply of money and short-term, moneylike debt claims as a fraction of GDP on a quarterly basis from 2003:Q4 to 2015:Q4. Data on currency in circulation and reserves held by depository institutions are from Table 3.5 of the H.4.1 Release. To smooth over the large seasonal swings in the mix between RRP and reserves, we take quarterly averages of the weekly quantities. Data on outstanding Treasury bills are quarterly averages of month-end quantities, net of month-end Federal Reserve holdings. Data on outstanding volumes for the overnight reverse repurchase agreement (ON RRP) program are available from the Federal Reserve Bank of New York; we plot quarterly averages of daily outstanding volumes in order to smooth out the large quarter-end spikes.

T-bills, with those bills maturing in less than 30 days broken out separately. As of the fourth quarter of 2015, the outstanding quantity of interest-bearing Fed liabilities (reserves and RRP) was over seven times that of the shortest-maturity T-bills. Specifically, on average over the fourth quarter of 2015, there were only $381 billion of outstanding T-bills with a maturity of 30 days or less. However, depository institutions held $2,566 billion of interest-bearing reserves at the Fed, and the outstanding quantity of Fed overnight RRP averaged $127 billion.[23]

---

[23]Our figures for overnight repo do not exactly match end-of-quarter numbers reported in the Financial Accounts of the United States because we purposefully take quarterly averages of daily outstanding

Of course, this does not prove that the Treasury could not supply far more in the way of short-term bills if it were prodded to do so. It only shows that, for whatever reason, it has not done so in the past, even in the face of a strong economic incentive, while the Fed has demonstrably had no problem in expanding its short-term liabilities very rapidly. We suspect that a differential exposure to auction risk lies at the heart of this marked divergence, though this is admittedly hard to prove.

The thrust of our argument thus far is that it may be attractive for the Fed to maintain a large balance sheet even when there is no longer a need for any QE-type monetary accommodation. This is because, in doing so, it can produce short-term safe claims more effectively than the Treasury. In other words, if we decided that we wanted an extra $3 trillion of government-provided short-term claims in order to crowd out private-sector maturity transformation, this may be more efficiently accomplished by having the Fed buy $3 trillion of longer-term bonds from the Treasury and finance these bonds with reserves and RRP, as opposed to having the Treasury retire the same amount of long-term debt and replace it with one-week T-bills. In the former case, there is no issue of auction risk to worry about, while in the latter case the increase in the size and frequency of bill auctions would be unprecedented.

3.2. *The Fed's comparative disadvantage: Taking on fiscal risk*

There is an important caveat to this line of reasoning, however. When the Fed maintains a large balance sheet, thereby converting a significant quantity of longer-term Treasuries into short-term interest-bearing claims, it is effectively taking over part of what has been the Treasury's traditional debt management role, along with the associated interest-rate risk. While the Fed purposefully took on this kind of fiscal risk with its QE programs in the wake of the financial crisis, it did so in the explicit pursuit of its congressionally-mandated objective of returning the economy to full employment while constrained by the ZLB. It would arguably be a bigger stretch relative to the Fed's traditional role to maintain this level of fiscal

---

volumes; we do this to avoid overemphasizing quarter-end spikes in reverse repo that we discussed above.

exposure once the economy has fully recovered, and the ZLB constraint no longer binds.[24]

Indeed, a natural way to interpret the arguments of those who would like to see the Fed's balance sheet revert to its pre-crisis size is that they believe the proper role for an independent Federal Reserve is to take the minimum level of fiscal risk consistent with its dual mandate.[25] According to this view, the fiscal risk-taking associated with debt maturity choice ought to properly be lodged with the executive branch in the Treasury Department, and to deviate from this approach absent a compelling logic grounded in the Fed's monetary-policy mandate runs the risk of jeopardizing the Fed's independence.

While these political-economy concerns deserve to be taken seriously, there are reasons to think that they can be managed to a significant extent. For our purposes, there is a crucial distinction between *the size of the liability side of the Fed's balance sheet and the total dollar duration of the bonds it holds on the asset side.* This is a key difference relative to QE, where it was important for the Fed to buy long-duration bonds so as to depress term premiums. By contrast, if the goal is simply to supply a large quantity of very short-term liabilities, this can be done even if the assets backing these liabilities have a shorter weighted average maturity of, say, two to five years. Thus, even if the nominal size of the Fed's balance sheet was kept at its current level of roughly $4.5 trillion, it should be possible to significantly reduce the amount of fiscal risk that a balance sheet of this size poses.

Chart 3.8 provides some illustrative calculations of how our proposal might work. Panel A shows the current maturity breakdown of marketable Treasury securities, based on data from the Center for Research in Securities Prices (CRSP) and the December 2015 Monthly Statement of the Public Debt. As of December 31, 2015, the outstanding quantity of Treasury debt, consisting of bills, notes, bonds, TIPS and FRNs, totaled $13.2 trillion.

---

[24] Some have suggested that the Fed's large balance sheet, and the associated risk of remittances turning negative, may limit its willingness to raise rates in the future (Woodford, 2012; Bhattarai, Gafarov and Eggertsson, 2015).

[25] Mishkin (2010), Rudebusch (2011) and Dudley (2013) all argue that low or negative remittances could put political pressure on the Fed. See also Del Negro and Sims (2015). Hall and Reis (2013), Christensen, Lopez and Rudebusch (2015), and Carpenter, Ihrig, Klee, Quinn and Boote (2013) explore simulations of remittances and the Federal Reserve's balance sheet under different paths of interest rates.

Chart 3.8.   Marketable Treasury Debt under Different Federal Reserve Balance Sheet Scenarios.

Panel A: Status Quo $2.5 Trillion Treasury Holdings
Fed portfolio WAM = 8.6 years

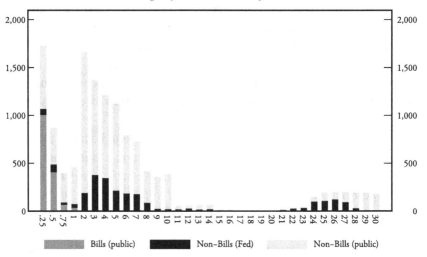

Panel B: Use MBS Proceeds to Expand Treasury Holdings to $4.5 Trillion
Fed portfolio WAM = 8.7 years

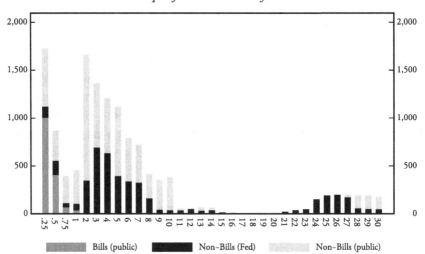

Chart 3.8.   (*Continued*)
Panel C: $4.5 Trillion Portfolio that holds all Treasuries in Proportion to Total Outstanding
Fed portfolio WAM = 6.4 years

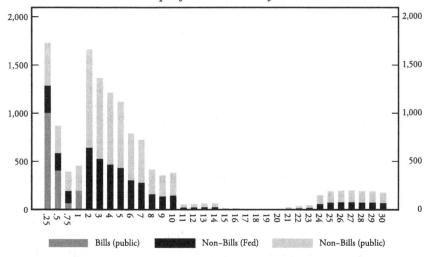

Panel D: $4.5 Trillion Portfolio that holds Treasuries Maturing in ≤ 5 years in Proportion to Outstanding
Fed portfolio WAM = 2.2

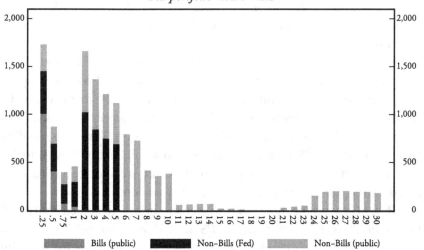

←——

(*caption continued*)   Note: This chart provides a breakdown of marketable Treasury debt as of December 31, 2015, under different Federal Reserve balance sheet scenarios described in the text. Data are based on CRSP and Bloomberg. Since our attention is on the duration exposure of the Fed's portfolio, we classify FRNs based on their next quarterly interest rate reset even though they have an initial contractual maturity of two years. Panel A shows the Fed's actual Treasury holdings at year-end 2015 when the Fed held $2.5 trillion in Treasuries. Panel B assumes that the Fed reinvests its roughly $2 trillion of MBS holdings in Treasuries, bringing its Treasury holdings to $4.5 trillion and maintaining the current maturity structure of its holdings. In Panel C, we assume that the Fed holds $4.5 trillion of Treasury notes and bonds (holding no T-bills), with each bond or note held in proportion to total outstanding. In Panel D, we assume that the Fed holds $4.5 trillion of Treasury notes and bonds but no T-bills, with maturities less than or equal to five years, in proportion to outstanding. For each scenario, we separately mark T-bills, non-bills held by the Fed, and non-bills held by the public.

The public debt had a weighted average maturity of 5.7 years. The black bars in the chart denote the distribution of the Fed's $2.5 trillion of Treasury holdings, which are tilted toward longer-term issues and have a weighted average maturity of 8.6 years. T-bills are marked separately in the chart; note that the Fed currently does not hold any bills. The $1.9 trillion of the Fed's holdings of mortgage-backed securities (MBS) are not shown.

The three remaining panels in Chart 3.8 show alternate scenarios which maintain the current size of the Fed's balance sheet, while varying the weighted average maturity of its Treasury holdings. Each of these scenarios assumes that the Fed runs off its portfolio of MBS and reinvests the proceeds in Treasuries, keeping its balance sheet at $4.5 trillion.

Panel B shows an extreme scenario in which the Fed scales up its current portfolio, reinvesting its MBS proceeds so as to maintain the weighted average maturity of its Treasury holdings at 8.7 years. This scenario would involve large purchases of long-term Treasuries, leading to the Fed owning 100 percent of the outstanding amount of 21-year to 26-year bonds. In this case, for purposes of the chart, we allocate any residual amount over 100 percent to 29-year and 30-year bonds.

Panel C shows the more realistic scenario in which the Fed holds $4.5 trillion of Treasury notes, bonds, TIPS and FRNs — but not T-bills — in proportion to their outstanding amount, thereby mimicking the maturity distribution of outstanding Treasury debt. The Fed currently does not hold any T-bills, and the thrust of our crowding-out argument suggests that this would be a desirable policy going forward: all else equal, the Fed should aim to maximize the amount of short-term government debt available to the public. This scenario takes the average maturity of Treasuries held by the Fed down to 6.4 years, a reduction of 2.2 years from the status quo in Panel A. Since the Fed would own only 39 percent of each outstanding issue in this scenario, such a reconfiguration of the balance sheet seems feasible; by way of comparison, in some longer maturity buckets, the Fed currently owns more than 65 percent of all outstanding issues.

Panel D presents a more aggressive shortening of the Fed's balance sheet: we assume that the Fed concentrates its holdings in all issues (again excluding T-bills) with a remaining maturity of less than five years, holding those securities in proportion to the amount outstanding. This would reduce the weighted average maturity of the Fed's portfolio from 8.6 years to just 2.2 years but would still preserve the Fed's ability to issue a large amount of very short-term claims in the form of excess reserves and reverse repo. To maintain this maturity structure on a \$4.5 trillion balance sheet would involve the Fed owning 62 percent of the outstanding amount of shorter maturity notes and bonds. So while it represents quite a dramatic reduction of the Fed's duration position, even a maturity profile of the sort shown in Panel D does not seem to be pushing the envelope any more so than the Fed's current asset mix, at least in terms of the metric of fractional ownership of individual Treasury issues.

In Table 3.3, we present estimates of how these different configurations of the Fed's balance sheet might impact long-run fiscal risk. We report nine different Fed balance sheet scenarios: three different balance sheet sizes — \$1.5 trillion, \$3 trillion and \$4.5 trillion — and three different asset-side maturity structures — portfolios with weighted average maturities of 2.2, 6.4 and 8.7 years, corresponding to the maturity profiles in Chart 3.8. For each of these scenarios, we present estimates of the long-run volatility of (1) the consolidated government's interest expense, and (2) the net interest income that the Federal Reserve remits to the Treasury. The former is our preferred measure of fiscal exposure, as it captures the more economically relevant notion of taxpayers' overall exposure to rising rates.

The consolidated federal interest expense is the interest that the government pays on its liabilities that are held by the public (i.e., net of Fed holdings), including both publicly held Treasury debt and interest-bearing

Table 3.3: Long-Run Volatility of Consolidated Federal Interest Expense and Federal Reserve Remittances under Different Fed Balance Sheet Profiles.

	Volatility of Consolidated Federal Interest Expense			Volatility of Federal Reserve Remittances		
	WAMFED = 2.2 yrs	WAMFED = 6.4 yrs	WAMFED = 8.7 yrs	WAMFED = 2.2 yrs	WAMFED = 6.4 yrs	WAMFED = 8.7 yrs
	(1)	(2)	(3)	(4)	(5)	(6)
Panel A: $4.5 Trillion Fed Balance Sheet (financed with 1/3 non-interest bearing currency, 2/3 interest bearing reserves)						
St Dev (percent of Treasury debt or percent of Fed assets)	1.09%	1.42%	1.54%	1.28%	1.87%	2.00%
St Dev ($ billion)	$ 141.2	$ 185.0	$ 200.1	$ 57.4	$ 84.3	$ 90.1
Panel B: $3.0 Trillion Fed Balance Sheet (financed with 1/2 non-interest bearing currency, 1/2 interest bearing reserves)						
St Dev (percent of Treasury debt or percent of Fed assets)	1.01%	1.20%	1.29%	1.23%	1.40%	1.48%
St Dev ($ billion)	$ 130.8	$ 156.5	$ 167.1	$ 37.0	$ 42.0	$ 44.5

(Continued)

Table 3.3: (*Continued*)

	Volatility of Consolidated Federal Interest Expense			Volatility of Federal Reserve Remittances		
	WAMFED = 2.2 yrs	WAMFED = 6.4 yrs	WAMFED = 8.7 yrs	WAMFED = 2.2 yrs	WAMFED = 6.4 yrs	WAMFED = 8.7 yrs
	(1)	(2)	(3)	(4)	(5)	(6)
Panel C: $1.5 Trillion Fed Balance Sheet (financed with 100% non-interest bearing currency)						
St Dev (percent of Treasury debt or percent of Fed assets)	0.97%	1.05%	1.09%	2.24%	1.05%	0.76%
St Dev ($ billion)	$126.4	$136.4	$141.7	$33.6	$15.8	$11.4

Note: The table presents estimates of how different configurations of the Fed's balance sheet might impact long-run fiscal risk. The consolidated federal interest expense is defined as the interest on Treasury debt minus the net interest income the Federal Reserve remits to the Treasury. The Federal Reserve's remittances are defined as the interest income the Fed earns on its assets minus the interest that it pays on interest-bearing liabilities. In this table, we assume total Treasury debt of $13 trillion with a weighted average maturity 5.75 years; we assume non-interest bearing currency in circulation of $1.5 trillion. To compute our long-run volatility measures, we simulate the term structure of interest rates using 100,000 years of monthly term structure data, compute the consolidated federal interest expense and remittances using equations (3), (4), and (5), and then take the standard deviation of these series. Term structure data is based on simulations of the model in Greenwood, Hanson and Vayanos (2015) (GHV). We simulate paths of interest rates using the parameters that GHV lists in Table 3.1 of their paper. Their key parameters are chosen to match the time-series volatility and persistence of nominal short rates from 1961 to 2015. Our simulation methodology and the GHV model are described in the online Appendix. The table reports long-run volatilities both in $ billion and as a percentage of the $13 trillion debt (for the consolidated interest expense) and as a percentage of Fed assets (for Fed remittances).

Fed liabilities. The consolidated interest expense in dollars is

$$INT_t^{TOT} = INT_t^{UST} - REMIT_t^{FED}(\tau_{FED}, Z) \tag{3}$$

where INT_t^{UST} is the dollar interest expense on Treasury debt, and $REMIT_t^{FED}(\tau_{FED}, Z)$ is the Fed's remittance to the Treasury in dollars. To simulate the Treasury's interest expense, INT_t^{UST}, we assume a total Treasury debt of $D = \$13$ trillion with a weighted average maturity (WAM) of $\tau_{UST} = 5.7$ years. We assume that the Treasury uses a uniform issuance "ladder." For example, if the Treasury's weighted average maturity was five years, we would assume that each month the Treasury refinances the maturing 10-year bonds that it issued 10 years ago by issuing new 10-year bonds. This implies that the percentage interest expense on a five-year WAM portfolio is just a 120-month moving average of 10-year yields, i.e., $\sum_{j=1}^{120} y_{t-(j-1)}^{(10)}/120$, where $y_t^{(n)}$ denotes the n-year yield at time t. More generally, the interest expense (in dollars) on a total debt of D when the Treasury follows a uniform issuance ladder with a weighted-average maturity of τ_{UST} years is given by:

$$INT_t^{UST} = D \times \frac{\sum_{j=1}^{12 \times \tau_{UST}} y_{t-(j-1)}^{(2 \times \tau_{UST})}}{12 \times \tau_{UST}}. \tag{4}$$

We simulate Fed remittances similarly, assuming that the distribution of maturities in the Fed's portfolio is uniform — i.e., that the Fed follows a simple ladder investment strategy. Remittances, in dollars, for a balance sheet of size A that invests in Treasuries with a weighted average maturity of τ_{FED} years and is financed with fraction Z of interest-bearing reserves are:

$$REMIT_t^{FED}(\tau_{FED}, Z) = A \times \left(\frac{\sum_{j=1}^{12 \times \tau_{FED}} y_{t-(j-1)}^{(2 \times \tau_{FED})}}{12 \times \tau_{FED}} - Z \times r_t \right). \tag{5}$$

We simulate the term structure of interest rates using 100,000 years of monthly term structure data, compute the consolidated federal interest expense and remittances using Equations (3), (4) and (5), and then obtain long-run volatilities by taking the standard deviation of these series. Term structure data is based on simulations of the model in Greenwood, Hanson and Vayanos (2015) (GHV), adopting parameters from Table 3.1 of their paper. Our simulation methodology and the GHV model are described in the online Appendix.

Consider Panel A of Table 3.3, where we assume that the Fed's balance sheet remains at $4.5 trillion. Throughout Table 3.3, we assume that non-interest bearing currency in circulation is fixed at $1.5 trillion. Thus, we assume that a $4.5 trillion Fed balance sheet is financed with one-third of non-interest bearing currency and with two-thirds of interest-bearing reserves and RRP.

Columns (1), (2), and (3) of Table 3.3 show how the volatility of the consolidated federal interest expense varies across Fed balance sheet scenarios. Looking at each of the three panels in Table 3.3, we see that, for a given balance sheet size, the Fed's contribution to consolidated fiscal risk is always increasing in the weighted average maturity of its asset holdings. For example, if the Fed maintains a $4.5 trillion balance sheet with a WAM of 8.7 years, the volatility of consolidated interest expense is $200 billion or 1.54 percent of the $13 trillion debt. If the Fed reduces the maturity of its holdings to 2.2 years, the volatility of consolidated interest expense drops considerably, to $141 billion per year. The intuition is straightforward: the longer the Fed's assets portfolio, the greater is the quantity of short-term debt that the consolidated government needs to refinance each period, and therefore the more volatile is the government's consolidated interest expense.

Table 3.3 makes it clear that, by reducing the WAM of its Treasury holdings aggressively enough, a Fed with a $4.5 trillion balance sheet can make roughly the same modest contribution to consolidated fiscal risk as one that maintains a much smaller pre-crisis-style balance sheet but that holds a more representative mix of Treasuries. Concretely, as shown in column (2) of Panel C, a Fed with a $1.5 trillion balance sheet that holds a pro-rata fraction of all outstanding Treasuries (excluding bills) delivers a consolidated interest expense with a long-run volatility $136 billion. This is very close to the $141 billion figure that one gets with a $4.5 trillion balance sheet when the Fed holds only Treasuries maturing in less than five years. Simply put, varying the WAM of the Fed's Treasury portfolio is a potent tool for adjusting its contribution to fiscal risk, and — unlike changing the nominal size of the balance sheet — is one that allows the quantity of Fed-produced safe short-term claims to be kept constant.

Columns (4), (5), and (6) of Table 3.3 show the corresponding volatility of Federal Reserve remittances to the Treasury. In Panel A and Panel B, our conclusion remains the same: reducing the WAM of U.S. Treasury bonds held by the Fed reduces remittance volatility in much the same way that reducing WAM reduces overall fiscal risk. In Panel C, however, the result flips: reducing the WAM of Federal holdings *increases* remittance volatility.[26] In this case, where the two metrics produce opposing results, we believe that looking at the volatility of consolidated interest expense is more meaningful, particularly if the ultimate point is to ask what the Fed's behavior implies for overall fiscal risk, defined as taxpayer exposure to rising interest rates.

The message from our analysis is that one can easily envision an outcome in which the Treasury still does much of the economically meaningful decision making with respect to the overall duration risk exposure of the government debt, and the Fed is only left with responsibility for the "last mile," with relatively little consequence for the consolidated government's exposure to interest-rate risk. Moreover, if it so desired, the Treasury could always raise the weighted average maturity of its issuance to offset any increase in fiscal risk posed by a large Fed balance sheet. In other words, the consolidated government could implement the kind of "barbell" strategy discussed in Section 3 by having the Treasury term out further at the same time that the Fed issues more short-term liabilities.

4. Implementation Issues

Having argued that the Federal Reserve should maintain a larger balance sheet to expand the supply of safe short-term claims, we now turn to a series of implementation issues. The first concerns the precise nature of the liabilities that the Fed should supply and, in particular, the choice between interest-bearing reserves and overnight RRP. The next set of issues concerns the ways in which the Fed's balance sheet interacts with two of the most prominent post-crisis regulatory innovations, namely the heightened SLR that now applies to the largest U.S. bank holding companies and the LCR. We consider these issues in turn.

---

[26]What explains this counterintuitive finding? In the scenario considered in Panel C, the Fed maintains a balance sheet of $1.5 trillion that is entirely financed by currency. Since currency is effectively a long-duration liability (the rate it pays is a constant at zero) the volatility of net income is minimized by matching it with long-duration assets.

Table 3.4:   Federal Reserve Balance Sheet as of 2015:Q4.

Assets ($ billion)		Liabilities ($ billion)	
Treasury Securities	2,462	Currency (Federal Reserve notes)	1,361
GSE Debt and GSE-Backed MBS	1,782	Depository Institution Reserves	2,566
Other Assets	245	ON RRP Facility	127
		Other Liabilities and Capital	435
Total	4,489	Total	4,489

Note: This table presents data on the Fed's Balance sheet as 2015:Q4. To smooth over the large seasonal swings in the mix between RRP and reserves, we take quarterly averages of the weekly quantities from Table 5 of the H.4.1 Release, "Factors Affecting Reserve Balances." For the overnight RRP facility, we take quarterly averages of the daily outstanding amount based on data from the Federal Reserve Bank of New York available at https://www.newyorkfed.org/ markets/omo/dmm/temp/file/Reverse Repo Data by Counterparty Type.xlsx.

4.1. *The optimal mix of reserves and RRP*

Table 3.4 presents a stylized version of the Fed's balance sheet as of the fourth quarter of 2015. To smooth over the large seasonal swings in the mix between RRP and reserves, we present quarterly averages of weekly and daily quantities. Total assets, predominantly in the form of Treasury securities and agency MBS, total roughly $4.5 trillion. On the liability side, the two largest categories are paper currency, at $1.36 trillion, and reserve balances, which are deposits at the Fed by depository institutions, at $2.57 trillion. The volume of overnight RRP outstanding is about $127 billion, although this amount tends to rise around quarter-ends. Thus the quantity of reserves outstanding is nearly 20 times that of overnight RRP.

To understand how these quantities are determined in equilibrium, one needs to know the interest rates paid on both reserves and RRP, as well as the counterparties eligible to receive these rates. Depository institutions (DIs) as well as government-sponsored enterprises (GSEs) are allowed to make deposits at the Fed — i.e., to hold reserves balances. However, only DIs are paid IOR, which is currently set by the Fed at 50 basis points. By contrast, while the rate paid on the RRP program is set 25 basis points lower than the IOR rate, there is a wider set of counterparties eligible to receive this rate. In addition to DIs and GSEs, there are currently more than 100 money market funds that are approved counterparties for the RRP program.

The Fed directly sets the IOR rate and the RRP rate and thereby influences both market-determined rates, such as the federal funds rate, as well as the relative quantities of reserves and RRP outstanding. Consider the fed funds rate, which has recently traded in the neighborhood of 37 basis points. At first glance, it might seem odd that the fed funds rate lies below the IOR, as this configuration appears to allow for an immediate riskless arbitrage: a DI could borrow in the funds market at 37 basis points, deposit those funds with the Fed at 50 basis points and pocket the 13 basis point difference. However, there are two types of costs associated with this arbitrage, which allow the wedge between the fed funds rate and the IOR rate to be sustained in equilibrium. The first of these is the Federal Deposit Insurance Corp.'s (FDIC) deposit-insurance assessment, which applies to the total liabilities of all domestic DIs. A domestic bank that engages in IOR arbitrage expands its balance sheet and, in so doing, increases its FDIC assessment; this is a marginal cost of undertaking the trade. Notably, branches of foreign banks do not face this FDIC assessment because their deposits are not insured, and hence they are at a comparative advantage in performing the IOR arbitrage. In part for this reason, more than a third of total reserves are now held by foreign banking organizations.

A second cost associated with IOR arbitrage stems from the leverage ratio, which requires banks to maintain a minimal level of equity to all assets, including riskless assets like reserves. Because IOR arbitrage necessarily expands a bank's balance sheet, if a bank perceives its leverage ratio to be a binding constraint, it will be reluctant to engage in IOR arbitrage unless the trade is sufficiently profitable to compensate for the shadow value of the constraint.

Thus, the existence of a sizable spread between IOR and market-determined rates suggests that the banking system is glutted with reserves. On one hand, almost all the reserves in the system will be held by banks in equilibrium, because they are the only institutions who can earn the IOR rate. On the other hand, because banks find it costly to further expand their balance sheets — both because of FDIC assessments and the perceived tightness of the leverage-ratio constraint — banks have to be offered an IOR rate that is well in excess of market-determined rates in order to be willing to absorb such a large quantity of reserves.

By contrast, the Fed can finance itself at a considerably lower rate by making use of the RRP facility. This is because the market for RRP is not restricted to DIs who are subject to various regulatory frictions and hence is more competitive. In effect, Fed RRP is a very close substitute for overnight T-bills, as both are riskless claims that can be bought by money funds.

This observation begs a question in the spirit of Friedman (1969): taking the asset side of its balance sheet as given, why should not the Fed structure the liability side so as to minimize its total interest expense? As a practical matter, this could be accomplished simply by raising the RRP rate toward the IOR rate and thereby — assuming there is not a cap on the size of the RRP facility — encouraging a shift in the equilibrium mix of reserves and RRP. For example, instead of maintaining a 25 basis-point differential between the IOR and RRP rates, this wedge could be narrowed to, say, 10 basis points or perhaps even less, depending on how elastically the equilibrium quantities of reserves and RRP adjust.

Reducing the IOR-RRP spread and shifting the Fed's funding mix to the more open and competitive RRP market would potentially create social value in two related ways. First, and most obviously, it would save taxpayers a meaningful amount of money. With over $2.5 trillion of reserves outstanding, even a modest 10 basis-point reduction in the Fed's total funding cost amounts to $2.5 billion of taxpayer savings per year. Moreover, these savings effectively come directly out of the rents earned by banks — to a large extent foreign banks — as a result of the imperfectly competitive and frictional nature of the market for reserves. Second, this taxpayer savings is the flip side of a more efficient allocation of the Fed's liabilities to those who value them most at the margin — i.e., money market funds in this case, as opposed to depository institutions.

This second point gets to the heart of our crowding-out approach. Recall that our main argument is that the consolidated government should supply more short-term safe claims because, with an expanded government supply of short-term safe claims, institutions like money market funds will not bid as aggressively for private-sector substitutes such as asset-backed commercial paper, thereby crowding out the amount of maturity transformation by private financial intermediaries. When the Fed expands the supply of RRP, this is almost like the Treasury issuing more T-bills, since it increases the supply of a government-provided short-term safe claim that can be held by money market funds. By contrast, when the Fed supplies reserves, it pays more interest but does not come as close to replicating T-bills, because the reserves cannot be held outside the regulated banking system. Hence, from our crowding-out perspective, one would not expect reserves to be as effective as RRP in reducing the incentives for private-sector maturity transformation.

Our contention that the RRP facility is likely to be a useful tool over the long run is at odds with the Fed's public statements on the topic, which have repeatedly expressed a desire to minimize the use of this facility. For example, the minutes of the January 2016 FOMC meeting mention that: "...participants reiterated that the Committee expects to phase out the [RRP] facility when it is no longer needed to help control the federal funds rate, and they unanimously expressed the view that it would be appropriate to reintroduce an aggregate cap on [overnight] RRP operations at some point."

One reason for this difference is that the Fed does not appear to be attaching much weight to the sorts of financial-stability considerations that we have been emphasizing. Rather, they seem to view the RRP facility more narrowly as an instrument of monetary control. That is, they see RRP primarily as a device for establishing a more reliable floor under the federal funds rate in light of the frictions in IOR arbitrage discussed above. Indeed, the January 2016 minutes went on to state that: "In making these judgements, most policymakers emphasized the primacy of maintaining monetary control in setting the appropriate capacity of the [overnight] RRP facility for the time being; participants indicated that the Committee's future decisions regarding the size and ultimate longevity of the facility should be largely driven by considerations of monetary control, although other factors, such as financial stability, should also be taken into account."

Beyond these differences in perspective, observers who have been skeptical of the RRP program have worried that if the Fed supplies a safe asset in elastic quantity at a fixed rate — as would be the case with a completely uncapped RRP facility — this could exacerbate flight-to-safety dynamics in a stressed crisis scenario. To be concrete, consider a money market fund whose portfolio is a mix of government securities and financial commercial paper. In a crisis situation, the fund is likely to try to shift toward safe government securities and away from risky commercial paper. If the quantity of government paper is in fixed supply, T-bill yields must decline in equilibrium. If, however, the Fed allows the supply of RRP to expand elastically at a fixed interest rate, the yields on government securities cannot fall, and the only remaining equilibrating mechanism must therefore be a sharper upwards spike in the yields on commercial paper, which might further destabilize markets.

This observation strikes us as valid. However, it is also straightforward to address. The solution is to cap the size of the RRP facility, but not at some arbitrary ex ante value. Rather, the cap should be made explicitly dynamic, so that the volume of RRP outstanding can find its natural level in normal times but cannot increase too much in a stressed scenario. Suppose that, per our earlier recommendation, the spread between the IOR and RRP rates is cut to 10 basis points, and — that during a calm market environment — the quantity of RRP supplied by the Fed is left uncapped, thereby finding its natural equilibrium level. Suppose further that this value has averaged $1 trillion over the past six months. The dynamic capping mechanism that we have in mind would then specify that the quantity of RRP on any given day cannot exceed (say) 120 percent of this trailing six-month average, or $1.2 trillion. This approach would help to dampen the sort of crisis dynamics described above, while still allowing the RRP facility to be far more responsive to the demand for short-term safe claims in normal times.[27]

Finally, we should note that the logic in Sections 2 and 3 suggests that the *ideal* crowding-out policy would be for the Fed to issue large quantities of short-term securities — i.e., "Fed bills" — that could be held by all investors.[28] Our proposal to significantly expand the Fed's RRP program should be seen as a second-best approximation that takes as given the legal

---

[27] The design of the capping mechanism has already been worked out by the Fed in its implementation of the RRP facility. At each auction, each participant submits a complete price-quantity demand curve. If, at the posted RRP rate, total demand lies below the cap, the posted rate prevails, and quantities are allocated accordingly. If, at the posted RRP rate, total demand is above the cap, the mechanism flips over into an auction for the fixed cap amount and the demand curves are used to set the market clearing rate. Relative to this established design, we are merely suggesting that the value of the cap be a function of past usage of the facility, rather than a predetermined dollar value. See Frost *et al.* (2015) for a detailed discussion of design issues related to the RRP facility.

[28] The Fed currently lacks the legal authority to issue securities, although many foreign central banks have this power. If granted this authority, the Fed could offer very short term (e.g., one day or one week) bills using a fixed rate facility. Unlike an expansion in T-bill supply, an expansion in Fed bill supply would not increase auction risk because short-term fluctuations in the quantity of Fed bills would be perfectly offset by changes in bank reserves.

constraint that only the Treasury can issue short-term securities. However, one can imagine other ways that the Fed and Treasury could work together to increase the supply of short-term government claims, though these, too, bump up against existing institutional constraints. For example, if the debt ceiling were not binding, the Treasury could offer large amounts of one-day or one-week T-bills using a fixed rate facility similar to that currently used for RRP, deposit the proceeds in its account at the Fed, and have the Fed back these deposits with a portfolio of long-term Treasury securities (see Stella (2015) for a related proposal).[29] This arrangement is identical to an expansion of the Fed's RRP program from the perspective of consolidated fiscal risk and would yield similar financial stability benefits. However, it might better safeguard Fed independence as it would make it clear than the Fed was simply acting as the Treasury's agent, rather than taking on the fiscal risk of a large balance sheet in its own right.

4.2. Using the Fed's balance sheet to mitigate regulatory frictions

Our overarching theme in this paper has been that there is a complementarity between the Federal Reserve's balance sheet and its regulatory tools, and that by using its balance sheet intelligently, the Fed can achieve better financial stability outcomes than by relying on regulation alone. For much of the paper, the implicit model has been one in which regulation is generally helpful, but imperfectly effective in its coverage — say because some activity can always migrate from the more-regulated banking sector to the less-regulated shadow-banking sector. A related, but logically distinct case, is one in which regulation imposes costly side effects on the more-regulated sector itself. We now discuss two leading examples of this point.

4.2.1. The supplementary leverage ratio

One way the private sector performs maturity transformation is by engaging in Treasury repo. Specifically, when a hedge fund puts on a carry

---

[29]The Treasury recently took some small steps in this direction. In May 2015, the Treasury announced that it planned to raise the size of its regular T-bill auctions and to hold larger deposits balances at the Fed. However, the Treasury's efforts to expand bill supply have been limited by maneuvering necessitated by the debt ceiling (Stella, 2015).

trade by buying a long-term Treasury bond and financing this purchase with short-term repo borrowing, it increases the supply of short-term safe assets available to the nonfinancial sector and reduces the supply of long-term safe assets. In other words, the hedge fund is effectively doing the same transaction — and bearing the same duration risk — that we have been arguing that the government should otherwise do more of, say, by shortening aggregate Treasury debt maturity. Moreover, as far as private-sector maturity-transformation activities go, this Treasury carry trade is at the benign end of the spectrum, as compared to, say, funding much more risky and illiquid assets (such as private-label securitizations) with runnable short-term funding.

However, recent regulatory changes have put a significant crimp in private-sector Treasury repo. The most important of these changes is the introduction of the SLR, which was finalized by the U.S. banking agencies in September 2014. The SLR requires the largest U.S. bank holding companies to maintain a ratio of equity to total assets (irrespective of risk weights) of 5 percent, or 2 percent above the global standard. To the extent that the SLR is perceived to be a binding constraint on the activities of these firms, it will tend to discourage relatively low-risk activities that consume a lot of balance-sheet capacity. One example of such a low-risk activity that appears to have been noticeably impacted is so-called "matched-book repo." This is when a dealer bank acts as an intermediary to facilitate the type of carry trade by a hedge fund just described. For example, the dealer bank would borrow from a money fund in the tri-party repo market and then turn around and lend to the hedge fund in the bilateral repo market. Again, this type of matched-book activity on the part of the dealer is effectively taxed under a binding SLR, because the loan to the hedge fund increases the raw size of the dealer's balance sheet.

Chart 3.9 presents some evidence which suggests that the SLR has indeed increased intermediation frictions in the Treasury repo market. In Panel A, we plot the spread between the rate on 10-year plain-vanilla interest-rate swaps and 10-year Treasury yields. Because levered investors like hedge funds need to obtain dealer financing for their Treasury positions but not for their swap positions, the spread between swap rates and Treasury rates will, in part, reflect the shadow value of dealers' SLR constraint. As can be seen, the swap spread has declined significantly into negative

Chart 3.9.   Selected Market Spreads.

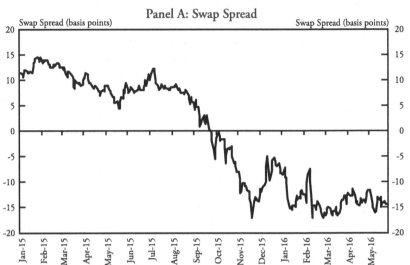

Panel A: Swap Spread

Panel B: Repo Outstanding and the GCF-Triparty Repo Spread

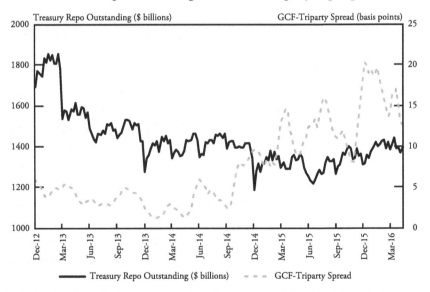

Note: Panel A shows the 10-year swap-minus-Treasury spread. Panel B plots total repurchase agreements outstanding alongside the GCF-Triparty spread.
Source: Bloomberg, DTCC and the New York Fed Primary Dealer Survey.

territory over the past year, meaning that the Treasury yield has gone up sharply relative to the swap rate. This is indirect evidence, but it is consistent with the idea that it has become expensive for levered investors to finance their holdings of long-term Treasury securities.

More directly relevant for the hypothesis, Panel B of Chart 3.9 shows the spread between the tri-party repo rate (the rate at which dealer banks borrow) and the GC repo rate (the rate at which they lend). This spread is quite literally the intermediation spread in the repo market and should, in principle, be driven exactly the sort of regulatory frictions like those due to the SLR. As can be seen, this spread has widened considerably, from a range of 5 to 7 basis points in late 2012 to over 20 basis points at the end of 2015. The chart also shows that this widening of the intermediation spread has happened at roughly the same time that the outstanding quantity of Treasury repo has declined.

To be clear, none of this evidence implies that a heightened SLR is a bad idea in any absolute sense. It may well create additional frictions in the Treasury repo market, but one might argue that its benefits outweigh the costs. However, the evidence does suggest that it is important to think about the complementarities between different policies. If one accepts that a side effect of the SLR is to inhibit the ability of private-sector intermediaries to convert long-term Treasuries into short-term safe claims, and if one also believes that such short-term safe claims are highly valued in the marketplace, it is natural to ask whether the SLR raises the burden on the public sector to take over some of the work that was previously being done by the private sector.

Thus, we believe that the frictions associated with the SLR — and the associated reduction in the vibrancy of the private-sector Treasury repo market — strengthen the general case for the Fed to step in and do essentially the same activity, by holding more Treasuries and financing these Treasuries with its own repo borrowing, via the RRP facility. This discussion also hints at one of the risks that may arise if the Fed chooses not take up this role. One might expect that the relative scarcity of Treasury repo, and the corresponding high returns to the Treasury carry trade, would lead private-sector actors to try to find a workaround. That is, eventually the function of doing matched-book repo intermediation might migrate from the balance sheets of regulated dealer banks, to some sort of entity that is not subject to the SLR. Perhaps this would involve a small number of very large hedge funds acting as a conduit between money funds and a larger number of other smaller hedge funds, much in the way that dealer banks do today. Or perhaps it would take some other form. But if an evolution like this does happen, it will be harder to say that overall systemic risk has been reduced by the SLR. So, if by maintaining a relatively large balance sheet, the Fed can help to reduce the incentives for this kind of regulatory arbitrage, it would be supporting the initial goals of the SLR regulation.

4.2.2. *The liquidity coverage ratio*

Another important piece of the post-crisis regulatory framework is the LCR, which was also finalized in 2014. The LCR requires each large bank to hold enough high-quality liquid assets (HQLA) to meet its net cash outflows in a 30-day liquidity stress scenario, under specific assumptions about how different classes of liabilities and off-balance-sheet commitments behave in such a stress scenario. The LCR applies in full force to firms with $250 billion or more in assets, and in a less stringent form to those with between $50 billion and $250 billion in assets.

Key to the design of the LCR is the choice of what kinds of assets can be used to satisfy the HQLA requirement. In its current implementation, there are three categories of assets that can count as HQLA. Level 1 assets, the most pristine category, include Treasury securities and central bank reserves; each dollar of these counts as $1 of HQLA, and they can be used without limit to satisfy the requirement. Next come Level 2 assets, which include agency MBS. These are subject to a 15 percent "haircut," so a dollar of MBS only counts as 85 cents of HQLA; moreover, Level 2 assets can only be used to satisfy 40 percent of the HQLA requirement. Finally, there are Level 2B assets, including corporate stocks and bonds. These are subject to a 50 percent haircut and can only be used to satisfy 15 percent of the requirement.

For the purposes of what follows, it is useful to focus attention just on the Level 1 part of the requirement: that a given bank must hold a certain minimum level of Treasuries and reserves. Two points are worth noting here. First, as many observers have pointed out, the LCR may exacerbate an overall scarcity of safe assets, to the extent that the induced demands for Level 1 assets are quantitatively large (Hannoun, 2011; IMF Stability Report, 2012: 100).[30]

Second, the Level 1 HQLA constraint is analogous to an expanded set of reserve requirements, but with a crucial difference. With traditional reserve requirements, and under the pre-crisis operating framework, if reserves became scarce — leading to an undesired increase in the federal funds rate — the Fed could choose to offset this scarcity with a standard open-market operation in which it purchased Treasuries with reserves, thereby increasing the supply of reserves. Thus, the level of the funds rate could be insulated from shocks to reserve demand. By contrast, the way the LCR is designed, if Level 1 assets become scarce, leading to unusually pronounced yield spreads between Treasuries and those near substitutes not classified as Level 1, the simplest open-market operation cannot loosen the constraint. This is because, by purchasing Treasuries with reserves, the Fed would leave *the sum of the two available to the public unchanged*, and it is the sum that is relevant for the Level 1 HQLA requirement.[31]

Thus, there is the risk that, given: (1) the rigidity of the regulation itself; (2) unpredictable shocks to the supply and demand for Level 1 HQLA; and (3) the Fed's inability to offset these shocks through open-market operations, the LCR could create undesirable volatility in various yield spreads relative to Treasuries, particularly in periods of market stress. One way to address this problem, and to introduce a "safety valve" role for the Fed, would be to tinker with the relative treatments of reserves and Treasury securities in the rule. For example, one could make it so that Treasuries — but not reserves — were haircut by, say, 10 percent in the computation of Level 1 HQLA. In this case, a dollar of reserves would buy more headroom under the rule than a dollar of Treasuries, and an open-market operation that purchased Treasuries with reserves would leave the financial system with more total available Level 1 HQLA. As a result, the Fed would be able to accommodate shocks to HQLA demand, much as it can accommodate shocks to reserve demand under a simple reserve-requirement regime.

---

[30] See BCBS (2010) and Elliott (2014) for more details of the LCR.
[31] Because agency MBS does not count as Level 1 assets, the Fed can ease a shortage of Level 1 HQLA by undertaking an open-market operation in which it purchases agency MBS instead of Treasuries. However, such an operation might be unattractive because, say, it represents an explicit shift in the stance of monetary policy toward the housing market.

If this avenue were to be pursued, it would be another reason to be open minded about the Fed maintaining a relatively large balance sheet. In addition to ensuring an adequate supply of short-term safe claims, as we have been arguing all along, a larger balance sheet might also allow the Fed to vary the quantity of Level 1 HQLA in the financial system, and thereby temper some of the volatility that might otherwise be associated with the LCR.[32]

5. Looking Forward: Crowding Out as the Economy Leaves the ZLB

We have argued that the Federal Reserve should use its balance sheet to help reduce financial intermediaries' tendency to engage in excessive amounts of maturity transformation. As the economy returns to full employment in the years ahead, and the Fed begins raising the policy rate, will the need to crowd out maturity transformation subside, or will it instead become a more pressing consideration?

In this section, we argue that the crowding-out motive is likely to apply with even greater force as the Fed's policy rate moves away from the ZLB. Our argument is based on the observation that, as short-term interest rates rise, savings tend to flow out of stable retail deposit products offered by insured banks and into the more run-prone claims such as money market fund shares and wholesale deposits.

In recent decades, these cyclical outflows appear to stem from the fact that banks have considerable market power over retail depositors — either because deposit markets are concentrated or because some depositors face high search costs. As a result, banks choose to pass through only a small fraction of increases in short-term money-market rates (e.g., the fed funds rate) into the rates they pay to retail depositors; therefore the spread between money-market rates and retail deposit rates widens as money-market rates

---

[32] See Pozsar (2016) for a similar argument. Pozsar does not raise the issue of differential regulatory haircuts for Treasuries and reserves. However, he suggests that some banks have an intrinsic preference for holding reserves relative to Treasuries to meet the LCR requirement. This has a similar effect, in that an increase in reserves matched one for one with a decrease in Treasuries may be perceived as easing the cost of the constraint for banks.

rise.[33] In response, more sophisticated households and nonfinancial firms tend to substitute away from stable retail bank deposits and toward more run-prone shadow banking liabilities, which pay rates that more closely track the fed funds rate. This logic suggests that maturity transformation migrates to the shadow banking sector as interest rates rise, strengthening the argument for increased provision of short-term claims by the Fed.

In Table 3.5, we provide evidence that private money creation rises following increases in the fed funds rate. We present regressions of the four-quarter percentage change in moneylike claims on the level as well as the four-quarter change in the fed funds rate. Formally, we estimate

$$\Delta_4 \log(Q_t) = a + b \cdot (r_t - r_{t-4}) + c \cdot r_{t-4} + \varepsilon_t, \qquad (6)$$

where Q_t is the amount of moneylike financial claims in quarter t expressed as a percentage of GDP. We show results for the 1960–2015 period, the 1960–1989 subperiod, and the 1990–2015 period. Our series on moneylike claims — including checking deposits, Treasury bills, money market fund shares and other private moneylike debt (open market paper, repurchase agreements and foreign deposits) are the same as those that we plotted earlier in Panel A of Chart 3.1.

We start by looking at increases in all forms of moneylike financial claims. Column (1) shows that in aggregate, total demand for moneylike claims rises modestly when short-term rates are high. Columns (2) and (5) show that as rates rise, there is a significant substitution away from checking deposits and toward money market fund shares. As a result, columns (6) and (7) show that as a result, the *share* of moneylike assets supplied by the shadow banking sector — defined as the sum of money market funds and other private moneylike debt — responds strongly to the level of and changes in the fed funds rate.

Chart 3.10 displays this result graphically, showing for each year from 1990 to 2015 how moneylike claims supplied by shadow banks have grown relative to total moneylike claims. The regression, shown in column

---

[33] For studies linking the weak pass-through to retail deposit rates to market concentration, see Hannan and Berger (1991), Neumark and Sharpe (1992), and Drechsler, Savov and Schnabl (2016). See Sharpe (1997) and Hannan and Adam (2011), who show that consumer switching costs help explain the low rates on deposits, and Yankov (2014), who argues that heterogeneity in customer sophistication plays a key role in explaining deposit pricing dynamics.

Table 3.5:   Growth of Moneylike Claims and the Nominal Interest Rate.

	(1)	(2)	(3)	(4)	(5)	(6)	(7)
		Changes in Quantities of Moneylike Claims				Relative Changes in Shadow Money Claims	
	$\Delta_4 log\left(\frac{TOT_t}{GDP_t}\right)$	$\Delta_4 log\left(\frac{CHECK_t}{GDP_t}\right)$	$\Delta_4 log\left(\frac{TBILL_t}{GDP_t}\right)$	$\Delta_4 log\left(\frac{OTH_t}{GDP_t}\right)$	$\Delta_4 log\left(\frac{MMF_t}{GDP_t}\right)$	$\Delta_4 log\left(\frac{SHAD_t}{PRIV_t}\right)$	$\Delta_4 log\left(\frac{SHAD_t}{TOT_t}\right)$
			Panel A: Full Sample 1960:Q1–2015:Q4				
$r_t - r_{t-4}$	-0.239	-1.522	-1.642	3.582	3.616	3.974	4.242
	(-0.84)	(-3.15)	(-1.69)	(2.28)	(0.93)	(4.69)	(4.71)
r_{t-4}	0.319	-0.570	0.466	-0.130	4.573	1.006	0.973
	(2.41)	(-2.13)	(1.13)	(-0.19)	(3.29)	(3.55)	(3.33)
T	224	224	224	224	164	224	224
R^2	0.10	0.22	0.09	0.21	0.22	0.38	0.39
			Panel B: 1960:Q1–1989:Q4				
$r_t - r_{t-4}$	0.316	-0.684	-0.003	2.879	4.595	3.952	4.046
	(1.16)	(-3.12)	(-0.01)	(1.56)	(0.83)	(3.61)	(3.50)
r_{t-4}	0.716	0.150	0.919	-1.057	5.124	0.088	0.039
	(6.81)	(1.46)	(2.29)	(-1.33)	(2.47)	(0.18)	(0.07)
T	120	120	120	120	60	120	120
R^2	0.31	0.25	0.09	0.26	0.08	0.37	0.37

(Continued)

Table 3.5:   (Continued)

	(1)	(2)	(3)	(4)	(5)	(6)	(7)
	Changes in Quantities of Moneylike Claims					Relative Changes in Shadow Money Claims	
	$\Delta_4 log\left(\frac{TOT_t}{GDP_t}\right)$	$\Delta_4 log\left(\frac{CHECK_t}{GDP_t}\right)$	$\Delta_4 log\left(\frac{TBILL_t}{GDP_t}\right)$	$\Delta_4 log\left(\frac{OTH_t}{GDP_t}\right)$	$\Delta_4 log\left(\frac{MMF_t}{GDP_t}\right)$	$\Delta_4 log\left(\frac{SHAD_t}{PRIV_t}\right)$	$\Delta_4 log\left(\frac{SHAD_t}{TOT_t}\right)$
			Panel C: 1990:Q1–2015:Q4				
$r_t - r_{t-4}$	−0.991	−4.194	−6.144	4.445	0.648	2.426	3.266
	(−2.04)	(−3.71)	(−2.18)	(1.54)	(0.51)	(4.08)	(3.59)
r_{t-4}	0.360	−2.123	0.250	0.708	2.958	1.697	1.693
	(1.18)	(−5.34)	(0.26)	(0.75)	(4.24)	(5.06)	(4.03)
T	104	104	104	104	104	104	104
R^2	0.22	0.50	0.32	0.17	0.41	0.55	0.49

Note: This table reports quarterly time-series regressions relating four-quarter growth in short-term, safe, and liquid claims to four-quarter changes in the federal funds rates and the four-quarter lagged level of the federal funds rate:

$$\Delta_4 \log(Q_t) = a + b \cdot (r_t - r_{t-4}) + c \cdot r_{t-4} + \varepsilon_t$$

where r_t denotes the average federal funds effective rate during the quarter. Columns (1) to (5) examine percentage changes in quantities (expressed as percentage of GDP) of moneylike claims. The series in column (1) to (5) are shown in Panel A of Chart 3.1. Column (1) shows total moneylike claims, column (2) shows checkable deposits, column (3) shows Treasury bills, column (4) shows other moneylike claims (open market paper, repurchase agreements, and foreign deposits), and column (5) shows money market fund shares. Columns (6) and (7) show the changes in shadow money claims relative to private moneylike claims (all claims except Treasury bills) and total moneylike claims. t-statistics are based on Newey-West (1987) standard errors, allowing for serial correlation at up to eight quarterly leads and lags.

Chart 3.10. Growth of Moneylike Claims and the Level of Short-Term Nominal Interest Rates.

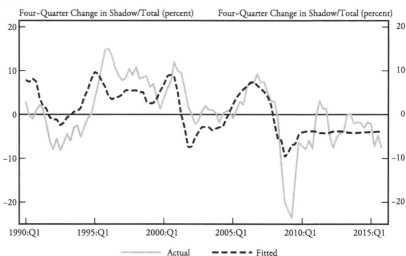

Note: The chart plots four-quarter log changes in the ratio of shadow banking moneylike claims — the sum of money market shares and other short-term safe private debt (open market paper, repurchase agreements, and foreign deposits) — to total moneylike claims, which are the sum of shadow banking claims, Treasury bills, and checking deposits. The chart shows the actual four-quarter changes from 1990:Q1 to 2015:Q1 as well as the fitted change from estimating the specification shown in column (7) of Panel C of Table 3.5:

$$\Delta_4 \log \left(\frac{SHAD_t}{TOT_t} \right) = \underset{(t=-4.86)}{-0.04} + \underset{(t=3.59)}{3.27} \cdot (r_t - r_{t-4})$$
$$+ \underset{(t=4.03)}{1.69} \cdot r_{t-4}, \quad R^2 = 0.49.$$

(6) of Panel C in Table 3.5, is:

$$\Delta_4 \log \left(\frac{SHAD_t}{TOT_t} \right) = \underset{(t=-4.86)}{-0.04} + \underset{(t=3.59)}{3.27} \cdot (r_t - r_{t-4})$$
$$+ \underset{(t=4.03)}{1.69} \cdot r_{t-4}, \quad R^2 = 0.49. \qquad (7)$$

As shown in Chart 3.10, the fitted values from this regression closely track a combination of the fed funds and recent changes in the fed funds rate.

Thus, money market funds and other shadow banking players are flush with funds when short rates are high. Consistent with this view, Nagel (2016) shows that the premiums on safe, short-term securities prized by these funds also tend to be high when short rates are high. As a result, financial intermediaries may find it increasingly attractive to finance themselves using uninsured forms of short-term debt as short rates rise.

Moreover, recent changes to the Securities and Exchange Commission's (SEC) Rule 2a-7, which governs money market funds, may intensify the relationship between private maturity transformation and short-term interest rates that we have documented here. The SEC's 2010 amendments to Rule 2a-7 require money market funds to shorten the weighted average maturity of their assets.[34] As a result, a given dollar flow into money market funds during the next tightening cycle may create an even greater demand for the very shortest-maturity claims and, as a result, may elicit even more aggressive maturity transformation by the private sector.

A corollary of this observation is that the Fed should be willing to allow its balance sheet to adjust over time to accommodate the above-described changes in the demand for moneylike claims. In particular, our analysis makes the following prediction: as short rates rise, if the Fed maintains a fixed spread between the IOR rate and the RRP rate, the take-up of the RRP facility should be expected to increase, perhaps quite substantially, mirroring the inflows into money funds. From a normative perspective, our logic suggests that this change in the composition of the Fed's liabilities in a rising-rate environment — away from reserves and toward RRP — is a helpful stabilizing influence and should be welcomed, rather than resisted.[35]

6. Conclusions

Our basic point is that even as the need for QE-style monetary accommodation wanes, the size and composition of the Federal Reserve's

---

[34]The 2010 Amendments to Rule 2a7 require money market funds to maintain a weighted average asset maturity below 60 days (the prior requirement was 90 days); to hold 10 percent of their assets in cash, Treasury securities, or private claims that can be redeemed within a day; and to hold 30 percent of their assets in Treasuries, cash, or private claims that can be redeemed within five business days.

[35]As a logical matter, if the IOR-RRP spread were kept fixed at a narrow value, and if the demand for safe claims from money funds were to increase dramatically enough, it is possible that the Fed would have to expand its balance sheet beyond the current size of roughly $4.5 trillion in order to fully accommodate the demand for RRP. In other words, both the composition and size of its balance sheet might ultimately be in play if it were determined to both keep the IOR-RRP spread constant and small and to fix the funds rate at a given value. To be clear, this is just an articulation of constraints, not a policy recommendation: if a growing balance sheet became a cause for discomfort, the IOR-RRP spread could be widened, thereby tamping down the demand for Fed-provided safeclaims.

balance sheet will continue to be important policy tools that can be enlisted to help mitigate the financial-stability risks associated with excessive private-sector maturity transformation. Notably, our approach draws attention away from the asset side of the Fed's balance sheet and toward the liability side. In other words, while during the QE era much of the focus was on the allocation of the Fed's asset holdings between Treasuries and MBS, and on the duration of its investments in each of these categories, a financial-stability orientation leads one to ask instead about the nature of the claims that the Fed issues against these assets, and in particular about the appropriate mix of reserves and RRP.

A number of concrete policy recommendations flow from our framework.

First, the Fed should keep a large balance sheet indefinitely going forward, even as rates rise well above the ZLB. While we do not attempt to pin down an exact dollar number, the current size of approximately $4.5 trillion strikes us as a plausible baseline.

Second, in order to reduce its impact on the consolidated government's interest-rate exposure, the Fed can wind down its investment in MBS and reduce the weighted average maturity of its Treasury holdings. Our calculations suggest that by doing so, the Fed's contribution to the overall interest-rate risk position of the federal government can be reduced significantly, even at a nominal balance sheet size of $4.5 trillion. Moreover, once monetary policy has normalized, there will no longer be a QE motive for the Fed to be overweight longer-maturity securities.

And finally, the Fed should meaningfully reduce the spread — which currently stands at 25 basis points — between IOR and the rate on its RRP facility. In addition to saving taxpayers billions of dollars a year, reducing this spread will lead to an expansion in the volume of RRP, which we argue is likely to be more effective than reserves at crowding out maturity transformation. Moreover, independent of the exact level of the spread, we expect that the RRP facility will have a more important role to play in the coming years as policy rates rise above the ZLB. We would urge the Fed to embrace this role, rather than seeking to phase out the RRP program.

Authors' note: We thank Matteo Maggiori, Adi Sunderam, and Matt Rutherford for helpful conversations and Randall Kroszner for his discussion. An online appendix is available at http://www.people. hbs.edu/rgreenwood/JH2016_IA.pdf

References

Adrian, Tobias and Nellie Liang. 2016. "Monetary Policy, Financial Conditions, and Financial Stability," Federal Reserve Bank of New York, Staff Reports No. 690.

Aiyagari, S. Rao, Albert Marcet, Thomas J. Sargent and Juha Seppälä. 2002. "Optimal Taxation Without State Contingent Debt," *Journal of Political Economy*, Vol. 110, pp. 1,220–1,254.

Barro, Robert J. 1979. "On the Determination of the Public Debt," *Journal of Political Economy*, Vol. 87, pp. 940–971.

Basel Committee on Banking Supervision (BCBS). 2010. *Basel 3: International Framework for Liquidity Risk Measurement, Standards and Monitoring* (Basel: Bank for International Settlements, December 16). www.bis.org/publ/bcbs188.pdf

Bates, Thomas W., Kathleen M. Kahle and Rene M. Stulz. 2009. "Why do U.S. Firms Hold So Much More Cash?" *Journal of Finance*, Vol. 64, pp. 1,985–2,021.

Bernanke, Ben S. 2015a. "Should Monetary Policy Take Into Account Risks to Financial Stability?" Ben Bernanke's Blog, April 7.

_____. 2015b. "Monetary Policy in the Future," Ben Bernanke's Blog, April 15.

_____. 2005. "The Global Saving Glut and the U.S. Current Account Deficit," Sanbridge Lecture, Virginia Association of Economists, Richmond, Va., April 14.

_____. 2002. "Asset-Price "Bubbles" and Monetary Policy," speech at the New York Chapter of the National Association for Business Economics, New York, N.Y., October 15.

Bhattarai, Saroj, Gauti B. Eggertsson and Bulat Gafarov. 2015. "Time Consistency and the Duration of Government Debt: A Signaling Theory of Quantitative Easing," National Bureau of Economic Research, NBER Working Papers 21336.

Board of Governors of the Federal Reserve System. 2014. Open Market Committee statement on "Policy Normalization Principles and Plans," September 17. http://www.federalreserve.gov/newsevents/press/monetary/20140917c.htm.

Bohn, Henning. 1990. "Tax Smoothing with Financial Instruments," *American Economic Review*, Vol. 80, pp. 1,217–1,230.

Borio, Claudio, and Mathias Drehmann. 2009. "Financial Instability and Macroeconomics: Bridging the Gulf," Paper prepared for the Twelfth Annual International Banking Conference, "The International Financial Crisis: Have the Rules of Finance Changed?" at the Federal Reserve Bank of Chicago, Chicago, September 24–25.

Caballero, Ricardo J., and Emmanuel Farhi. 2016. "The Safety Trap," working paper.

Caballero, Ricardo, Emmanuel Farhi and Pierre-Olivier Gourinchas. 2008. "An Equilibrium Model of Global Imbalances and Low Interest Rates," *American Economic Review*, Vol. 98, No. 1, pp. 358–393.

Carlson, Mark, Burcu Duygan-Bump, Fabio Natalucci, Bill Nelson, Marcelo Ochoa, Jeremy Stein and Skander Van den Heuvel. 2016. "The Demand for Short-Term, Safe Assets and Financial Stability: Some Evidence and Implications for Central Bank Policies," *International Journal of Central Banking*, forthcoming.

Carpenter, Seth B., Jane E. Ihrig, Elizabeth C. Klee, Daniel W. Quinn and Alexander H. Boote. 2013. "The Federal Reserve's Balance Sheet and Earnings: A Primer and Projections," Federal Reserve Board Finance and Economics Discussion Series, No. 2013-01.

Cecchetti, Stephen G. 1988. "The Case of the Negative Nominal Interest Rates: New Estimates of the Term Structure of Interest Rates During the Great Depression," *Journal of Political Economy*, Vol. 96, pp. 1,111–1,141.

Christensen, Jens H.E., Jose A. Lopez and Glenn D. Rudebusch. 2015. "A Probability-Based Stress Test of Federal Reserve Assets and Income," *Journal of Monetary Economics*, Vol. 73, pp. 26–43.

Del Negro, Marco, and Christopher A. Sims. 2015. "When Does a Central Bank's Balance Sheet Require Fiscal Support?" Federal Reserve Bank of New York Staff Reports No. 701.

Drechsler, Itamar, Alexi Savov and Philipp Schnabl. 2016. "The Deposits Channel of Monetary Policy," New York University working paper.

Dudley, William C. 2013. "Unconventional Monetary Policies and Central Bank Independence," remarks at the Central Bank Independence Conference — Progress and Challenges, Mexico City, Mexico.

Elliott, Douglas J. 2014. "Bank Liquidity Requirements: An Introduction and Overview," Bookings Institution, working paper, June 23.

Friedman, Milton. 1969. *The Optimum Quantity of Money*. London: Macmillan.

_____. 1964. Comment on "Collusion in the Auction Market for Treasury Bills," *Journal of Political Economy*, Vol. 72, No. 5, pp. 513–514.

Frost, Josh, Lorie Logan, Antoine Martin, Patrick McCabe, Fabio Natalucci and Julie Remache. 2015. "Overnight RRP Operations as a Monetary Policy Tool: Some Design Considerations," Federal Reserve Board of Governors, Finance and Economics Discussion Series 2015-010.

Gagnon, Joseph E., and Brian Sack. 2014. "Monetary Policy with Abundant Liquidity: A New Operating Framework for the Federal Reserve," Petersen Institute for International Economics, Policy Brief Number PB14-4.

Gallin, Joshua. 2013. "Shadow Banking and the Funding of the Nonfinancial Sector," Federal Reserve Board of Governors, Finance and Economics Discussion Series working paper 2013-50.

Garbade, Kenneth D. 2004. "The Institutionalization of Treasury Note and Bond Auctions, 1970–75," *Economic Policy Review*, Vol. 10, pp. 29–45.

Garbade, Kenneth D. 2012. *Birth of a Market: The U.S. Treasury Securities Market from the Great War to the Great Depression*. Cambridge: MIT Press.

Gensler, Gary. 1998. "Treasury Assistant Secretary for Financial Markets Gary Gensler addresses the President's Commission to Study Capital Budgeting," Presentation at the U.S. Department of the Treasury, Washington, D.C., April 24.

Gorton, Gary. 2016. "The History and Economics of Safe Assets," NBER Working paper 22210.

Gorton, Gary, and Andrew Metrick. 2012. "Securitized Banking and the Run on Repo," *Journal of Financial Economics*, Vol. 104, pp. 425–451.

Gorton, Gary, Andrew Metrick and Stefan Lewellen. 2012. "The Safe-Asset Share," *American Economic Review: Papers and Proceedings*, Vol. 102, No. 3, pp. 424–451.

Greenwood, Robin, Samuel G. Hanson and Jeremy C. Stein. 2015. "A Comparative Advantage Approach to Government Debt Maturity," *Journal of Finance*, Vol. 70, pp. 1,683–1,722.

Greenwood, Robin, Samuel G. Hanson and Dimitri Vayanos. 2015. "Forward Guidance in the Yield Curve: Short Rates versus Bond Supply," NBER Working Paper, No. 21750.

Greenwood, Robin, Samuel Gregory Hanson, Joshua S. Rudolph and Lawrence Summers. 2015. "The Optimal Maturity of Government Debt," in *The $13 Trillion Question: How America Manages Its Debt*, David Wessel, ed., pp. 1–41. Washington: Brookings Institution Press.

Gürkaynak, Refet S., Brian Sack and Jonathan H. Wright. 2007. "The U.S. Treasury Yield Curve: 1961 to the Present," *Journal of Monetary Economics*, Vol. 54, pp. 2,291–2,304.

Hall, Robert E., and Ricardo Reis. 2013. "Maintaining Central-Bank Solvency under New-Style Central Banking," manuscript.

Hannan, Timothy H., and Robert M. Adams. 2011. "Consumer Switching Costs and Firm Pricing: Evidence from Bank Pricing of Deposit Accounts," *Journal of Industrial Economics*, Vol. 59, No. 2, pp. 296–320.

Hannan, Timothy H., and Allen N. Berger. 1991. "The Rigidity of Prices: Evidence from the Banking Industry," *American Economic Review*, Vol. 81, pp. 938–945.

Hannoun, Hervé. 2011. "Sovereign Risk in Bank Regulation and Supervision: Where Do We Stand?" Speech at the Financial Stability Institute High-Level Meeting, Abu Dhabi, United Arab Emirates, October 26.

Hanson, Samuel G., David S. Scharfstein and Adi Sunderam. 2015. "An Evaluation of Money Market Fund Reform Proposals," *IMF Economic Review*, Vol. 63, pp. 984–1,023.

Juselius, Mikael, Claudio Borio, Piti Disyatat and Mathias Drehmann. 2016. "Monetary Policy, the Financial Cycle, and Ultra-Low Interest Rates," Bank for International Settlements, working paper.

Krishnamurthy, Arvind, and Annette Vissing-Jorgensen. 2015. "The Impact of Treasury Supply on Financial Sector Lending and Stability," *Journal of Financial Economics*, Vol. 118, No. 3, pp. 571–600.

———— and ————. 2012. "The Aggregate Demand for Treasury Debt," *Journal of Political Economy*, Vol. 120, No. 2, pp. 233–267.

Mishkin, Frederic S. 2010. "Don't Monetize the Debt," *The Wall Street Journal*, p. A7, September 9.

Nagel, Stefan. 2016. "The Liquidity Premium of Near-Money Assets," *Quarterly Journal of Economics*, forthcoming.

Neumark, David, and Steven A. Sharpe. 1992. "Market Structure and the Nature of Price Rigidity: Evidence from the Market for Consumer Deposits," *Quarterly Journal of Economics*, Vol. 107, No. 2, pp. 657–680.

Newey, Whitney K., and Kenneth D. West. 1987. "A Simple, Positive Semi-definite, Heteroskedasticity and Autocorrelation Consistent Covariance Matrix," *Econometrica*, Vol. 55, pp. 703–708.

Pozsar, Zoltan. 2016. "What Excess Reserves," *Global Money Notes #5*, Credit Suisse Economic Research, April 13.

Ramanathan, Karthik. 2008. "Overview of U.S. Treasury Debt Management," Presentation at the U.S. Department of the Treasury, Washington, D.C., June.

Rudebusch, Glenn D. 2011. "The Fed's Interest Rate Risk," Federal Reserve Bank of San Francisco, *Economic Letter* 2011-11.

Sharpe, Steven A. 1997. "The Effect of Consumer Switching Costs on Prices: A Theory and its Application to the Bank Deposit Market," *Review of Industrial Organization*, Vol. 12, No. 1, pp. 79–94.

Stein, Jeremy C. 2014. "Incorporating Financial Stability Considerations into a Monetary Policy Framework," Speech at the International Research Forum on Monetary Policy, Washington, D.C., March 21.

_____. 2013. "Overheating in Credit Markets: Origins, Measurement, and Policy Responses," Speech at the Restoring Household Financial Stability After the Great Recession, Federal Reserve Bank of St. Louis Research Symposium, St. Louis, Mo., February 7.

_____. 2012. "Monetary Policy as Financial-Stability Regulation," *Quarterly Journal of Economics*, Vol. 127, pp. 57–95.

Stella, Peter. 2015. "Exiting Well," Stellar Consulting working paper.

Sunderam, Adi. 2015. "Money Creation and the Shadow Banking System," *Review of Financial Studies*, Vol. 28, No. 4, pp. 939–977.

Svensson, Lars E.O. 2016a. "Cost-Benefit Analysis of Leaning Against the Wind: Are Costs Larger Also with Less Effective Macroprudential Policy?" IMF Working Paper, no. WP/16/3, January.

_____. 2016b. "A Simple Cost-Benefit Analysis of Using Monetary Policy for Financial-Stability Purposes," in *Progress and Confusion: The State of Macroeconomic Policy*, Olivier J. Blanchard, Raghuram Rajan, Kenneth S. Rogoff and Lawrence H. Summers eds. Cambridge: MIT Press.

_____. 2015. "Monetary Policy and Macroprudential Policy: Different and Separate," presentation at the Federal Reserve Bank of Boston's 59th Economic Conference, Boston, Mass., October 2–3.

_____. 1995. "Estimating Forward Interest Rates with the Extended Nelson & Siegel Method," Sveriges Riksbank, *Quarterly Review*, 1995: 3, pp. 13–26.

Woodford, Michael. 2012. "Methods of Policy Accommodation at the Interest-Rate Lower Bound," in *The Changing Policy Landscape*, Federal Reserve Bank of Kansas City, Jackson Hole Economic Policy Symposium, August 30–September 1.

Yankov, Vladimir. 2014. "In Search of a Risk-free Asset," Federal Reserve Board of Governors, Finance and Economics Discussion Series 2014–2108.

Yellen, Janet. 2014. "Monetary Policy and Financial Stability," Michel Camdessus Central Banking Lecture, International Monetary Fund, Washington, D.C.

Chapter Four

Lessons from the U.S. Experience with Quantitative Easing

Eric S. Rosengren*

Federal Reserve Bank of Boston

The expansion of the Federal Reserve's balance sheet ended with the completion of the tapering process last October, but we still are a long way from normalizing either short-term interest rates or our balance sheet. As a result, it may be some time before a full assessment of the effects of our quantitative easing policies can be made, since a full evaluation will require a successful return to a normalized monetary policy. Nonetheless, I think it is quite possible and appropriate at this point to consider which design features of the Federal Reserve's asset-purchase program were effective, and which were less successful, in achieving our monetary policy goals.

In addition to considering the design features, I will also consider the equally important communications strategy. Communications, often referred to as forward guidance, are an increasingly important component of monetary policy, especially when short-term interest rates are at the zero lower bound.

---

*Eric Rosengren is President and Chief Executive Officer at the Federal Reserve Bank of Boston. This speech was presented on February 5, 2015, at The Peterson Institute for International Economics and Moody's Investors Service's *8th Joint Event on Sovereign Risk and Macroeconomics* in Frankfurt, Germany. It is published with permission from the Federal Reserve Bank of Boston. The author thanks Adam Posen, President of the Peterson Institute for International Economics, for the invitation to provide his perspective on the quantitative easing programs in the United States. The views expressed are the authors, not necessarily those of my colleagues at the Federal Reserve's Board of Governors or on the Federal Open Market Committee (the FOMC).

An important caveat here is that institutional, structural, and governance differences across the world's central banks can make comparisons of policy actions (and their efficacy) quite difficult. Perhaps the most important difference between the Fed in the United States (U.S.) and most central banks in developed countries is that Congress assigned the Federal Reserve a "dual mandate" — the twin goals of achieving maximum sustainable employment as well as stable prices — rather than a single mandate related only to inflation.

However, another important difference involves the restrictions on securities that the Fed can purchase for its open market account. We are limited to securities that have the full backing of the U.S. government, and thus have purchased government-guaranteed mortgage-backed securities (MBS) and U.S. Treasury securities. Such restrictions vary significantly across the world's central banks.

Reflecting on the financial crisis and its aftermath, I have become convinced that the dual mandate is one reason why the U.S. Federal Reserve moved more aggressively than many other central banks to address the significant undershooting of inflation that we saw in the U.S., and that many other countries have experienced. Given the imperfect understanding of inflation dynamics, even a string of quarters in which inflation significantly undershoots its target may be reasonably interpreted as a temporary shortfall, since deviations of this magnitude and persistence still lie well within the accuracy of current inflation forecasting models. However, the substantial increase in *unemployment* throughout the developed world, in combination with the below-target inflation rates, indicates that significant output gaps do exist. How aggressively a central bank reacts to this situation depends on whether that central bank's mandated goals involve inflation alone or, as in the U.S., a dual mandate that includes employment.

However, I would argue that regardless of mandate, delays by central banks in moving to address the undershooting on inflation can be costly — especially if such delays lead households and firms to *expect* very low inflation rates.

In the United States, the decline in inflation during the recession afforded us more latitude to aggressively focus on the employment side of our dual mandate. Given the painful disruptions in labor markets that the U.S. experienced, this emphasis seemed appropriate, and does so with hindsight, and with all due consideration to the possibility of structural shifts in labor markets. I felt it was important that the focus on weak labor markets, as well as the undershooting of inflation, together provided important support for U.S. monetary policymakers to decide to move aggressively during the financial crisis, and indeed its long aftermath.

Of course today, after significant labor market improvement, and with the horizon over which inflation will return to its target being uncertain, inflation has taken on a more prominent role in our deliberations.

Currently, an obvious caveat in interpreting the low inflation rate in the U.S. is the supporting role played by the recent decline in energy prices. Oil shocks have been associated with major changes in monetary policy before. The failure to control inflation in the United States during the 1970s, in the presence of an adverse oil supply shock, highlighted a serious dilemma facing monetary policy at that time. Importantly, in that case, what might have been a *temporary* pass-through of oil to non-oil prices turned into a more lasting problem with overall inflation, as wage and price dynamics at that time helped turn increases in oil prices into fairly protracted increases in overall inflation. Former Federal Reserve Board Chairman Volcker is rightfully recognized for taking forceful action to address the situation and ultimately tame inflation in the United States.

Currently, a concern is that central banks are facing the mirror image of the problem in the 1970s. The problem of significantly *under*shooting inflation — a dynamic which could well keep interest rates at the zero lower bound — is likely to be a key challenge to central bankers in the first two decades of the 21st century. And I would say that as with the oil shock in the 1970s, the current shock has served to accentuate a potential monetary policy pitfall–in this case, the failure to quickly and vigorously address a significant undershooting of inflation targets, potentially leaving economies stagnant at the zero lower bound.

There are three observations I will make today. First, that a significant *under*shooting of the inflation target should be treated with the same policy urgency as a significant *over*shooting of the inflation target. Second, that *open-ended* quantitative easing tied to policy goals is likely to be much more effective than limited quantitative easing programs. Third, that clarity on monetary policy communications is difficult to achieve, but critically important for the success of the program. I would add that this final point is as critical to how we *normalize* policy as it is to how we *initiate* quantitative easing policies.

The Design of Large-Scale Asset Purchases in the United States

While there were three separate large-scale asset purchase programs in the United States, I will only briefly focus on the first one, since it was at least partly designed to address dysfunctional markets during the height of the financial crisis. In addition to addressing the shortfall in macroeconomic goals, this program was focused on purchases of mortgage securities, and sought to relieve the weak demand for mortgage-backed securities when markets became quite illiquid and risked becoming much more so. This program has generally been viewed as a successful way to stabilize markets, but isolating its effects is complicated because it occurred in the midst of the financial crisis.

Figure 4.1 provides details of the large-scale asset purchase programs commonly referred to as "QE1," "QE2," and "QE3." QE1 was announced on November 25, 2008, with purchases beginning shortly thereafter.[1] Initial purchases were of agency debt and agency mortgage-backed securities (MBS), "to provide support to the mortgage and housing markets."[2] Additional agency debt and MBS purchases were announced in March 2009, along with the purchase of longer-term Treasury securities, all to "provide greater support to mortgage lending and housing markets" and "to help improve conditions in private credit markets."[3] The program concluded in March 2010. Purchases totaled $1.25 trillion in agency MBS, $175 billion in agency debt, and $300 billion in longer-term Treasury securities.[4]

QE2 began in November 2010, and ended in June 2011. The program committed to purchase $600 billion of longer-term securities by the

---

[1] The Federal Reserve's press release announcing the action on November 25, 2008 stated: "This action is being taken to reduce the cost and increase the availability of credit for the purchase of houses, which in turn should support housing markets and foster improved conditions in financial markets more generally." http://www.federalreserve.gov/newsevents/press/monetary/20081125b.htm.

[2] See the statement from the December 16, 2008 FOMC meeting: http://www.federalreserve.gov/newsevents/press/monetary/20081216b.htm.

[3] See the statement from the March 18, 2009 FOMC meeting: http://www.federalreserve.gov/newsevents/press/monetary/20090318a.htm.

[4] See the statement from the March 16, 2010 FOMC meeting: http://www.federalreserve.gov/newsevents/press/monetary/20100316a.htm.

Program	Announcement Date	Targeted End Date	Targeted Total Purchase	Composition of Purchases	Program Details as Announced
Quantitative Easing 1 (QE1)	November 25, 2008	Over Several Quarters	Agency Debt: Up to $100 bil Agency MBS: Up to $500 bil	Agency Debt and Agency MBS	Purchase up to $100 bil of agency debt and up to $500 bil of agency MBS. Purchases expected to take place over several quarters.
	March 18, 2009	Treasury Securities: September 30, 2009 Agency Debt and MBS: December 31, 2009	Agency Debt: Additional $100 bil Agency MBS: Additional $750 bil Longer-Term Treasuries: $300 bil	Agency Debt, Agency MBS, and Longer-Term Treasury Securities	Total purchases of agency MBS will now be to up to $1.25 trillion, and agency debt up to $200 bil. Purchase up to $300 bil of longer-term Treasury securities over next 6 months.
Quantitative Easing 2 (QE2)	November 3, 2010	June 30, 2011	$600 bil	Longer-Term Treasury Securities	Purchase $600 bil of longer-term Treasury securities by the end of the second quarter of 2011, a pace of about $75 bil per month.
Maturity Extension Program (Operation Twist)	September 21, 2011	June 30, 2012	$400 bil	Longer-Term Treasury Securities[1]	Purchase, by the end of June 2012, $400 bil of Treasury securities with remaining maturities of 6-30 years and sell an equal amount of Treasury securities with remaining maturities of 3 years or less.
	June 20, 2012	December 31, 2012	Amount Limited by Remaining Shorter-Term Treasury Securities[1]	Longer-Term Treasury Securities[1]	Purchase Treasury securities with remaining maturities of 6-30 years at the current pace and sell or redeem an equal amount of Treasury securities with remaining maturities of approximately 3 years or less.
Quantitative Easing 3 (QE3)	September 13, 2012	None Given	None Given	Agency MBS and Longer-Term Treasury Securities	Purchase agency MBS at pace of $40 bil per month and continue Twist through yearend, increasing holdings of longer-term securities in aggregate by $85 bil.
	December 12, 2012	None Given	None Given	Agency MBS and Longer-Term Treasury Securities	Purchase agency MBS at a pace of $40 bil per month and longer-term Treasury securities initially at a pace of $45 bil per month after Twist ends at yearend.

Fig. 4.1.   Monetary Policy: Large-Scale Asset Purchase Programs — QE1, QE2, QE3, and Operation Twist.

[1]Shorter-term Treasury securities are sold or redeemed while an equal amount of longer-term Treasury securities are purchased, resulting in no net increase in balance-sheet size.

middle of 2011.[5] Unlike QE1, it was focused solely on purchasing long-term Treasury securities, and did not include the purchase of mortgage securities — which had been the focus of that first large-scale asset purchase program.

The purchase program did not fully meet expectations in terms of achieving monetary policy goals. As a result, in September of 2011 — only three months after the end of QE2 — the Federal Reserve announced the Maturity Extension Program (commonly referred to as "Operation Twist"). This program was designed to lengthen the average maturity of the Fed's Treasury securities portfolio, by purchasing long-term securities and selling an equal amount of short-term securities. The program removed duration from private holdings of Treasury securities, but did not increase the overall amount of the securities portfolio held by the Federal Reserve. The goal was to decrease the longer-term rates that tend to affect the real economy; in fact, the FOMC statement at the time highlighted that the program should "put downward pressure on longer-term interest rates."[6]

The initial program was a purchase of $400 billion in long-term Treasury securities, and clearly had the intended effect on long term rates. The program was extended in June 2012, at which point the program was limited by the lack of short-term securities to sell, and ended in December 2012.[7] At the time, this eliminated our holdings of T-bills and very short term notes.

The third quantitative easing program began in September 2012.[8] The program began as a monthly purchase of $40 billion in agency mortgage-backed securities, in addition to the Treasury securities that were being purchased (or swapped) under the "Twist" program. Unlike QE2, QE3 was an open-ended program. The continuation of the program was tied to substantial improvement in labor markets, consistent with price stability. In this way, the communication emphasized the need to achieve the policy

---

[5]See the statement from the November 3, 2010 FOMC meeting: http://www.federalreserve. gov/newsevents/press/monetary/20101103a.htm.
[6]See the statement from the September 21, 2011 FOMC meeting: http://www.federalreserve. gov/newsevents/press/monetary/20110921a.htm.
[7]See the statement from the June 20, 2012 FOMC meeting: http://www.federalreserve. gov/newsevents/press/monetary/20120620a.htm.
[8]See the statement from the September 13, 2012 FOMC meeting: http://www.federalreserve. gov/newsevents/press/monetary/20120913a.htm.

goals rather than a given size of the program. Communications also emphasized that the program would "put downward pressure on longer-term interest rates" and "support mortgage markets." When the Maturity Extension Program ended in December 2012 because of a lack of short-term Treasury securities remaining in the portfolio, the program was adjusted to the outright purchase (rather than exchange or swap) of $45 billion per month in longer-term Treasury securities, in addition to the purchase of $40 billion per month in mortgage-backed securities.[9]

Figure 4.2 shows the growth of the Federal Reserve's balance sheet over this period. QE2 expanded the Federal Reserve's balance sheet by $600 billion, to a little below $3 trillion. Operation Twist did not influence

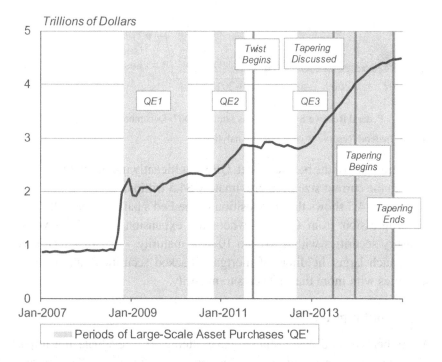

Fig. 4.2. Federal Reserve System Assets January 2007–December 2014.

Source: Federal Reserve Board, Haver Analytics.

---

[9]See the statement from the December 12, 2012 FOMC meeting: http://www.federalreserve.gov/newsevents/press/monetary/20121212a.htm.

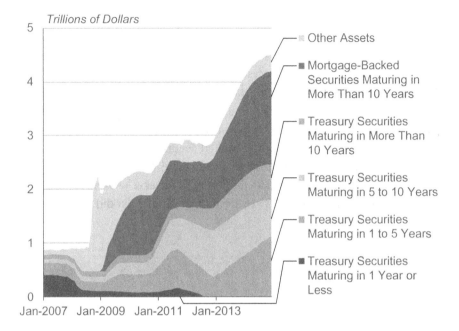

Fig. 4.3.   Federal Reserve System Assets January 2007–December 2014.

Source: Federal Reserve Board, Haver Analytics.

the overall size of the balance sheet. QE3 significantly increased the balance sheet to the current size of approximately $4.5 trillion.

Figure 4.3 shows the composition of the Fed's balance sheet. It shows the progression from QE2 — where the expansion primarily involved Treasury securities with a five- to 10-year maturity — to a balance sheet with much larger holdings of mortgage backed securities, and Treasury securities with more than 10 years to maturity.

Impact of Programs

A number of good event studies have attempted to evaluate the impact of the purchase programs in a narrow time window around the program-announcement dates.[10] In general, the studies find roughly a 20- to 25-basis

---

[10]See, for example: Gagnon, Joseph, Matthew Raskin, Julie Remache and Brian Sack. 2011. "Large-Scale Asset Purchases by the Federal Reserve: Did They Work?" *Federal Reserve Bank of New York Economic Policy Review*, 17 (1), pp. 41–59; Hancock, Diana, and Wayne Passmore. 2011.

point reduction in long-term rates associated with a purchase of $500 billion in long-term assets, although there is a high degree of imprecision involved.

In particular, with numerous Federal Reserve officials publicly discussing possible policy options, the timing of *exactly when the market came to expect* a new program is hard to pinpoint. It is very difficult to isolate the extent of the "news" contained in any announcement — news about either the timing or magnitude of a program.

Figure 4.4 shows 10-year Treasury yields around the time of announcements related to the three quantitative easing programs. QE1 was

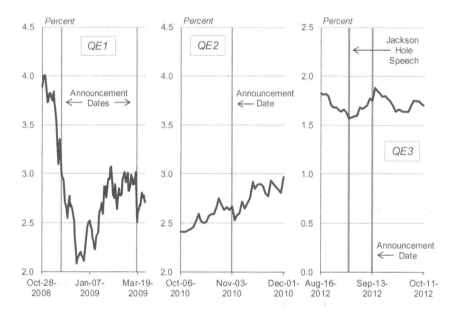

Fig. 4.4. Quantitative Easing Announcements and Ten-Year Treasury Yields.

Source: Federal Reserve Board, Haver Analytics.

"Did the Federal Reserve's MBS Purchase Program Lower Mortgage Rates?" *Journal of Monetary Economics*, 58 (5), pp. 498–514; Hamilton, James D., and Jing Wu. 2010. "The Effectiveness of Alternative Monetary Policy Tools in a Zero Lower Bound Environment," University of California, San Diego, working paper; Krishnamurthy, Arvind, and Annette Vissing-Jorgensen. 2011. "The Effects of Quantitative Easing on Interest Rates: Channels and Implications for Policy," *Brookings Papers on Economic Activity*; Fuhrer, Jeffrey and Giovani Olivei. 2011. "The Estimated Macroeconomic Effects of the Federal Reserve's Large-Scale Treasury Purchase Program." *Federal Reserve Bank of Boston Public Policy Brief* No. 11-2, (2011).

announced on November 25, 2008, with the announcement reiterated in the FOMC statement on December 16, 2008. Additional purchases were announced in the FOMC statement released on March 18, 2009. The 10-year Treasury yield fell 24 basis points on the day of the November announcement, and an additional 12 basis points on the following day. On the day of the March announcement of additional purchases, the 10-year Treasury rate fell 51 basis points.

Treasury yields, at much lower levels by the November 3, 2010 announcement of QE2, fell by 14 basis points the day following the announcement, but drifted slightly upward over the next couple of weeks.

As QE3 was contemplated, 10-year Treasury yields hovered at historic lows well under two percent. (Because of the low levels, please note that the scale on the chart for QE3 is different than the scale for the QE1 and QE2 charts.) QE3 was announced in the FOMC statement on September 13, 2012. However, shortly prior to the announcement, on August 31, 2102, Chairman Bernanke spoke at the annual Jackson Hole symposium hosted by the Federal Reserve Bank of Kansas City.[11]

On the day of Bernanke's speech, the 10-year Treasury yield declined by 6 basis points. However, on the day after the QE3 announcement, the 10-year Treasury yield rose 13 basis points but then adopted a downward trend, falling over 20 basis points over the next two weeks, easing the initial jump. Through the announcement of QE3, 10-year Treasury rates had fallen approximately 200 basis points, which was the immediate goal of the program.

While measuring the reduction in rates is one way to capture the impact of the program, the real goal is to have a significant impact on economic variables more generally. QE1 was meant to stem the tide of the deepening recession; the economy's momentum was highly contractionary and QE1 was meant to moderate the resulting decline in output. On the other hand, the latter two QEs were meant to stimulate the economy.

---

[11] See the full text of Chairman Bernanke's speech: http://www.federalreserve.gov/newsevents/speech/bernanke20120831a.htm.

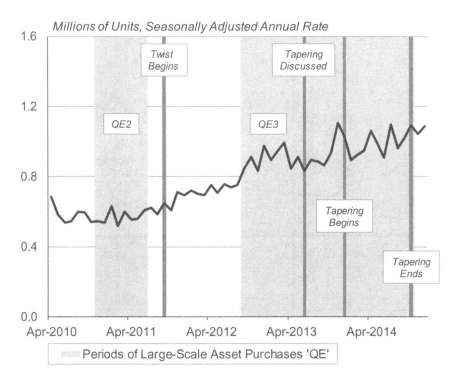

Fig. 4.5. Housing Starts April 2010–December 2014.

Source: Census Bureau, Haver Analytics.

The FOMC statement announcing QE3 highlighted the desire to support mortgage markets. Figure 4.5 shows that there was no notable change in housing starts during the period of QE2. However, housing starts did improve over the period of Operation Twist and QE3. After averaging 569,000 units during QE2, starts averaged 708,000 units from early on in Operation Twist through August 2012. During the past six months, starts have improved to averaging over one million units.

Figure 4.6 shows the path of housing prices. With housing prices declining, it was very hard to see or generate momentum in the housing market. Housing prices continued to decline during QE2, but began to rise somewhat steadily — albeit modestly — in late 2011, with Operation Twist underway for several months. Housing prices continued their upward trend during QE3.

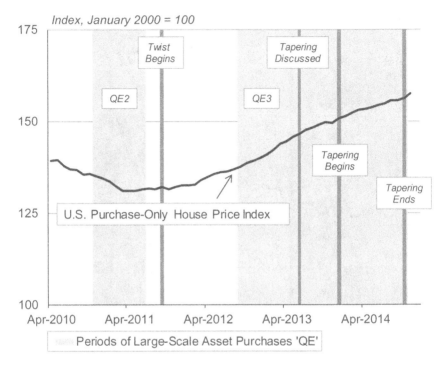

Fig. 4.6.   U.S. House Price Index April 2010–November 2014.

Source: FHFA, Haver Analytics.

Figure 4.7 shows that QE2 did not generate much momentum in auto and lightweight truck sales, which did pick up during Operation Twist and QE3. During QE2, auto and light truck sales were averaging 12.4 million units. Midway through Operation Twist, and as QE3 began, auto sales had risen to an average of nearly 15 million units and, over the past six months, auto sales have averaged nearly 17 million units.

One of the transmission mechanisms is to alter asset prices other than interest rates. Figure 4.8 illustrates that while there was not much momentum in stock prices from QE2, there was a substantial improvement over the period of Operation Twist and QE3.

Figures 4.9 and 4.10 illustrate what happened to measures of the two goals embedded in the Fed's dual mandate over this period. The

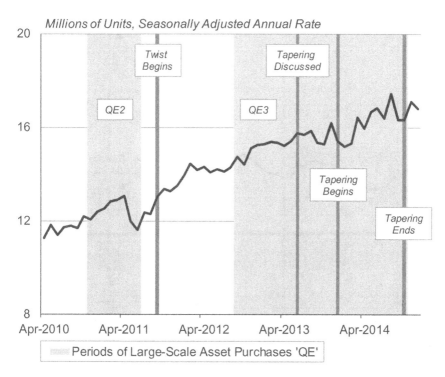

Fig. 4.7. Auto and Light-Weight Truck Sales April 2010–December 2014.

Source: BEA, Haver Analytics.

unemployment rate fell appreciably over the period. Core PCE inflation reached two percent during Operation Twist, but has generally been persistently below the two percent target. In part, the presence of full employment in the mandate, and the pain being felt in U.S. labor markets — coupled with core inflation below two percent — provided plenty of support for aggressive policy actions. The FOMC statements noted the need for substantial improvement in labor markets, and the statements related to QE3 eventually incorporated an unemployment threshold.

In sum, in the absence of the *dual* mandate, some significant and, I would say, needed policy actions may not have occurred — Operation Twist when core PCE was relatively close to the two percent target, and

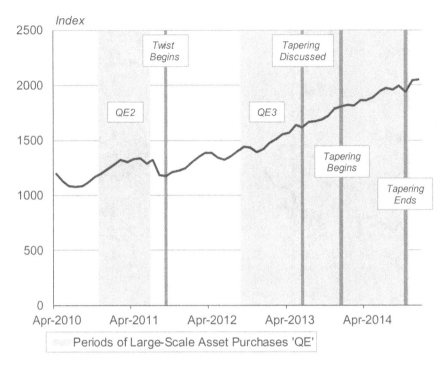

Fig. 4.8.   S&P 500 Composite Stock Price Index April 2010–December 2014.

Source: S&P, Haver Analytics.

QE3 when core inflation trended at roughly 50 basis points below two percent. Had these policy actions not occurred, it would in my view have prevented what was ultimately important preemptive action against a persistent undershooting of the inflation target that could have become much worse, as in some other parts of the globe.

QE2 was limited in scope. It had a fixed purchase amount and was not communicated in a manner tied to goals. Moreover, it was focused on Treasury securities rather than on areas with larger spreads, such as mortgages. And there is little evidence it had the desired impact on rates or real variables.

In contrast, QE3 was limited only by the progress made against the goals. The purchases were open-ended, and the communication was firmly

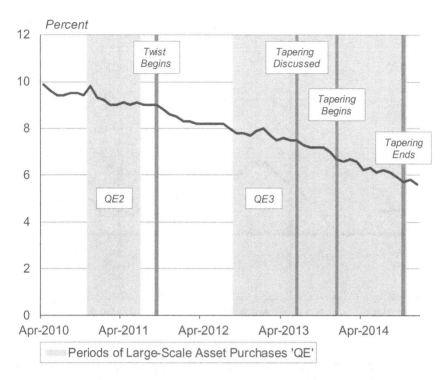

Fig. 4.9.   Civilian Unemployment Rate April 2010–December 2014.

Source: BLS, Haver Analytics.

tied to goals. It included areas with larger spreads such as mortgages. And both financial variables and real variables showed improvement with this program.

In summary, program design, and communication, both matter. A program that is open-ended and focused on areas where spreads are large — in conjunction with a communication strategy tied to goals — seems to have made a material difference in outcomes. While the transmission channels of large-scale asset purchases are still not completely understood, it seems to me that the signaling and communication tied to a large-scale asset purchase are an important channel — but one that unfortunately is hard to accurately quantify.

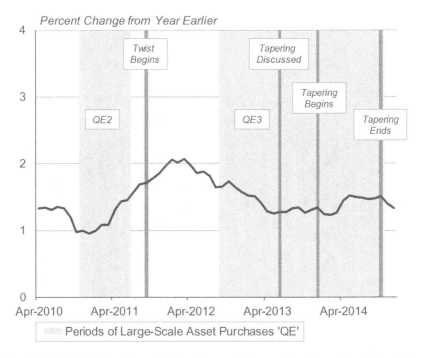

Fig. 4.10.   Inflation Rate: Change in Core Personal Consumption Expenditures Price Index April 2010–December 2014.

Source: BEA, Haver Analytics.

Exit Strategies

At this point, no central bank has fully normalized its policy stance. However, as my discussion has highlighted, communication and actions around *exit* are likely to be as important as they were at *initiation*. I am pleased that the United States has experienced much improved labor markets and inflation rates that, while below target, are higher — less close to dangerously low or negative rates — than in some, if not many, developed countries.

Nonetheless, policy should not be focused on progress from where we have been, but should instead be focused on meeting the ultimate goals in a timely fashion. At this time, there is insufficient evidence that U.S. inflation is clearly trending toward the two percent goal. While labor markets have continued to improve, the employment cost index (ECI) overall, and

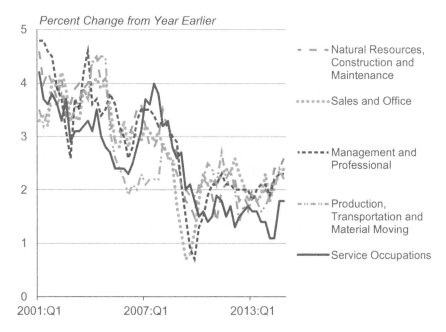

Fig. 4.11.   Employment Cost Index for Total Compensation for Private Industry Workers by Occupational Group 2001:Q1–2014:Q4.

Source: BEA, Haver Analytics.

the occupational breakdown of the ECI shown in Figure 4.11, show little evidence of trending to pre-crisis levels.

While disentangling the impact of positive energy shocks on prices will be difficult, we know that the PCE core inflation rate remains well below the Federal Reserve's two percent target. Given how low total and core inflation have fallen in most developed countries, a policy of patience in the United States continues to be appropriate. This is particularly true given the inherent asymmetry that we face at the zero lower bound — meaning, while we have all kinds of room to respond to an unexpectedly favorable shock, we remain quite limited in our ability to respond to negative shocks.

Concluding Observations

My remarks have focused on the United States experience. Given the different places central banks in developed countries are on policy at this time, it is likely premature to draw hard and fast conclusions for the global context. Certainly, the Japanese experience of raising the rate of inflation with a broad open-ended program tied to its policy goal is encouraging. Similarly, we will all learn from recently announced programs being initiated in Europe.

The relatively recent focus among central banks around the world on addressing the problem of persistently low inflation rates is in my view very encouraging. Just as high inflation in the 1970s was a pernicious problem for central banks, the problems generated by low inflation and interest rates settling at the zero lower bound were underestimated by professional economists and central bankers alike. The broad focus on meeting central bank mandates is important, and actions being taken to achieve inflation targets should result in a more robust global economy.

Chapter Five

Macroprudential Regulation and Supervision: Different Strokes for Different Folks

Gillian Garcia

International Monetary Fund (Retired)

Abstract

FDICIA's prompt corrective action did not prevent a subsequent financial crisis. After the 2007–2008 crisis, the international financial community turned to macroprudential regulation/supervision to forestall future financial crises. While many countries enthusiastically adopted macroprudential policies, U.S. adoption is thwarted by its clumsy supervisory system. Aided by its unshared responsibility for overseeing financial holding companies, the Federal Reserve is working with the Basel Committee and other international bodies to increase the resilience of large systemically important financial institutions by raising their capital standards, imposing liquidity requirements, testing their ability to withstand stress, requiring them to make plans for recovery and resolution, and revamping supervision. The Fed's efforts can be criticized, however. First, its actions are still largely micro- rather than macroprudential. Second, its confidential rules are open to court challenge when they do not conform to the Administrative Procedures Act. Third, by dovetailing regulatory requirements to banks' stress tests, the Fed violates the American presumption that similar institutions will face identical regulatory requirements. Fourth, while FDICIA favored rules over discretion, Fed discretion now rules according to the Board and the staff's best judgment. Fifth, the Fed's rules have become so complex and its supervisory actions so opaque that accountability to the press, Congress and the public is deficient. These developments are not healthy in a democracy.

1. Introduction

Prompt Corrective Action (PCA) was the mantra after the U.S. savings and loan (S&L) crisis of the late 1980s, and "Never Again" was the slogan for the subsequent rules-based 1991 FDIC Improvement Act (FDICIA), as people hoped that PCA would prevent a crisis recurrence. This did not happen. Instead, the U.S., and subsequently many other advanced countries, suffered the worst financial crisis and recession since the Great Depression. International regulators and policymakers turned to macroprudential regulation and supervision, especially for systemically important financial institutions (SIFIs), to deter future crises. Macroprudential policies have been enthusiastically embraced in many parts of the world but less so in the U.S., which is plagued by complex and opaque yet hardly macroprudential implementation.

This chapter first examines the origin of macroprudential policies, their objectives, and subsequently the adoption of macroprudential instruments around the world. The rest of the paper explores macroprudential policy implementation in the U.S., where the Federal Reserve has taken the lead through heavier SIFI regulation and supervision, which nevertheless still appear to be more micro- than macroprudential. In doing so, the Fed has reasserted its discretion and appears to be using it to an exceptional extent. PCA still exists for insured depository institutions, but one rarely hears of it now.

2. Macroprudential Origins

In what proved to be a precursor to its later macroprudential policies, the IMF concluded that a strong economy needs a sound financial system and strong macroeconomic policies to promote a stable financial system. This duality was embraced by the IMF's message (Lindgren, Garcia and Saal, 1996) and it reminds the author of Frank Sinatra singing:

> "Love and marriage go together like a horse and carriage. You can't have one without the other."

The duality between bank soundness and macroeconomic strength was used in IMF programs throughout the East Asian financial crisis that began in the summer of 1997, and which later spread to Russia and Latin America. Although the IMF has changed many policies, the macroeconomic/ financial nexus was the foundation of its programs in those days and remains so today, where it is enshrined in the Financial Sector Assessment Program (FSAP).

2.1. The early days of macroprudential policies

The term macroprudential was first used in the internal documents of the Cooke Committee, the precursor to the Basel Committee of Banking Supervision (BCBS), and the Bank of England in the late 1970s (Clement, 2010). It did not appear publicly until 1986, and was then dormant until the late 1990s. The Bank for International Settlements (BIS) advocated macroprudential policies in the early 2000s, but its message was ignored until the 2007–2008 financial crisis,[1] when the IMF, BIS, Financial Stability Board (FSB), BCBS, and G20 began to see macroprudential regulation as a panacea for financial instability and to promote it vigorously.

These bodies appear to have placed less emphasis on macroprudential supervision. Although the BCBS revised its Core Principles for Effective Banking Supervision in 2012, these principles still appear to be oriented toward supervising individual institutions rather than financial markets or the financial system as a whole.[2] At the start of the new century, attention had been focused on microprudential supervision, especially for banks. The BIS's Andrew Crockett understood, however, that microprudential supervision needed to be supplemented by macroprudential insights, and it was his agency's (largely ignored) theme in the early 2000s (Crockett, 2000; Borio, 2003).

At that time, the U.S., and most other countries, did not pay much attention to either macroprudential regulation or supervision. They, and the international supervisory agencies, indulged in a fallacy of composition by believing that by ensuring that individual institutions meet strong capital standards and have regular onsite inspections, it would keep the financial system safe and stable.

Since its enactment in 1991, U.S. regulatory agencies have not been enthusiastic about PCA, and have given the impression that they thought

---

[1] Internet searches for the term macroprudential began to rise on Google in the middle of the 2000s and rose sharply there and on Lexis-Nexis, Factiva and in the academic literature in 2007 and especially in 2008 (Hamilton, Surane and Onaran, 2016).

[2] "Each Core Principle applies to the supervision of all banks," so the Basel Committee did not include a separate principle for systemically important banks (Basel Committee, 2012: 5–6). Moreover, it observes that a "broad financial system perspective is integral to many of the Core Principles" and so did not include a specific stand-alone Core Principle on macroprudential issues."

it called their integrity into question, and diminished their discretion and independence. Regulated institutions also pushed back against PCA and other regulations, so deregulation became the vogue and microprudential supervision became weak because of regulatory capture and/or a policy-driven quest for economic growth (Financial Crisis Inquiry Commission, 2011). Furthermore, the Fed believed that a central bank should not try to curb financial bubbles, but should clean up any mess after they burst by relaxing monetary policy via the Greenspan and Bernanke puts (Bernanke, 2002; Bernanke and Gertler, 1999, 2001). There was little attempt to moderate a cyclical build-up of risk, except perhaps by belated monetary tightening.

With the exception of the IMF, the international community and the U.S. thus had no macroprudential apparatus before the crisis, and applied few or no macroprudential policies and instruments in either prudential regulation or supervision. In addition, microprudential supervision had significant deficiencies.

2.2. Pre-crisis microprudential deficiencies

After the crisis, a number of authors along with the bank regulatory agencies' Inspectors General (IG) criticized U.S. prudential supervision in the pre-crisis period (Bernanke, 2009; Garcia, 2009). Prudential supervision had proceeded procyclically institution-by-institution, and did not respond to the buildup of common overexposures to similar assets, new financial instruments, and short-term wholesale funding. These deficiencies were later revealed in the material loss reviews conducted by each supervisor's IG, as mandated under FDICIA.

When supervisors looked across institutions in peer review analysis, they mistakenly criticized those banks that did something different from their peers, and so departed from whatever was the common industry pattern. When the author asked supervisors why they ignored asset concentrations and common overexposures to new financial products like collateralized debt obligations (CDOs) and credit default swaps (CDSs), she was told they were following instructions from above. Perhaps the political-appointee bosses did not want to thwart economic expansion by supervisory actions that discouraged risk-taking, or were suffering from regulatory capture (Stigler, 1971).

PCA's reliance on individual banks' book capital ratios made it a backward-looking indicator of soundness, and was blind to liquidity problems and the build-up of risks across institutions (Goodhart, 2016). In addition, the shadow banking system ran free, and PCA did not distinguish between institutions that maintained adequate capital by raising new equity when needed and those that attained it by reducing assets, which raised the risks of destructive fire-sales and credit crunches — noteworthy financial crisis accelerants and detriments to economic recovery and growth.

Before the crisis, the BCBS neglected interlinkages among banks and the nexus between solvency and liquidity risks, i.e., it failed to see either the buildup of risks or bank reactions to stress in non-bank sectors. The Committee has attempted to remedy these deficiencies after the financial crisis.

3. Macroprudential Objectives

In general, macroprudential policies seek to promote financial stability, however that is defined — there is still no commonly agreed definition — in two ways. First, they aim to prevent cyclical systemic risk from building up within the system by "leaning against the wind." This would require the use of time-varying macroprudential tools. Second, macroprudential policies seek to strengthen financial institutions by building robustness to external shocks that do occur and resilience to shocks that arise endogenously (Minsky-like) within the financial system. This can partly be achieved by structural regulatory policies that strengthen individual institutions (Tarullo, 2015). Resilience would mean limiting the risks of financial distress that have adverse macroeconomic consequences, thus ensuring that the financial system is able to continue providing the financial services that a successful economy needs. "The objective of macroprudential policy is to reduce systemic risk by explicitly addressing the inter-linkages between, and common exposures of, all financial institutions, and the pro-cyclicality of the financial system. That is, systemic risk is to be reduced in its cross-sectional dimension and time series dimension, respectively." (Caruana, 2010: 3). This insight prompted the IMF, the Basel Committee, and academics to design and measure indicators of financial soundness for SIFIs based on, for example, the institution's asset size, complexity, inter-connectedness, substitutability, and cross-jurisdictional activity.

In the IMF's judgment, macroprudential regulation should focus on thwarting both the time-series and cross-sectional dimensions of perceived problems in financial institution behavior arising from both procyclical behaviors and common cross-sectional exposures. The IMF has used its soundness indicators consistently in its FSAPs, and vigorously recommended macroprudential policies and tools to cure discerned deficiencies. It is unclear whether different countries' tools would be rules-based or discretionary, how they would be calibrated, and whether they would be based on predictions from data-based models or on judgements made by policymakers or regulators.

4. Macroprudential Tools

IMF ideas regarding macroprudential tools evolved in the short time span between 2011 and 2013 (Cerutti, Claessens and Laeven, 2015; Claessens, 2014; Lim *et al.*, 2011).[3] In 2011, tools were almost entirely countercyclical. By 2013, the IMF also considered tools to decrease systemic risk and increase resilience by requiring SIFIs to hold more capital and by constraining institution size. Some countries responded enthusiastically to the IMF's recommendations of macroprudential tools (Cerutti *et al.*, 2015; Claessens, 2014; Lim *et al.*, 2011). Table 5.1 shows that less developed countries typically used one or more tools, while 11 of the 49 countries in the 2011 study, including the U.S. (and almost all other advanced countries), then used none of the macroprudential tools listed.[4] Most of the IMF's 2011 tools were then time-varying, and so were precluded by the slow comment period necessary for U.S. regulatory rule changes. Table 5.2 shows that countries at different stages of economic development adopted different macroprudential instruments. While concentration limits were popular worldwide, reserve requirements were no longer used in advanced

---

[3] In 2011, IMF tools included limits on: loan-to-value and debt-to-income ratios, borrowing and lending foreign exchange, open currency positions or mismatches, maturity mismatches, and profit distributions; ceilings on credit and/or credit growth; reserve requirements; countercyclical capital ratios; and dynamic provisioning (Lim *et al.*, 2011). The 2013 list also included: bank leverage ratios, capital surcharges for SIFIs, taxes on financial institutions, limits on interbank exposures, and concentration limits (Cerutti *et al.*, 2015).

[4] The U.S. is surprisingly omitted from the analysis of 57 countries' use of macroprudential instruments (Akinci and Olmstead-Rumsey, 2016).

Table 5.1:   Early Macroprudential Tool Adopters.

Tools	Countries	Countries
0	11	Australia, Belgium, Czech Republic, Finland, Germany, Japan, Netherland, the Philippines, Switzerland, U.K., U.S.
1	6	Austria, Canada, Ireland, New Zealand, Spain, Sweden
2	7	Chile, France, Indonesia, Italy, Norway, Slovakia, South Africa
3	7	Hong Kong, Lebanon, Mexico, Peru, Portugal, Singapore, Uruguay
4	9	Bulgaria, Hungary, India, Mongolia, Nigeria, Poland, Russia, Thailand, Turkey
5	4	Argentina, Brazil, Korea, Malaysia
6	2	China, Serbia
7	1	Croatia
8	2	Colombia, Romania
9/10	0	

Source: Lim *et al.*, 2011.

Table 5.2:   Percentage Use of Macroprudential Tools in 120 Countries 2000–2013.

Tools	All Countries	Advanced Countries	Emerging Markets	Developing Countries
Limits on loan-to-value ratios (LTV)	29	49	30	6
Limits on debt-to-income ratios (DTV)	16	13	24	0
Dynamic provisioning (DP)	11	5	7	28
Counter-cyclical capital buffers (CTC)	3	6	3	1
Leverage ratio (LEV)	19	13	20	22
Capital surcharge on SIFIs (SIFI)	6	11	4	6
Limits in interbank exposures (INTER)	30	33	33	22
Concentration Limits (CONC)	77	69	80	79
Limits on foreign exchange exposure (FX)	15	9	16	18
Reserve requirements (RR)	25	0	29	37
Limits on domestic currency loans (CG)	13	0	12	31
Tax/levy on financial institutions (TAX)	17	14	17	21

Source: Cerutti *et al.*, 2015.

countries. Basel's counter-cyclical capital buffer had been rarely adopted during the sample period.

Limits on LTV ratios in real estate lending had fallen into disuse in the U.S. Despite this, they were used in almost half of the advanced countries and almost one-third of emerging markets. Dynamic provisioning and limits on domestic currency lending were popular in developing countries.

5.   U.S. Macroprudential Strokes

When a financial crisis strikes the U.S., Congress and the Administration frequently create a new federal agency to address the problem. The result has been a plethora of U.S. financial prudential regulatory agencies that are difficult to coordinate. Moreover, it takes a potentially extended period of time to formulate a crisis response because the new agency has to get up and running. At the same time, Congress needs to allocate oversight responsibility to committees in both the House and Senate that need to gear up to monitor the new agency and fit oversight hearings into their busy schedules.

The 2010 Dodd–Frank Act (DFA) enacted macroprudential objectives for the U.S. but provided an inadequate apparatus for achieving them. Title I of the Act created the inter-agency Financial Sector Oversight Committee (FSOC), headed by the Treasury Department and including representatives from 15 financial regulatory agencies (10 voting) to set macroprudential policies and coordinate the responses in the multitude of U.S. financial regulatory agencies. The amorphous nature of the FSOG makes it unconvincing as the originator of macroprudential policies and regulations.

Before the crisis, some analysts saw gaps in the availability of financial data, such as repurchase agreements (referred to as RPs or repos), CDOs, and CDSs, as contributing to the severity of the financial crisis. If an institution or market was not federally regulated, it was then unlikely that relevant data were available. In response, the DFA created the Office of Financial Research (OFR) within the Treasury Department to fill the data gaps. The OFR's October 2016 website states that its mission is to "promote financial stability by delivering high quality financial data, standards and analysis for the Financial Stability Oversight Council and public," but its last congressional testimony was in March 2014. Thus, the press pays little attention to it and the public knows little about it. Hence, there is little evidence as to whether the FSOC and the OFR are succeeding in their missions of formulating and executing macroprudential policies, and providing high quality financial data. They remain largely unknown and untested bodies.

The Federal Reserve has stepped into this macroprudential breach. Unlike some other central banks, the Fed does not have an explicit financial stability mandate in its charter. Nevertheless, "safeguarding financial stability is ingrained in its mission and culture" (Brainard, 2014), so it created an Office of Financial Stability Policy and Research in 2010, and elevated it to Division status in May 2016, where it works to identify, analyze, and research potential threats, monitors financial markets, institutions and structures, and recommends policies to address the threats it identifies. Each quarter, the Fed's interdisciplinary staff assesses a set of financial vulnerabilities in the broad financial system by viewing asset valuations, risk appetites, leverage, maturity and risk transformations, interconnectedness, and borrowing by households and businesses, in order to identify credit booms before they end in distress.

The Fed has also gained supervisory dominance through its authority to oversee financial holding companies — an authority it does not share with other financial regulatory agencies. Moreover, the Fed has acquired the ability to supervise SIFI insurance companies to ensure their robustness. They had previously been subject only to state oversight.[5]

The process of regulatory rule-making is protracted because a proposing authority is legally obligated to expose its proposals to public comment and to make appropriate revisions. In addition, it needs to coordinate with the many other U.S. and international financial regulators, including the Fed, the Office of the Comptroller of the Currency (OCC), the Federal Deposit Insurance Corporation (FDIC), the Securities and Exchange Commission (SEC), the Commodity Futures Exchange Commission (CFTC), National Credit Union Administration (NCUA) and the Consumer Financial Protection Bureau (CFPB), which thwarts the use of counter-cyclical macroprudential regulations.

---

[5] The DFA authorized a Federal Insurance Office (FIO) within the Treasury Department to monitor the industry for the FSOC.

5.1. Institution size

The S&L crisis involved a large number of small institutions, whose failures threatened the integrity of the FDIC fund, so that PCA was enacted to control the many misadventures of small banks and thrifts. In contrast, the international community judged that, during the 2007–2008 financial crisis, it was the largest SIFIs that posed the greatest threat to countries' financial stability and fiscal solvency. The FSB, BCBS, and G20 subsequently focused attention on SIFIs, and invented a new regulatory/supervisory environment for them.

Regulators and policymakers in the U.S. also concluded that "the failures and near failures of SIFIs were key drivers of the 2007–2008 financial crisis and resulting recession" (Board of Governors, 2015b), and currently focus their attention on large institutions, especially holding companies, rather than their insured depositories.[6] While the U.S. participated in forming the international crisis response, it has varied the new rules, typically strengthening them to suit its own particular circumstances and judgments. U.S. regulators have divided institutions into five size groups that face different regulations and differing intensity of supervisory oversight. In an ascending order of size and systemic importance, they are as follows:

1. community banks and holding companies,
2. intermediate banks and holding companies,
3. SIFI banks and holding companies that are not "advanced approach institutions" (that is, they do not use their internal models to determine their capital requirements);
4. institutions that use advanced approaches but are not globally systemically important banks (G-SIBs), and
5. G-SIBs.[7]

---

[6]The DFA designates all domestic bank holding companies with $50 billion or more in consolidated assets as SIFIs, foreign subsidies whose parents have at least $50 billion in consolidated assets and nonbank holding companies chosen by the FSOC (Board of Governors, 2015b). Some SIFI banks are active globally and are designated as GSIBs by the Basel Committee and in the U.S. by the Fed.

[7]There is no agreed size limit for a community bank but capital regulations give latitude to BHCs with less than $15 billion in assets. Intermediate banks and holding companies might be measured as having assets more than or equal to $15 billion, but less than $50 billion. BHCs with assets at $50 billion or above but less than $250 billion, are large non-advanced approach institutions. Advanced approach institutions are those with total consolidated assets at or above $250 billion, or $10 billion in foreign exposures. G-SIBs are the largest most internationally active advanced approach institutions.

The chapter next discusses five arms of U.S. macroprudential oversight that aim to reduce the risk that a SIFI will fail, or threaten to fail, and harm the nation's economy:

1. capital standards,
2. liquidity standards;
3. stress testing;
4. recovery and resolution planning; and
5. enhanced supervision.

5.2. Capital standards

Before the financial crisis, capital requirements in the U.S. were relatively straightforward. Section 131 of FDICIA on "Prompt Regulatory Action" in microprudential fashion focused on individual depository institutions and divided them into five groups according to strength of their book-capital ratios, and set regulatory rewards and punishments accordingly. It did so in just nine pages and, until recently, set the same standards regardless of the institution's size.

To make capital regulations more macroprudential after the financial crisis, U.S. regulators helped to create the Basel III capital standards and in 2013 adopted them to provide "a harmonized, codified regulatory capital framework" for banks, saving associations and their bigger holding companies (Board of Governors of the Federal Reserve System and Comptroller of the Currency, p. 62,021). Basel III aims to aid financial stability by:

1. improving the quality of measured capital by, for example, excluding some debt-like items that had previously been included in Tier 1 capital[8];
2. revising the definition of risk-based assets;
3. increasing the amounts of capital required;
4. introducing required leverage ratios;
5. ending reliance on credit ratings provided by rating agencies;
6. requiring SIFIs and G-SIBs to meet higher capital standards; and
7. introducing a counter-cyclical capital buffer.

---

[8]Trust Preferred Securities and cumulative perpetual securities, for example, are now excluded from Tier 1 capital.

In the process, Basel III capital standards have become extremely lengthy and complex.

Researchers have concluded that PCA capital standards had not succeeded in closing failing institutions before they incurred large losses to the FDIC, partly because book capital is a lagging indicator and bank regulators were lax in applying it (Garcia, 2010; Government Accountability Office, 2015). Moreover, by aligning it with Basel III, U.S. regulators have now foregone PCA's simplicity. So, while depository institutions, both large and small, remain subject to PCA, you rarely hear of it now.

The Basel Committee's capital standards set additional capital requirements for large institutions based on their systemic importance score that is derived from their size, interconnectivity, complexity, cross-jurisdictional activity, and substitutability. The Fed has chosen to also assess systemic importance by two measures — the Basel measure, and another that replaces the BSCS's substitutability by reliance on short-term wholesale funding, which it believes is more relevant in assessing the riskiness of U.S. financial institutions. The Fed then requires institutions to use whichever systemic importance measure is larger. In practice, using wholesale funding produces a larger measure of risky assets, the denominator in the measured capital ratios, so its use has required the largest U.S. institutions to hold more capital.

As mentioned above, the Fed now divides banks into five size categories. Starting from the smallest institutions, the groups face increasingly demanding capital standards as they ascend in size and systemic importance. Institutions that use advanced approaches, or are G-SIBs, in particular are required to meet more and higher capital ratios. Table 5.3 summarizes the current complex U.S. capital requirements.

The Fed considered several methods for calibrating capital surcharges for G-SIBs, including cost-benefit analysis and compensating for the measured too-big-to-fail funding advantage. It chose instead to use an expected impact approach (Board of Governors, 2015b). In it, the Fed aims to place a capital surcharge on each G-SIB, so that its probability of failure falls far enough to lower its expected loss[9] to that of a reference SIFI that is

---

[9]The expected loss is the product of the probability of failure and the loss given default.

Table 5.3: Capital Ratios for U.S. Banks [%].

Minimum Capital Ratios for Non-Advanced Approach Institutions[1]	2016	2017	2018	2019
Minimum Common Equity Tier 1 [CET1] to Risk-Based Assets	4.5	4.5	4.5	4.5
Capital Conservation Buffer	0.625	1.25	1.875	2.5
CET1 + the Capital Conservation Buffer	*5.125*	*5.75*	*6.375*	*7.0*
Tier 1 Capital to Risk-Based Assets	6.0	6.0	6.0	6.0
Tier 1 Risk-Based Capital + the Capital Conservation Buffer	*6.625*	*7.25*	*7.875*	*8.25*
Total Capital to Risk-Based Assets	8.0	8.0	8.0	8.0
Total Risk-Based Capital plus the Capital Conservation Buffer	*8.625*	*9.25*	*9.875*	*10.5*
Leverage Ratio [Tier 1 capital to average consolidated assets]	4.0	4.0	4.0	4.0
ADDITIONAL MINIMUM CAPITAL RATIOS FOR ADVANCED APPROACH INSTITUTIONS				
Minimum Common Equity Tier 1 [CET1] to Risk-Based Assets	4.5	4.5	4.5	4.5
Capital Conservation Buffer	0.625	1.25	1.875	2.5
Minimum CET1 plus the Capital Conservation Buffer	*5.125*	*5.75*	*6.375*	*7.0*
Maximum Countercyclical Capital Buffer	0.625	1.25	1.875	2.5
Minimum CET1 + Capital Conservation + maximum Countercyclical Capital Buffers	5.75	7.0	8.25	9.5
Minimum Tier 1 capital	6.0	6.0	6.0	6.0
Minimum Tier 1 capital + Capital Conservation Buffer	6.625	7.25	7.875	8.5
Maximum Counter-Cyclical Capital Buffer[4]	0.625	1.25	1.875	2.5
Minimum Tier 1 Capital + Capital Conservation + maximum Countercyclical Buffers	7.25	8.5	9.75	11.0
Total Capital to Risk-Based Assets	8.0	8.0	8.0	8.0
Total Risk-Based Capital + the Capital Conservation Buffer	*8.625*	*9.25*	*9.875*	*10.5*
Total Capital + Capital Conservation + Maximum Countercyclical Capital Buffers	*9.25*	*10.5*	*11.75*	*13.0*
Leverage Ratio [Tier 1 capital to average consolidated assets]	4.0	4.0	4.0	4.0

(*Continued*)

Table 5.3: (*Continued*)

Minimum Capital Ratios for Non-Advanced Approach Institutions[1]	2016	2017	2018	2019
Supplementary Leverage Ratio [Tier 1 capital to on- and off-balance sheet assets][3]	3.0	3.0	3.0	3.0
FURTHER ADDITIONAL MINIMUM CAPITAL REQUIREMENTS FOR G-SIBs[2]				
Minimum CET1 + Capital Conservation + maximum Countercyclical Capital Buffers	5.75	7.0	8.25	9.5
Minimum CET1 + Conservation + Counter Cyclical Buffers + G-SIB surcharge[5]	5.75+	7.0+	8.25+	9.5+
Minimum Tier 1 Capital + Conservation + Counter Cyclical Buffers + G-SIB surcharge[5]	7.25+	8.5+	9.75+	11.0+
Minimum Total Capital + Conservation + Countercyclical Buffers plus G-SIB surcharge	9.25+	10.5+	11.75+	13.0+
Long-term Debt to RWA				6.0
G-SIB Long-term Debt Surcharge to RWA[6]				varies
Total Loss Absorbing Capacity [TLAC] to RWA[7]				18%

Source: Board of Governors, 2015c; Board of Governors and Office of the Comptroller of the Currency, 2013.

Note:
[1] "If a banking organization failed to hold capital above the minimum capital ratios and proposed capital conservation buffer (as potentially expanded by the countercyclical capital buffer), it would be subject to certain restrictions on capital distributions and discretionary bonus payments" (Board of Governors and Office of the Comptroller of the Currency, 2013: 62,022).
[2] Ratios in addition to those applicable to non-advanced approach institutions.
[3] Tier 1 capital to both on- and certain off-balance sheet assets.
[4] The Countercyclical Capital Buffer would measure the ratio of CET1 capital to risk-weighted assets. Set at 0% in 2016, it could rise if regulators judge that credit growth in the economy has become excessive.
[5] The applicable GSIB surcharge varies with the institution's systemic importance.
[6] Long-term debt could alternatively be required to be greater than 4.5% of total leverage exposure (Board of Governors, 2015c).
[7] TLAC has four components: (1) the 4.5% CET1 minimum capital; (2) an additional 1.5% of Tier I capital to RWA; (3) the capital conservation buffer of 2.5% plus a GSIB surcharge; and (4) long-term unsecured debt (6% of RWA plus a G-SIB surcharge) that could be converted to equity on resolution. The TLAC minimum could alternatively be measured as 9.5% of total leverage exposure (Board of Governors, 2015c).

not quite as large as a G-SIB (Board of Governors, 2015b; Tarullo, 2011). The Fed's surcharges increase according to a bank's position in increasing bands of G-SIB systemic importance scores.[10]

5.3. Complexity

In contrast to PCA's simplicity, the Basel III capital rules, including the preamble, cover 970 pages. The Federal Register notice (Board of Governors and Office of the Comptroller of the Currency, 2013) that describes U.S. capital requirements spans 273 pages. The DFA covers 2,319 pages and has required 22,200 pages of rule-making, and complying with them is expensive (Grind and Glazer, 2016). Herring (2016) identifies four different asset denominators, five different capital numerators, and 36 required capital ratios for G-SIBs. Complying with all of these is costly and detracts from financial stability because it makes oversight by supervisors, Congress, the press, and the markets so much more difficult (Government Accountability Office, 2015). For these reasons, Haldane (2011) criticized the international Basel II and III standards, which should be simple, robust, and timely, but are not. Hoenig (2013: 1) opposing the FDIC's adoption of Basel III, argued that "a capital standard, to be useful, must be understandable and enforceable and must be sufficient to absorb unexpected loss. Unfortunately, the Basel III interim final rule, as proposed, fails to fully meet these criteria." Thus, capital standards have become lengthy, extremely complex, and opaque. This is stark raving bonkers.

Moreover, if U.S. banks failed or were rescued because their unethical/illegal behavior caused investors and depositors to lose confidence and run from them, the global focus on raising bank capital is misdirected.

5.4. Liquidity requirements

The international community judged that bank illiquidity had been an important contributor to bank problems during the financial crisis and Great Recession, so the Basel Committee initiated two liquidity standards for banks — the Liquidity Coverage Ratio (LCR) and the Net Stable Funding Ratio (NSFR) — as part of the after-the-crisis Basel III banking standards

---

[10]Current U.S. G-SIBs surcharges range from 1.0% for the Bank of New York Mellon to 4.5% for JPMorgan Chase.

(Elliot, 2014). The Fed has added an additional test — the largest banks must pass the confidential Comprehensive Liquidity Analysis and Review (CLAR).

5.4.1. *The liquidity coverage ratio*

The LCR requires banks to hold enough liquid assets to withstand a 30-day market crisis. That is:

The Amount of High Quality Liquid Assets/Total Net Cash Outflows over a 30-day period $>= 100\%$

The Basel Committee used its judgment to divide assets into three liquidity groups and assign haircuts. Level 1 assets can be quickly used or sold and so can be included in the liquidity tally without a haircut. Level 2A assets are considered somewhat less liquid and so require modest haircuts, and may not contribute more that 40% of the numerator. Level 2B assets are seen to be less liquid and so have higher haircuts, and are restricted to no more than 15% of Level 2 assets. The Fed initiated the LCR for the SIFIs in 2012, and will extend its application to other banks in 2017 and subsequently to non-bank SIFIs.

5.4.2. *The net stable funding ratio*

The Basel Committee's NSFR seeks to ensure that a bank's assets would be adequately supported by its sources of funding. That is, it aims to ensure that the bank does not overindulge in maturity transformation. While regulators acknowledge that banks themselves will want to maintain adequate liquidity and that markets will penalize them if they do not, regulators note that holding liquid assets is costly, so banks' business models may encourage them not to hold enough liquid assets and rely too much on wholesale short-term funding. Therefore, the NSFR requires that:

The Available Amount of Stable Funding/Required Amount of Stable Funding $>= 100\%$

The Basel Committee divides bank assets into six groups according to their perceived ability to provide the required stable funding (RSF), and applies a RSF factor that ranges from 0 to 100 percent to them. Off-balance sheet commitments are also taken into account. At the time of writing, the Fed had not yet started to use the NSFR in the U.S., but on May 3, 2016, the three banking regulators issued proposals to implement the Basel NSFR in the U.S. at the start of 2018 (Board of Governors and Office of the Comptroller of the Currency, 2016). The proposals would apply most stringently to the biggest holding companies and depositories,[11] which must publish their results quarterly, and demand fewer liquid assets from the next lower tier of institutions.[12] The rule would not apply to smaller holding companies or to community banks.

5.4.3. *Comprehensive Liquidity Analysis and Review (CLAR)*

The Fed has the Comprehensive Liquidity Analysis and Review (CLAR), an additional periodic confidential liquidity test for the largest banks. It provides a detailed and institution-specific review of each large institution's liquidity management processes. Each bank runs a liquidity test using its own scenarios and assumptions about the behavior of its staff and clients, and its own models. The Fed provides guidance on banks' stress scenarios and can adjust the bank's test results. The Fed evaluates the institution's liquidity planning processes and governance, and uses the confidential results in its SIFI supervisory oversight. The tests were first undertaken by the largest banks in 2012 (Elliot, 2014).

There has been much criticism of the vast amount of judgment used in creating and calibrating the LCR and the NSFR. Like the process of risk-weighting assets in capital requirements, the new liquidity ratios direct lending towards some assets (sovereign bonds) and away from others (municipal debt and longer-term repos). In Fall 2016, the liquidity requirements were shortening the tenor of bank asset portfolios, increasing banks' demand for cash and reserves at the Fed, decreasing their supply of loans, and raising U.S. short-term interest rates and spreads, even though the Fed had deferred raising its policy rate (Pozsar, 2016). Interest rates are currently being driven by macroprudential rather than monetary policies.

---

[11] Institutions with at least $250 billion in total consolidated assets or $10 billion in on-balance sheet foreign exposure, plus subsidiary depositories with assets of $10 billion or more in on-balance sheet foreign exposures.

[12] Holding companies with between $50 billion and $250 billion in total consolidated assets, and less than $10 billion in on-balance sheet foreign exposure.

5.5. *Stress testing*

Before the financial crisis, a bank's condition was judged by its call reports and other reported data and by its regular onsite examinations. In the mid-1990s, mega-banks built internal (VaR) models to assess the risks they were taking and judge their resiliency in a precursor to stress testing. The IMF and World Bank began to use stress testing in their FSAPs in the late 1990s. On the regulatory front, Basel II subsequently allowed banks to assess their capital requirements using their own internal models.[13] After the financial crisis, the BCBS issued its *Principles of Sound Stress Testing Practices*, and BCBS (2015) attempted to make the stress tests more macroprudential. Basel III strengthened stress testing for regulatory capital, while Pillar 2 allowed supervisors to review banks' internal models for capital assessment. However, stress testing did not take off until 2009, when the U.S. began to test SIFI's capital adequacy with Supervisory Capital Assessment Program (SCAP) stress tests. These tests were regarded as successful in restoring public confidence in the country's banks, and subsequently became a feature of U.S. prudential supervision. Stress tests have also been adopted in the European Union and the United Kingdom (U.K).

Today, institutions operating in the U.S. face two kinds of forward-looking stress tests for capital. Section 165(i)(2) of the DFA requires banks and savings associations with over $10 billion in assets to conduct company-run annual stress tests.[14] These DFA stress tests (DFASTs) assess whether institutions would have enough capital to continue operating during adverse economic conditions. In 2016, the three regulators provided three DFAST scenarios with baseline, adverse, and severely adverse conditions.

In the Comprehensive Capital Analysis and Review (CCAR) stress tests, each year, every BHC operating in the U.S. with over $50 billion in assets must demonstrate to the Fed that it will have sufficient capital to continue operating in baseline, stressed, and even severely stressed conditions, and that it has a robust forward-looking capital planning process

---

[13]Though banks' internal models did not foresee bank problems well before the crisis, in 2016 Basel III still allowed advanced-approach institutions to use their own internal models to assess the riskiness of their portfolios.

[14]Companies with more than $50 billion in consolidated assets have to conduct two DFAST tests a year.

that takes into account its unique risks. The Federal Reserve's severe stress test scenario for 2016 postulated that short-term Treasury rates would decline to a negative 50 basis points and stay there. The Fed expects banks to use quantitative models to make point estimates of their losses, revenues, expenses, and capital levels for each scenario over a nine-quarter horizon.[15] The Federal Reserve is open to allowing holding companies to use qualitative model overlays and expert judgment to overcome shortcomings in their models and the lack of historical data relevant to, for example, negative rates.[16]

Using the results of its DFAST tests, the banks' capital plans and supervisory materials, the Fed evaluates the BHC's capital adequacy, assessment processes, and the BHC's plans to make capital distributions and share buybacks (Bernanke, 2013). The Fed may disapprove the bank's plans for dividends and share buybacks, and has done so. There is also a stress test of the liquidity of major financial holding companies (CLAR) described above.

5.6. *Recovery and resolution planning*

There are two requirements regarding resolution plans (referred to as "living wills"). One living will requirement relates to financial holding companies and the other to insured depository institutions. Title I of the DFA identifies bankruptcy under the Bankruptcy Code as the preferred method for resolving failing financial holding companies.[17] The FDIC resolves insured commercial and savings institutions that fail.

5.6.1. *Living wills for holding companies*

The Fed and the FDIC implemented Section 165(d) of the DFA by requiring all domestic bank holding companies with $50 billion or more in consolidated assets, nonbank companies identified by the FSOC as able

---

[15]Holding companies are not required to provide standard errors of their estimates. Moreover, the quality of the data used by banks in their models and lack of progress in improving it is a concern (Senior Supervisors Group, 2014).

[16]Jensen (2016) suggests using Bayes theorem to update estimates using data from banks in countries (Denmark Japan, Sweden and Switzerland) that have experienced negative rates.

[17]Even though Title II of the Act makes provision for resolution by the FDIC under certain circumstances.

to pose a threat to U.S. financial stability, and foreign entities operating in the U.S. whose parent has more than $50 billion in global consolidated assets to each submit a living will annually. These 165[d] plans need to identify critical operations and core business lines, map these into the firm's legal entities, and identify obstacles to a rapid and orderly resolution in bankruptcy. Smaller holding companies face less demanding living will requirements.

The Act requires the Fed and the FDIC both to review these living wills. If they jointly determine that the plans submitted are not credible, they can require the company to submit a revised plan that changes its business operations and/or corporate structure. If the revised plan does not satisfy the two regulators, they may jointly impose additional capital, leverage, and/or liquidity requirements and can restrict the company's growth, activities, and operations. If the deficient company has not resolved the regulators' concerns within two years, after consulting with the FSOC, the two regulators can require it to divest assets or operations. Five of the top eight U.S. holding companies failed the test early in 2016 and all of their living wills showed deficiencies.

Scott (2016) notes that the Federal Reserve has not engaged in the formal rule-making process required under the 1946 Administrative Procedures Act, which requires an agency to publish its proposed rules, allow the public to comment on them and then publish a revised final version. While the regulators have published a general rule and guidance for preparing living wills, they have not revealed their standards for determining the credibility of living wills (Scott, 2016; U.S. Government Accountability Office, 2015). Instead, the Fed is keeping the criteria for its decisions confidential. This lack of transparency and failure to comply with the 1946 Administrative Procedures Act means that the regulators' living-will decisions and penalties are open to challenge in the courts. Even if the Fed were to publish its compliance standards, it would not be able to change/tighten them each year — as Tarullo has suggested the Fed will do with capital requirements in the stress tests for big banks (Hamilton *et al.*, 2016). Moreover, GAO notes that regulators have been so tardy in reviewing the banks' submissions that some banks have been forced to begin formulating the next living will before receiving feedback on their previous year's submission.

5.6.2. *Living wills for insured depository institutions*

In addition to the 165[d] resolution plans, the FDIC now requires all insured depository institutions with $50 billion or more in assets to file plans for their orderly resolution under the Federal Deposit Insurance Act.[18] This living will needs to show how the failed insured depository would provide depositors with access to their insured deposits within one day, maximize the net present value of the bank's assets, and minimize losses to its creditors, including the FDIC. The plan needs to demonstrate how the depository would separate itself and its subsidiaries from the parent company in a cost effective and timely manner, and how it would dispose of its deposit franchise, core business lines, and assets.

FDIC chairman Martin J. Gruenberg (2016) expresses confidence that the two complimentary living will requirements are sufficient to resolve failed banks without taxpayer support. Goodhart (2016) on the other hand, regrets that attention has been paid solely to resolution instead of graduated PCA-like recovery planning for weak but viable banks. As he notes, like Lehman Brother's Fuld and Royal Bank of Scotland's Goodwin, no CEO likes to admit his errors and plan for formal failure, but will rather over-confidently maintain course until too late. The author notes that living wills focus on individual institutions, rather than the financial system as a whole, so would strengthen the financial system institution-by-institution and so are microprudential.

5.7. *Supervision*

Post-crisis macroprudential attention in the U.S. has focused on reforming supervision. Federal Reserve stress tests, described above, present a sharp contrast to pre-crisis supervisory methods that relied on on-site and off-site supervision. In addition, the FDIC and OCC have revamped their systems for overseeing individual banks and thrifts, but most published reports on supervisory changes focus on the Federal Reserve Board and the New York Fed's supervisory revisions. Using authority from Section 5 of the BHC Act,

---

[18]The FDIC did adhere to the Administrative Procedures Act, did publish its proposals, did make them available for public comment and did publish its final rule.

the Fed in 2010 established nationwide the Large Institutions Supervision Coordination Committee [LISCC] reporting that

> "The financial crisis highlighted a need to improve the Federal Reserve's supervisory oversight of the largest, most systemically important financial institutions, to mitigate risks to the financial system and to ensure that financial institutions are able to support lending to businesses and households in times of economic stress." (Board of Governors, 2015a:1)

The LISCC conducts annually three horizontal reviews of SIFIs: (1) the Comprehensive Capital Analysis and Review (CCAR); (2) The Comprehensive Liquidity Analysis and Review (CLAR) and the Supervisory Assessment of Recovery and Resolution Preparedness (SRP).[19] It coordinates nationwide the Board's and the reserve banks' multi-disciplinary supervisors in horizontal analysis, stress testing, scenario analysis and collection of new data sets (Board of Governors, 2015a).

The FRBNY has also reformed its system of prudential supervision by creating the Financial Institution Supervisory Group (FISC) that has interdisciplinary staff divided into two groups; (a) institution-specific staff that rotate after five years and are less often housed onsite, and (b) roving specialists (Eisenbach, Lucca and Townsend, 2016). The New York Fed is relocating a third of its examiners from on-site locations to newly renovated central bank offices and the OCC has also substantially reduced the proportion of its examiners located on-site (Burne, 2016).

Horizontal reviews are supposed to, in a process that is not clear to this writer, search out developing trends and correct deficiencies. The author has been told that horizontal reviews have replaced peer analysis, and that stress tests have partly replaced or aided on-site examinations in order to gain a forward-looking perspective to supplement backward-looking capital rules.

The U.S. has influenced the creation of international standards for capital, liquidity and governance through its participation in the G-20, FSB and BCBS. Nevertheless, it has demanded that SIFIs operating in the U.S. attain higher capital and liquidity standards than those set by the Basel Committee. Regulations have become somewhat institution-specific by aligning regulatory requirements to the individual institution's stress tests results. This process gives the Federal Reserve some opportunity

---

[19] The Assessment of Recovery and Resolution Preparedness examines holding companies' living wills.

to be flexible, possibly even timely and modestly counter-cyclical, in its prudential oversight. In this way, it can legitimately escape the slow and inflexible regulatory proposal-and-comment process. However, it is not a transparent process. Regulation has become more discretionary and tailored to the results of each individual SIFI's stress tests and capital and liquidity requirements. Also, the Fed has become the dominant prudential regulator through its authority over financial holding companies. The author is not sure how the OCC has adapted to this new reality, but the FDIC has a new mission to provide technical assistance to the community banks it oversees.

5.8. A desk-top exercise

In mid-2015, the Federal Reserve conducted an exercise in which five Federal Reserve Bank presidents decided how to react to a financial stress scenario that could possibly occur over the next few years (Adrian *et al.*, 2015). The Presidents were allowed to use both macroprudential and monetary policy tools to reduce the likelihood and severity of financial disruptions that could arise from unwinding an overheated economy.[20] They sought to increase the regulators' ability to preempt a crisis and strengthen financial institutions' resilience should one occur.

Some presidents expressed preferences for certain of these tools, while others opted to use monetary policy to counteract the credit over extension. In general, stress tests, margin requirements on repo funding, and supervisory guidance were preferred over countercyclical capital, liquidity or credit-based instruments. Delays in implementation arising from the need to coordinate actions across regulators and from slow formal administrative processes discouraged use of these latter instruments. Several presidents found these impediments so strong that they considered that the overheating would best be countered by monetary policy tools, not by macroprudential instruments, despite the danger that prudential supervisory objectives could conflict with monetary policy goals under certain conditions, as was discussed above with respect to liquidity tools (Goodhart, 2010).

---

[20]The available tools included capital-based macroprudential instruments, such as leverage ratios, counter-cyclical capital buffers and sectoral capital requirements; liquidity tools such as the LCR and NSFR; credit-based tools such as LTV and DTI ratios and margin requirements; capital and liquidity stress testing; supervisory guidance and moral suasion.

6. Conclusions

The crisis and the Great Recession have caused a revolution in the regulation and oversight of financial institutions around the world. Many countries adopted with enthusiasm macroprudential policies in the hopes of discouraging a repeat calamity. Developing countries and some emerging market states have sufficiently nimble prudential regulatory systems that allow them to adopt countercyclical prudential tools, like time-varying capital requirements, dynamic provisioning, debt-to-income and loan-to-value ratios. They have adopted these instruments, sometimes in addition to, and sometimes instead of, the Basel Committee's and FSB's focus on large banks that the aim to increase their resilience to external shocks.

In the U.S., the focus has shifted away from the risk that individual banks and thrifts could bankrupt the deposit insurance fund towards the danger that SIFIs could threaten the health of the economy and the government's fiscal integrity. It was judged that government authorities had felt obliged in the financial crisis to expend vast amounts of taxpayer and central bank funds to support over-risky, possibly insolvent, institutions so that they could continue to provide financial services to the economy.

National and international authorities have acknowledged the fiscal cost of such actions, the moral hazard that the rescues offered to weak institutions, the competitive advantages they provided to too-big-to-fail institutions, and the unpunished opportunities proffered to individuals to engage in unethical, even illegal activities. The focus therefore has shifted to monitoring and restraining the anti-social activities of systemically important institutions, not just banks, but their holding companies and mega nonbank institutions. The DFA began an extended process of reforming regulation and supervision in the U.S. to focus more on SIFI health and activities. This process has shifted primacy among regulators to the Federal Reserve, which has sole responsibility for overseeing financial holding companies. The OCC and the FDIC have revised their supervisory processes, but their roles (especially the OCC's) have been diminished in comparison to that of the Federal Reserve.

Thus, the Federal Reserve has come to dominate supervisory process in the United States. There, supervision now attempts to look forward and rely less on lagging indicators of financial health, such as onsite inspections and capital adequacy ratios. Federal Reserve stress tests have become the flavor of the month. Regulations have become excessively lengthy and complicated with regulatory demands differing according to an institution's perceived importance, measured by its size, complexity, international activity, and vulnerability.

The regulatory system in the U.S. is too clumsy for it to embrace countercyclical macroprudential policies and tools. Instead, it is focusing on increasing the resilience of individual institutions, especially G-SIBs and other institutions that use the advanced approaches to measuring risk-based assets. The Federal Reserve is attempting to give itself greater flexibility and timeliness by tying the strength of its regulatory requirements for the largest financial firms to the results of their annual stress tests and other supervisory examinations.

This approach has several disadvantages, however. First, despite the regulatory and supervisory changes in the U.S., supervision here still has a decidedly microeconomic flavor. Huertas (2016) judges that stress tests have successfully improved microprudential supervision but that much needs to be done to make them macroprudentially useful. Capital and liquidity regulations still focus on individual banks. Stress tests and living wills are focused on individual banks, their solvency and liquidity. To make the tests useful for macroprudential action they would need to: [1] evaluate the impacts of macroprudential measures that the authorities take, [2] be more countercyclical, and [3] account for spillovers and for banks' reaction to being placed under stress. The countercyclical macroeconomic tools that the IMF has tabulated, and underdeveloped countries have adopted remain neglected in the U.S. The main concession to macroprudential supervision appears to be the replacement of peer review analysis by horizontal analysis, but how that is conducted, what are its objectives and outcomes are not clear to this writer.

Second, some Federal Reserve regulations have bypassed the legal requirement to expose proposed regulations to public scrutiny, comment, and revision. To the extent that the Fed and other regulators avoid these legal requirements, they expose themselves to the possibility of being challenged in court and having their decisions reversed. The Fed's intention to annually strengthen its confidential rules violates the Administrative

Procedures Act and exposes its supervisory decisions and penalties to court challenge (Scott, 2016).

Third, the current processes ignore the typical American presumption that similar institutions will face similar if not identical regulatory requirements. Instead, the Fed is aligning the capital and liquidity requirements that each systemically important institution must face to its systemic importance as evaluated by the regulators, according to criteria that they judge to be important. Further, the numerical values of the required ratios they face are set according to the regulators' perception of the strength of the institution's responses and its capital and liquidity management processes.

Fourth, whereas FDICIA attempted to move the supervisory dial in the direction of rules and away from discretion, the pendulum has now swung fully so that discretion has currently won the regulatory battle in the U.S. against rules. The Federal Reserve is in charge and is doing things according to the Board's and the staff's best judgment. Yet, the district court decision in favor of MetLife in over-ruling the FSOC's determination that MetLife is a SIFI may be a first step in turning the regulatory tide back towards rules and against discretion.

Fifth, the regulatory and supervisory scenes have become so complex that that their visibility is diminished. With diminished transparency, the ability of Congress, the press, the courts, the academic community, and the public to hold the regulators accountable has been greatly reduced. Who outside the Fed really knows or understands what is happening? Who is currently holding the regulators to account? Accountability lacunae are not healthy for a democracy. In order to do a better job at regulatory oversight, Congress needs to reorganize its committees and resources to enable it to more adequately oversee U.S. macroprudential policies and their execution. At present, Congress is far from reaching the DFA's objective of giving the same attention to financial stability as the Humphrey-Hawkins hearings give to monetary policy.

On these five counts, the current focus on individual institutions and their behavior, as evaluated by unaccountable regulators, is undemocratic. Warsh (2016) summarizes the Federal Reserve's current problems as follows; "central bank power is permissible in a democracy only when its scope is limited, its track record strong, and its accountability assured."

This author is concerned that the macroprudential paths adopted in the U.S. do not meet these standards that are required in a democracy.

References

Adrian, T, de Fontenouvelle, P, Yang, E and Zlate, A (2015). Macro-prudential Policy: Case Study from a Tabletop Exercise. *Federal Reserve Bank of New York Staff Report*, No. 742, September.

Akinci, O and J Olmstead-Rumsey (2016). How Effective Are Macro-prudential Policies? An Empirical Investigation. *International Finance Discussion Papers*, No. 1136, April.

Basel Committee on Banking Supervision (2009). *Principles for Sound Stress Testing Practices and Supervision,* Bank for International Settlements, May.

Basel Committee on Banking Supervision (2012). *Core Principles for Effective Banking Supervision*, Bank for International Settlements, September.

Basel Committee on Banking Supervision (2015). Making Supervisory Stress Tests More Macro-prudential: Considering Liquidity and Solvency Interactions and Systemic Risk. *BIS Working Paper*, No. 29, November.

Bernanke, BS (2002). *Asset-Price "Bubbles" and Monetary Policy*. New York Chapter of the National Association of Business Economics, 15 October.

Bernanke, BS (2009). *Financial Regulation and Supervision after the Crisis: The Role of the Federal Reserve*. Federal Reserve Bank of Boston, 54th Economic Conference. Chatham, Massachusetts, 23 October.

Bernanke, BS (2013). *Stress Testing: What Have We Learned*. Federal Reserve Bank of Atlanta, Maintaining Financial Stability: Holding a Tiger by the Tail [Conference]. 8 April.

Bernanke, B and M Gertler (1999). Monetary Policy and Asset Price Volatility. *New Challenges for Monetary Policy*, Federal Reserve Bank of Kansas City, pp. 77–128.

Bernanke, B and M Gertler (2001). Should central banks respond to movements in asset prices? *American Economic Review*, 91(2), pp. 253–257.

Board of Governors of the Federal Reserve (2015a). Governance Structure of the Large Institution Supervision Coordinating Committee (LISCC) Supervisory Program. *Supervisory and Regulatory Letters* SR-15-7, 17 April.

Board of Governors of the Federal Reserve (2015b). *Calibrating the GSIB Surcharge*. 20 July.

Board of Governors of the Federal Reserve (2015c). [Press release], 30 October.

Board of Governors of the Federal Reserve (2016). *Comprehensive Capital Analysis and Review 2016: Summary Instructions*. January.

Board of Governors of the Federal Reserve and the Office of the Comptroller of the Currency (2013). Regulatory capital rules. *Federal Register*, 78(198), pp. 62,018–62,291.

Board of Governors of the Federal Reserve and the Office of the Comptroller of the Currency (2016). *Agencies Propose Net Stable Funding Ratio Rule* [Press release]. 3 May.

Borio, C (2003). Towards a Macro-prudential Framework for Financial Supervision and Regulation. *BIS Working Paper*, No. 128, February.

Brainard, L (2014). *The Federal Reserve's Financial Stability Agenda*, Brookings Institution, 3 December.

Burne, K (2016). New York Fed Pulling Examiners Out of Banks. *Wall Street Journal*, 29 July, p. C1.

Caruana J (2010). *Macroprudential Policy: Working Towards a New Consensus*. Bank for International Settlement's Financial Stability Institute and the International Monetary Fund Institute, "The Emerging Framework for Financial Regulation and Monetary Policy" [Meeting]. Washington, D.C., 23 April.

Cerutti, E, S Claessens, and L Laeven (2015). The Use and Effectiveness of Macro-prudential Policies: New Evidence. *IMF Working Paper*, No. 15/61.

Claessens, S (2014). An Overview of Macro-prudential Policy Tools. *IMF Working Paper*, No. 14/214.

Clement, P (2010). The Term "Macro-prudential": Origins and Evolution. *Quarterly Review*, Bank for International Settlements, March.

Crockett, A (2000). *Marrying the Micro- and Macro-prudential Dimensions of Financial Stability*. Eleventh International Conference of Banking Supervisors, Basel, 20–21 September.

Eisenbach, T, D Lucca and R Townsend (2016). The Economics of Bank Supervision. *Federal Reserve Bank of New York Staff Report*, No. 769, March.

Elliot, DJ (2014). *Bank Liquidity Requirements: An Introduction and Overview*. Brookings Institution, 23 June.

Federal Deposit Insurance Corporation (2013). *Regulatory Capital Interim Final Rule*. 9 July.

Financial Crisis Inquiry Commission (2011). *Financial Crisis Inquiry Report*. Government Printing Office, January.

Garcia, GGH (2009). Ignoring the lessons for effective prudential regulation, failed bank resolution and depositor protection. *Journal of Financial Regulation and Compliance*, 17(3), pp. 186–209.

Garcia, GGH (2010). Failing prompt corrective action. *Journal of Banking Regulation*, 11(3), pp. 171–190.

Goodhart, CAE (2010). *The Role of Macro-Prudential Supervision*. Federal Reserve Bank of Atlanta, Up from the Ashes: The Financial System after the Crisis [Conference]. Atlanta, GA, 12 May.

Goodhart, CAE (2016). In Praise of Stress Tests. In Anderson, RW (Ed.), *Stress Testing and Macro-prudential Regulation: A Transatlantic Assessment*. London: The Center for Economic and Policy Research Press.

Grind, K and E Glazer (2016). Inside Enforcers Shake Up Bank Culture. *Wall Street Journal*, 31 May, p. A1.

Gruenberg, MJ (2016). *Speech to the Eurofinance High Level Seminar*. Amsterdam, 21 April.

Haldane, AG (2011) *Capital Discipline*. American Economic Association Annual Meeting, Denver, CO, 9 January.

Hamilton, J, J Surane and Y Onaran (2016). Fed's Tarullo says Stress Tests to Get Tougher for Big Banks. *Bloomberg News*, 2 June.

Herring, R (2016). *Evolving Complexity of Capital Regulation.* Federal Reserve Bank of Philadelphia, Conference on the Interdependence of Financial Regulation, Resilience, and Growth, 17 June.

Hoenig, T (2013). *Statement: Basel III Capital Interim Final Rule and Notice of Proposed Rule-Making.* 9 July.

Huertas, TF (2016). Do Stress Tests Pass the Test? In Anderson, RW (Ed.), *Stress Testing and Macro-prudential Regulation: A Transatlantic Assessment.* London: Center for Economic and Policy Research Press.

Jensen, MJ (2016). *Stress Testing with the Help of Bayes' Theorem.* Federal Reserve Bank of Atlanta Notes from the Vault, February.

Lim, C, F Columba, A Costa, P Kongsamut, A Otani, M Saiyid, T Wezel and X Wu (2011). Macroprudential Policy: What Instruments and How to Use Them? Lessons from Country Experiences. *IMF Working Paper,* No. 11/238.

Lindgren, CJ, G Garcia and M Saal (1996). *Bank Soundness and Macroeconomic Policy.* Washington, D.C.: International Monetary Fund.

Pozsar, Z (2016). What Excess Reserves? *Credit Suisse Global Money Note,* No. 5, April.

Scott, H (2016). Publish the Secret Rules for Banks' Living Wills. *Wall Street Journal,* 10 June, pp. A13.

Senior Supervisors Group (2014). *Progress Report on Counterparty Data.* Financial Stability Board, 15 January.

Stigler, G (1971). The theory of economic regulation. *Bell Journal of Economics and Management Science,* 2(1), pp. 3–18.

Tarullo, DK (2011). *Regulating Systemically Important Financial Firms.* Washington, D.C.: Peterson Institute for International Economics.

Tarullo, DK (2015). *Advancing Macroprudential Policy Objectives.* Office of Financial Research and Financial Stability Oversight Council, 4th Annual Conference on Evaluating Macroprudential Tools: Complementarities and Conflicts, Arlington, VA, 30 January.

United States Government Accountability Office (2016). *Resolution Plans: Regulators Have Refined Their Review Processes but Could Improve Transparency and Timeliness.* U.S. Government Accountability Office, pp. 16–341, April.

United States Government Accountability Office (2015). *Bank Regulation: Lessons Learned and a Framework for Monitoring Emerging Risks and Regulatory Response.* U.S. Government Accountability Office, pp. 15–365, June.

Warsh, K (2016). The Federal Reserve Needs New Thinking. *The Wall Street Journal,* 25 August, p. A11.

Chapter Six

The Costs and Benefits of Shrinking the Fed's Discount Window

Harvey Rosenblum

Southern Methodist University

Abstract

Most central banks share at least one common element in their design, the ability to serve as a Lender of Last Resort to banks, and sometimes, other financial institutions. By having this power, central banks can maintain credit flows to the financial system when the private sector, or other government entities, are unable or unwilling to provide credit. During the 2008–2009 Financial Crisis, the Fed provided massive flows of credit to a wider variety of financial institutions and businesses than it had ever done in its prior 93-year history. This likely shortened and reduced the impact of the Great Recession. However, the Fed's actions essentially made it appear to be the fourth branch of government that usurped the prerogatives and authorities of the Legislative Branch. In writing the Dodd–Frank Act, an angry and jealous U.S. Congress sought to curtail the Fed's abilities to serve as Lender of Last Resort in the future. In the name of ending bailouts and reducing moral hazard, the Congress has essentially eliminated the Fed's abilities to serve as First Responder in the next financial panic. This sets a dangerous precedent, akin to eliminating fire departments and emergency medical teams. The Fed's duties as First Financial Responder need to be restored long before the next financial crisis.

1. Overview

At the heart and center of most, if not all, central banks are the role of serving as a Lender of Last Resort (LOLR) for the commercial banking system of its country. During the Financial Crisis of 2008–2009, the Fed extended its LOLR activities beyond the traditional banking system by supporting the acquisition of Bear Stearns, an investment bank, by

173

JPMorgan Chase; and by lending to AIG, a global insurance company. Through other special credit arrangements, the Fed provided U.S. Dollar credit to several other central banks, and thereby to commercial banks and their customers throughout the global economy.[1] The Fed did what it was established to do.

In July 2010, Congress passed, and President Obama signed into law the Dodd–Frank Act (henceforth referred to as Dodd–Frank), which, among its many provisions, severely constrains the Fed's ability in the future to serve as LOLR. This is disconcerting because financial crises are extraordinarily expensive events, and if allowed to spin out of control, impose an enormous dead-weight burden on society. My own research suggests that the Financial Crisis of 2008–2009 cost U.S. citizens about one year of income, even after the Fed mitigated some of the potential costs of the crisis by its timely and inventive LOLR actions.[2] Had the Fed been seriously inhibited in serving its LOLR role, the costs of the Financial Crisis would, in all likelihood, have been much greater.

By restricting the ability of the Fed to serve as the LOLR, Dodd–Frank ties the hands of the Fed to act in a timely and aggressive way as the First Responder in the next financial crisis. This seems unwise and counter-productive, especially since Congress has not created a substitute institution to serve as LOLR.

2. The Central Tenet of Central Banking

Over the last 160 years, the essence of central banking can be described by the Bagehot Principle — in an emerging financial crisis, (1) lend freely (i.e., without limits); (2) to anyone and everyone, not just banks; (3) on good collateral, with haircuts; and (4) at a penalty rate. This is what Walter Bagehot, a journalist for the predecessor of today's *Economist* magazine, observed the Bank of England doing successfully in the 1850s and 1860s, to keep emerging financial crises from spinning out of control, thereby mitigating some of the negative spillovers from the banking and financial system from severely damaging the British economy.[3]

---

[1] See Willardson and Peterson (2010).
[2] See Luttrell, Atkinson and Rosenblum (2013).
[3] See Bagehot (1873).

In the early 1930s, the Fed was reluctant to use its full LOLR tools, and likely made the banking crisis worsen into what eventually became the 1930s Great Depression.[4] In 2008–2009, the Fed under Chairman Ben Bernanke responded with a full and expanded arsenal of LOLR tools to reduce the financial frictions that sapped the strength from the U.S. macroeconomy. In this sense, over the course of the 19th, 20th and early-21st centuries, there is nothing new in central banking. That is to say; the essence of central banking comes down to the judicious use of the discount window utilizing the Bagehot Principle. What is new and different, however, is the circumscribed authority of the Fed to serve as LOLR since the passage of Dodd–Frank, a change that has the potential to alter the course of economic history, and wreak havoc by reducing the Fed's ability to serve as first responder in the next financial crisis.

During the Financial Crisis of 2008–2009, the Fed tested and stretched the explicit and implied limits of its LOLR powers, according to former Fed Chairman Paul A. Volcker.[5] Initially the Fed expanded its LOLR function via the Term Auction Facility (TAF) in December 2007 to extend 28-day loans by auctioning funds to banks; this was done to loosen the "stigma" of borrowing from the Fed's traditional *lender of last resort* facility (Willardson and Peterson, 2010). During March 2008, the Fed extended its safety net beyond the commercial banking industry by lending to JPMorgan Chase to acquire Bear Stearns, the nation's fifth largest independent investment bank. In the next few days, the Fed established the Primary Dealer Credit Facility (PDCF), thereby codifying its willingness to lend to nonbank institutions on an ongoing basis (2010).

Some eight years later (in 2016, as this chapter was written), the Fed's provision of credit to non-banks does not seem extraordinary, but to many inside the Fed, including me, the PDCF was mind-boggling at the time. Prior to Spring 2008, the Fed would offer to lend only to commercial banks, letting them make the credit decision and bear the risk of loss, if they wished to extend credit to investment banks and other securities firms. This was the beginning of the Bernanke Fed's new attitude, followed by the decisive action necessary to "Do Whatever It Takes."[6]

---

[4] See Friedman and Schwartz (1963).
[5] See Michael S. Derby (2008).
[6] See Wessel (2009).

Essentially, the Fed became the Fourth Branch of Government (Wessel, 2009) when it unquestionably acted as the First Responder of First Resort. Moreover, unelected Fed officials engaged in fiscal policy actions (i.e., the power to tax and spend) with implied, but certainly not the explicit consent of the rest of the federal government. To this day, many in Congress remain resentful and vengeful about the extent and details of the Fed's response to the Financial Crisis, and the increased power displayed by the Fed.

3. The Limits of Market Mechanisms in a Financial Crisis

The Federal Reserve Act, which created the Fed, was enacted into law in December 1913, in large part because President Woodrow Wilson and the Congress recognized the limited ability of financial markets and the economy to self-correct within reasonable periods of time during a financial crisis if there were no central bank to provide the necessary liquidity to the financial system. In short, markets could be trusted to work well most of the time, until they did not, at which point the central bank was expected to swing into action. This trust in free markets — but with a recognition of the limits of private-sector firms to function in the face of economic downturns, credit contractions, deleveraging, and especially in the face of deflationary forces — is the Bagehot Principle, the bedrock of central banking and the Fed's original *raison d'être*. There are limits to what the market can handle without some form of government intervention, but we simply do not know the exact nature of these limits, a matter for (imperfect) judgement.

Over the Fed's 102-year history, Fed interventions in the private sector have been few and far between. In 1998, the New York Fed intervened to mitigate the negative spillovers from the downfall of Long Term Capital Management (LTCM), a hedge fund, by providing the coordination of LTCM's major creditors that allowed for, in Fed Chairman Alan Greenspan's words, "a private-sector solution to a private-sector problem."[7] The Fed's intervention enabled a simulated bankruptcy of LTCM without its creditors having to wait for a protracted proceeding in Federal Bankruptcy Court. Without lending as much a dime, the Fed was able to fulfill its role as

---

[7] See Greenspan (1998).

LOLR.[8] Whether the financial markets could or could not have handled the failure and bankruptcy of LTCM will never be known, and will be debated in business school case studies for years to come. What we do know is that the New York Fed, presumably with the consent of Chairman Greenspan, was unwilling to find out what these limits were. In the years leading up to the demise of LTCM, global financial contagion was prevalent. A banking crisis in Mexico in 1994, soon spread to other countries in Latin America, especially Argentina, and was dubbed the "Tequila Crisis." A small banking crisis in Thailand beginning in 1997 spread to many other countries in Asia in 1998, including Indonesia, Malaysia, South Korea, and the Philippines. The 1998 Asian Financial Crisis was still playing out in summer and autumn 1998, when the Fed decided the market's ability to absorb shocks had definite limits.

In March 2008, the Fed used and extended its LOLR power to intervene in the fall of Bear Stearns. By September 2008, U.S. financial markets and the Fed faced the prospect of five virtually simultaneous bankruptcies of financial firms that later would have been labeled "Systemically Important Financial Institutions." Andrew Ross Sorkin in the preface of his book, *Too Big to Fail*, describes the situation succinctly through a scene on Saturday morning, September 13, 2008, about a conference call that took place in the dining room of the apartment of Jamie Dimon, the chairman of JPMorgan Chase:

> "Then he dropped his bombshell. Here's the drill. We need to prepare right now for Lehman Brothers filing...and for Merrill Lynch filing...and for AIG filing. And for Morgan Stanley filing. And after an even longer pause, he added...and potentially for Goldman Sachs filing...There was a collective gasp on the other end of the phone."[9]

How efficiently and quickly could five simultaneous bankruptcies of major financial institutions have been handled by the financial markets and the Federal Bankruptcy Court? And by the U.S. and global economies? We will never know these answers.

Paul McCulley, Chief Economist for PIMCO, a mutual fund company, coined the term "paradox of deleveraging," to describe the situation where

---

[8] See Rosenblum, DiMartino. Renier and Alm (2008).
[9] See Sorkin (2010).

everyone in the private sector is trying to take the "sell-side," in the absence of "buy-side" bidders.[10] In such a situation, prices would go to zero, unless the Fed or some other government agency were willing and able to take the buy-side. At some point, you run out of deep-pocketed buyers like Warren Buffet. Again, it is a judgement call as to when that would occur.

4. Ben Bernanke's Viewpoint

Ben Bernanke became Fed Chairman in January 2006. During his first year and a half as Fed Chairman, Bernanke tended to underestimate the size and ramifications for the U.S. and global economies stemming from the housing bust that had begun in 2005. He incorrectly labeled the situation as being "contained." Once he realized that he had been wrong, he came to the conclusion that he had to: "Do whatever it takes." At the Kansas City Fed's Jackson Hole Symposium in August 2008, Bernanke's former colleagues from academia lectured and admonished him about his willingness to intervene in the Bear Stearns failure: "You should favor the market. Let them fail. The market will deal with it. Bernanke thought this was idiocy" (Wessel, 2009).

A few weeks later, Fannie Mae and Freddie Mac, the two quasi-government enterprises that dominated the U.S. home mortgage market, were nationalized by Treasury Secretary Hank Paulson. Roughly a week later, Lehman went into bankruptcy on September 15, 2008, despite enormous efforts by the Fed and the Treasury throughout the prior weekend to find a buyer for Lehman. Lehman had no collateral to support a loan from the New York Fed, so the Fed felt legally constrained and decided not to lend to Lehman. At the time, there seemed to be no legal way for the Fed or other parts of the government to recapitalize Lehman. The financial markets, both in the U.S. and elsewhere, had believed that Lehman would somehow be rescued, at least partially if not completely. Thus, the absence of a LOLR set off the beginning of a spiraling financial crisis.

The next day, September 16, AIG, the giant global insurance company was hemorrhaging losses in its London financial products subsidiary which had backed Credit Default Swaps on the belief that mortgage defaults would

---

[10]See McCulley (2008).

be limited. To honor its commitments, AIG needed a loan of $85 billion from the New York Fed. Taking a 79.9 percent ownership stake in AIG as collateral, the New York Fed served as AIG's LOLR.[11] This put the Fed over the line that divided monetary policy from fiscal policy. Taxing and government spending are the prerogative of the Congress under the U.S. Constitution. Bernanke and Paulson, following the suggestion of President George W. Bush, sought to inform Congressional leaders about their decision. It was too late to ask permission.

Bernanke's description of the late-evening meeting with the Congressional leaders on September 16, 2008, is very telling:

> "As the questions began to die down, I looked over and saw Senator Reid rubbing his face with both hands. Finally, he spoke. 'Mr. Chairman, Mr. Secretary [Paulson]' he said. 'I thank you for coming here tonight to tell us about this and to answer our questions. It was helpful. You have heard some comments and reactions. *But don't mistake anything anyone has said here as constituting Congressional approval of the action. I want to be completely clear. This is your decision and your responsibility*"
>
> (Emphasis added.) (2015: xii).

In short, no good deed goes unpunished.

Lending to AIG was a risky proposition, even with quasi-nationalizing the company to have collateral for the loan. The Fed is called the lender of *last* resort for a reason. Fortunately for the Fed and the taxpayers, AIG fully repaid its loan, with the New York Fed claiming to have actually booked a "profit." Nice, but not the Fed's motive for making the loan in the first place.

Bernanke goes on to provide a modern-day description of the role of the LOLR: "If we acted, nobody would thank us. But if we did not act, who would? Making politically unpopular decisions for the long-run benefit of the country is the reason the Fed exists as a politically independent central bank. **It was created precisely for this purpose: to do what must be done** *— to do what others cannot or will not do.*" (emphasis added) (p. xiii). The stakes for the U.S. financial and economic system in this endeavor were awesome. Bernanke concludes that: "*If we failed, an angry Congress might eviscerate the Fed.*" (emphasis added) (p. xiii). This raises an interesting

---

[11] See Wessel (2009), Chapter 11; and Bernanke (2015), Chapter 13.

and difficult question — when it is time for the Fed to "sound the general alarm, to put all hands on deck so as to serve its unique role as LOLR, to do "what others cannot and will not do," does it make sense to prevent or severely constrain the Fed from serving its role as LOLR?

5. Congressional Response

Dodd–Frank, like several other laws passed by Congress to deal with financial reform, was written in haste and anger, an unholy combination of factors that obscured the nation's need to effectively address the problems at hand (Dodd–Frank Wall Street Reform and Consumer Protection Act, 2010). Dodd–Frank was signed into law in July 2010, a little more than a year after the depths of the severe contraction in economic activity that followed the Financial Crisis. From the perspective of this chapter, the most serious flaw in Dodd–Frank was the curtailment of the Fed's power and ability to lend in emergency situations. Even more importantly, Dodd–Frank tried to create the false impression that it would eliminate future financial crises because it would end *Too Big to Fail* (TBTF). Dodd–Frank's goals were laudable — it sought to provide a healthier, more resilient, stable, and less crisis-prone financial system. To accomplish these goals, Dodd–Frank drastically increased the number and scope of regulations imposed on banks and other parts of the financial system; reduced the reliance on market discipline to regulate economic behavior of financial firms, and, in all likelihood, exacerbated many of the perverse incentives that precipitated the Financial Crisis.

6. The Dodd–Frank Act

Dodd–Frank was well-intentioned and contained many sections that, in the long-run, have the potential to improve the resilience and safety of the banking and financial system, but it tries to do so in a way that is not just inept, but creatively inept. Wherever there was a choice between trying to accomplish its goals in a simple, straightforward way versus a complicated and convoluted way, the drafters of Dodd–Frank chose the "Rube Goldberg" route. Had there not been so much at stake in getting financial regulation "right," the situation might be considered humorous.

To Dodd–Frank's credit, it did seek to address the need for higher capital requirements. However, the new requirements will not be fully phased in until 2019 at the earliest, a timeline that could be delayed should there be mitigating circumstances, such as a recession or adverse conditions in capital markets, in the U.S. or abroad. This is disconcerting because it would allow at least 10 years since the end of the Financial Crisis for systemically important financial institutions (SIFIs) to build the necessary capital cushions to withstand the next recession. The longest timeframe between recessions in U.S. history is just under 10 years; the average length of U.S. expansions has been closer to five years. Making matters worse is that the primary measure of capital adequacy will remain risk-weighted capital ratios, which can be subject to lots of gamesmanship. Moreover, the regulations implementing the new capital standards are still not complete, and run well over a thousand pages. It would have been preferable to require that all banks must have a capital-to-total assets ratio of, say, 10 percent or 12 percent, no later than, say, July 2015, five years following passage of Dodd–Frank.

Another virtue of Dodd–Frank is the central importance given to the need for banks, which serve as a key source of liquidity to the rest of the economy — and have access to the ultimate source of liquidity, the Federal Reserve's discount window — to have strong liquidity coverage ratios. However, it took until 2015 for the regulators to begin to agree on a working definition of liquidity coverage, a definition and implementation still under development in October 2016.

Another section of Dodd–Frank subjects the roughly 50 largest U.S. banks to an annual stress test. The penalty for failing the stress test is public censure from the Fed, including an inability of management to return capital to shareholders in the form of dividends. It worked. The CEO of Citigroup admonished his top management team that if Citi failed the stress test for a third time, he would resign, with the implicit threat that the rest of the management team would also be forced to resign. Subsequently, Citi passed a particularly tough stress test in 2016, as did most other banks that had shown stress test difficulties in prior years. The regulators should learn some lessons about imposing capital requirements from their experience with imposing stress tests.

In this regard, the regulators need reminding that tenacity on regulations that make bank management teams more accountable to shareholders through such mechanisms as dividend restrictions, can be extended to other parts of Dodd–Frank. As of Summer 2016, few if any banks seem to have been able to write a Living Will that satisfy both the Fed and the FDIC. What was wrong with this picture?

Another example of the lack of urgency in the implementation of Dodd–Frank displayed by the regulatory community is the failure of the Financial Stability Oversight Council (FSOC), the group of 16 financial regulators established by Dodd–Frank, to come up with a compelling definition or criteria for what constitutes a systemically important financial institution. The FSOC designated MetLife, a large insurance company, to be a SIFI. When MetLife sued to claim it was not systemic, the judge ruled that FSOC had never defined the term, so MetLife won its claim.[12] How can Dodd–Frank be "an act to end TBTF," if the regulatory bodies in charge cannot define systemically important? This is a critical issue because Dodd–Frank created the Orderly Liquidation Authority (OLA), which ordered the FDIC, not the Fed, to handle the failure of a nonbank SIFI, so that another situation like Lehman could not occur in the future. As of July 2016, only one-third of the necessary work to write the OLA regulations had been completed by the FDIC.[13]

In short, Dodd–Frank is an atonal, unfinished symphony in desperate need of a composer, an orchestrator and a conductor to come together to finish it under a tight deadline. So far, the implementing regulations are spread across over 22,000 pages and, overall, are about two-thirds complete. In this unfinished state, Dodd–Frank likely does more harm than good; this is especially shameful given the $15 trillion price tag of the 2008–2009 Financial Crisis. Do we wish to experience another crisis all over again?

To state it another way, Dodd–Frank is not ready to be used in prime time if a financial crisis were to occur in 2016, or at its current rate of implementation, before 2019. If Dodd–Frank is not ready for use, it may not have the full force of law that would allow it to function quickly and smoothly in the event of a financial crisis. In other words, we may have to rely on the laws and institutions that were in place prior to, and during, the 2008–2009 Financial Crisis, namely, the Fed and its old LOLR facility. The middle of a crisis is not the time to have to sort out the legal framework to be used to handle the crisis. Until Dodd–Frank's apparatus can truly be

---

[12] See Tracy and Holm (2016).
[13] See Davis and Polk (2016).

relied upon to function in a financial emergency, the Fed could likely be called upon to retain its role as the First Responder of First Resort, not by the Fed's own choice, but dictated by the circumstances of the time. This is not the best way to inspire confidence in the resiliency of our economic and financial system!

7. The Fed's Discount Window Prior to July 2010, and Currently

Going back to an amendment passed by Congress in 1932, creating Section 13[3] of the Federal Reserve Act, in the midst of the Great Depression, the Fed was enabled to extend emergency credit in "unusual and exigent circumstances" (Bernanke, 2015: 158). The Fed used this provision very sparingly from its inception. However, in March 2008, the Fed invoked the "unusual and exigent" clause as the legal foundation to lend to support JPMorgan Chase's acquisition of Bear Stearns, and six months later to lend to AIG, and eventually, to many others. To emphasize the significance of the Fed's use of its Section 13[3] powers, David Wessel characterized the 2008–2009 Financial Crisis as being composed of two phases: before Bear Stearns, and after Bear Stearns (Wessel, 2009: 147). Clearly, the use of Section 13[3] involved a judgement call that was to be used sparingly, as Congress originally intended.

Congress specified that the use of Section 13[3] required an affirmative vote by *five* of the members of the Fed's Board of Governors, no small task in the last six years when the usual complement of seven governors has been reduced to five by the unwillingness of the Senate to vote on the President's proposed nominations to fill vacant governor seats. In addition, the use of Section 13[3] requires that the borrower convince the lending Reserve Bank that: (a) credit is not available from other banks; and that (b) there is sufficient collateral to support the loan. Having served for many years as Secretary of the Dallas Fed's Discount Committee, I can attest that the directors of Federal Reserve Banks take their statutory requirements seriously; no Fed Board of Directors wants to endure the public's ignominy of making a discount window loan that cannot be repaid in full. These are hard-nosed business men and women, with a personal and business reputation at stake. Indeed, the conditions imposed by Congress were flexible enough to allow the New York Fed's Board of Directors to acquiesce to lending to AIG on September 16, 2008, but not to lend to Lehman over the weekend of September 12–14, 2008.

This flexibility, though limited, was circumscribed by Dodd-Frank, and the regulations the Fed has written to comply with the spirit and letter of the new law. Dodd–Frank specifies that the Fed: (a) can provide liquidity to an identifiable *market or sector of the financial system, **not** a single firm; (b) cannot allow through its lending for a firm to avoid bankruptcy or other resolution; and (c) to provide emergency credit to five or more firms, the Fed must have the prior approval of the Treasury Secretary. As should be required in a democratic society that wishes to foster transparency in government, Dodd–Frank specifies two further conditions: (1) to prevent abuses of this extraordinary use of the Fed's credit facility, Congress requires that the Board of Governors review any loans semi-annually and terminate the program unless the Board of Governors decides to publicly renew the program; and (2) in addition, the Fed's Board must promptly notify Congress of any emergency program or facility. For good measure, Dodd–Frank also specifies that any company operating under the OLA is ineligible for emergency credit from the Fed.

In short, the present-day status of the Fed's ability to serve as LOLR is back to where it was during the Panic of 1907, a full seven years prior to the Fed's formation! There is no LOLR, let alone a clearly-designated First Responder of First Resort. Backward time travel is alive and well. This is a shameful situation; 320 million U.S. citizens deserve a better solution from their elected representatives.

8. Lessons from 9/11

The U.S. recently commemorated the 15th anniversary of the September 11, 2001 attacks on the World Trade Center and the Pentagon. It would be useful to examine some parallels between the September 11 (9/11) event and the 2008–2009 Financial Crisis, since dealing with both events put the spotlight on the role of First Responders. Since I am a World Trade Center survivor, this is a matter of personal and paramount importance to me.

8.1. *First issue: Who's in charge?*

Using the 9/11 metaphor, it is completely unacceptable to have a shoving match between the police and fire departments over who is supposed to perform and lead certain tasks. Before and on 9/11, and at least eight years later, the New York City police and fire departments did not have a communication system that allowed them to coordinate their actions, and even if they did, they might not have spoken with one another because of deep-seated hostilities between the departments that went back a couple of generations. Similar issues exist between the Fed and the FDIC. One agency has to be in charge; in 2008–2009, the Fed was *de facto* in charge (together with the Treasury Secretary). After Dodd–Frank, the FDIC was granted the power to serve as the Orderly Liquidation Authority; the FDIC seems to be legally in charge, but it lacks the funds, expertise, and experience to perform its key tasks. As stated above, Congress needs to reinstate the Fed as being in charge, but with the assistance of the FDIC. In addition, Congress, the media, and the public need to demand that the Fed and FDIC communicate and coordinate their actions. This is easy to say, but difficult to do. However, first responders get better at their jobs through practice, practice, and still more practice, and better still by performing their practice exercises together in public demonstrations whenever possible. The police, fire, and EMTs in the tristate area of New York, New Jersey, and Connecticut practiced together following the 1993 bombing of the World Trade Center, and their efforts and jointly developed skills were transparent to me on 9/11. The Fed and the FDIC need to practice handling financial emergencies together, in public with media observation, as they hone their communications and skill sets.

8.2. *Second issue: Time is the enemy in a financial crisis*

The Fed and the FDIC share a common enemy in a crisis — time is one of the scarcest resources in a crisis. They need to unite to defeat the enemy of time; joint preparedness established through publicly-demonstrated practice in a variety of simulated crisis situations would help. Lastly, they need the resources to do their jobs; there is nothing like practice to reveal a shortage of critical resources. Just as we would not want the police to use toy guns to deal with narco-kingpins, we do not want the FDIC to have to use fake money to arrange the merger of a failed bank. The first rule in dealing with a person suffering from a possible heart attack or stroke is to get to a hospital emergency room as quickly as possible. A delay of only a few minutes can be the difference between life and death, or between a normal life and severe debilitation. The same principle applies to the analogous situation of the LOLR and the functioning of the U.S. economy.

In the early stages of the next financial crisis, it would be a shame if precious time is wasted to establish who has the authority to act in the public interest because of lack of legal clarity about the proper role of the LOLR versus the OLA, not to mention the pontification of competing ideologies emanating from Congress.

9.   The Costs and Benefits of the New Dodd–Frank LOLR Rules

9.1.   *The costs*

The most obvious cost of the new LOLR rules is that the Fed is seriously constrained in performing the primary duty it was created to do over a century ago. In the context of the 21st century, the Fed may not be able to provide temporary liquidity assistance to keep a systemic firm, or two or three systemic firms, alive long enough for an orderly resolution to be put together, in which case, we will suffer another Lehman Moment. When the Federal Reserve Act was passed in 1913, the U.S. likely had no financial institutions that would be deemed "systemically important." In 2016, the situation is very much the opposite; a handful of banks control over 50 percent of the assets of the banking industry. The failure of any single one of these institutions can decimate the U.S. financial system and the economy, with knock-on impacts on the global economy.

Dodd–Frank's proclamation of "no more bailouts" provides a false sense of security. No bailouts, but at what cost? Preventing bailouts is a worthy goal in a market-based capitalist economic system. However, there are tradeoffs in achieving this objective; namely, the increased likelihood of economic instability, together with prolonged recessions. In addition, the explicit standard of not allowing the Fed to lend to "an insolvent institution" increases the burden on the Fed to prove the unprovable, that it is only providing necessary liquidity. When markets are not functioning well, i.e., when liquidity is constrained for almost everyone, differentiating between liquidity shortages and solvency problems is difficult-to-impossible in real time.

Last, Dodd–Frank is vague enough to provide the Fed with escape clauses to do what is necessary. However, the Fed would have to break the new and explicit Section 13[3] rules in order to pursue its monetary policy goals of price stability and maximum employment, all in the highly charged environment of a microeconomic intervention in the midst of an impending financial crisis. This would put the credibility of the Fed as an institution of government at risk during a crucial and turbulent time. At minimum, this would be an unnecessary distraction, but it could exacerbate the impending disaster at hand.

9.2. The Benefits

The most obvious benefit of requiring the Fed to not lend to an individual financial institution under stress is that it would reduce moral hazard, but at the expense, as mentioned previously, of increasing the likelihood of financial instability and recession, not always the best set of tradeoffs. It should be noted in this regard that reducing moral hazard is a goal that has never been stated as part of the Federal Reserve Act. Economics and finance professors may desire the mitigation of moral hazard as an important goal, but it is a goal that has never been explicitly codified into statutes.

In drafting Dodd–Frank, Congress wished to reduce the Fed's tendency to provide a bailout for a private-sector financial institution under the guise of providing macroeconomic stability. At the same time, Congress sought to gain its own political cover by granting the Fed the flexibility to "break the rules" if it was necessary to save the financial system and the U.S. economy; while still allowing Congress the freedom to rave and rant about moral hazard and the Fed's interfering with the working of the market system. As a result, Congress is able to maintain "plausible deniability" for perpetuating moral hazard, TBTF, and bailouts; while at the same time, delaying and impairing the Fed's ability to engage in crisis management. This may be a benefit in the political sense of the term, but economically, it falls into the cost column.

10. Overall Assessment

We live in a dangerous world — militarily, financially, economically, and medically. In this environment, we need to rely on competent first responders. We may wishfully think otherwise in an effort to deny reality. However, to enact laws that severely curtail the ability of first responders to do their job is, if not criminal, then surely irresponsible, and, to the extent it entails living in denial of reality, it borders on insanity. In brief, the Fed's LOLR capabilities and First Responder of First Resort responsibilities should not be restricted.

References

Bernanke, B (2015). *The Courage to Act.* New York: W.W. Norton & Co.

Bagehot, W (1873). *Lombard Street: A Description of the Money Market.* New York: Armstrong & Co.

Davis Polk and Wardwell LLP (2016). *Dodd–Frank Progress Report: Six-Year Anniversary,* 19 July.

Derby, MS (2008). Volcker: Fed 'at Edge of Its Lawful and Implied Power.' *Wall Street Journal,* 8 April.

Dodd–Frank Wall Street Reform and Consumer Protection Act (2010). Public Law, pp. 111–203.

Friedman, M and AJ Schwartz (1963). *A Monetary History of the United States, 1867–1960.* (Princeton, NJ: Princeton University Press).

Greenspan A (1998). *Private-sector refinancing of the large hedge fund, Long-Term Capital Management,* Statement to the House, Committee on Banking and Financial Services, Hearing, 1 October.

Luttrell, D, T Atkinson and H Rosenblum (2013). Assessing the Costs and Consequences of the 2007–2009 Financial Crisis and Its Aftermath. *Economic Letter,* Federal Reserve Bank of Dallas, 8(7).

McCulley, P (2011). *The Paradox of Deleveraging.* Global Central Bank Focus, Pacific Investment Management Company, LLC, July.

Rosenblum, H, D DiMartino, J Renier and R Alm (2008). *Fed Intervention: Managing Moral Hazard in Financial Crises. Economic Letter,* Federal Reserve Bank of Dallas, 3(10), October.

Sorkin, AR (2010). *Too Big to Fail: The Inside Story of How Wall Street and Washington Fought to Save the Financial System — and Themselves.* New York: Penguin Books.

Tracy, R and E Holm (2016). Judge Curbs Oversight of MetLife. *Wall Street Journal,* 31 March, p. A1.

Wessel, D (2009). *In Fed We Trust: Ben Bernanke's War on the Great Panic.* New York: Crown Business.

Willardson, N and L Pederson (2010). *Federal Reserve Liquidity Programs: An Update, The Region,* Federal Reserve Bank of Minneapolis, June.

Chapter Seven

Stretching the Financial Safety Net to its Breaking Point

Edward J. Kane*

Boston College

What a government calls its financial safety net has three components: (1) actions officials take to restrict the risk of ruin that institutions assume; (2) measures officials take to limit the damage creditors, customers, employees, and stockholders suffer when and if an institution becomes hopelessly insolvent; and (3) an ability, in the event of financial turmoil, to make taxpayers and surviving institutions pay explicitly or implicitly for whatever rescue operations they undertake.

This definition casts a nation's safety net as a multiparty web of contractual duties and obligations. In a crisis, its most tangible features are explicit and implicit government guarantees and lender-of-last-resort credit facilities. The ideal safety net is one that would efficiently mitigate the particular monitoring, policing, and coordination difficulties that present themselves to financial institutions, counterparties, and taxpayers in the informational, ethical, legal, and economic environment of a particular country at a particular time. This mouthful of tasks means that a country's ideal safety net evolves with and partly causes changes in the market, legal, bureaucratic, and ethical/cultural problems that the net is intended to alleviate.

Safety nets have expanded over time for three reasons. First, formally uninsured firms (such as money-market mutual funds and clearinghouses) see a great advantage in making themselves too large, too complex, and too politically influential to supervise adequately, and too interconnected for authorities to comfortably risk letting them default on their obligations. Second, though their timing is irregular and unpredictable, crises inevitably occur. In the midst of a

---

*This chapter updates and refocuses material previously presented in Kane (2009), and Demirgüç-Kunt, Kane, and Laeven (2015). The author thanks the Institute for New Economic Thinking for financial support, George Kaufman for the title, and Robert Dickler and Thomas Ferguson for valuable comments on an earlier draft.

financial crisis, the immediate benefits of rescuing large classes of uninsured instruments by means of subsidized loans and blanket guarantees become dramatically more visible to regulators and politicians than the future taxpayer burdens that rescues generate. Finally, for a long while, explicit insurance was regarded to be part of "best practices" policy standards, and were promulgated as such in IMF policy reports during the last half of the 1990s (Lindgren, Garcia, and Saal, 1996; Garcia, 1999). It is now widely understood that these standards are not, in fact, "best practices" in environments where political institutions and regulatory accountability are weak (Demirgüç-Kunt and Kane, 2002). This is because, in poor informational and contracting environments, it is especially dangerous to undermine customers' and investors' ethical responsibility to look out for themselves. The ineffectiveness of contractual controls, and the ambiguous and unfunded nature of perceived implicit deposit guarantees lead depositors to demand a risk premium that is broadly commensurate with the risk-taking capacity of their bank.

Section 1 of the chapter introduces the idea that individual countries have had to confront what have been rapidly changing global and national contracting environments with slowly adapting national and global regulatory cultures. A contracting environment encompasses the degree to which relevant political and legal institutions and operative concepts of personal honor influence the transparency and accuracy of information flows and shape private methods of contract enforcement. A regulatory culture simultaneously authorizes and restricts *de jure* the ways in which a government or set of governments may exercise their supervision, rulemaking, and rescue powers, and expands them *de facto* as it copes with unforeseen difficulties in creative ways (Kane, 2016).

During the Great Financial Crisis, Fed officials used currency swaps and other creative procedures to rescue foreign (especially European) banks when they were in distress. The pride that these officials took in their action encouraged private counterparties and government officials to see the Federal Reserve — both then and going forward — as the global rescuer of last resort.

The conviction that the Fed has everybody's back emboldened authorities in other nations to expand their own system of guarantees, in many cases, beyond their likely capacity to pay for them. Drawing on Demirgüç-Kunt, Kane, and Laeven (2015), Section 2 discusses differences in safety net design and in how safety net support was expanded in different countries during the Great Financial Crisis.

Section 3 emphasizes the importance to U.S. taxpayers of seeing that accountability and disaster planning are incorporated into foreign safety nets and cross-country swap arrangements. The secular expansion of safety net liabilities will not stop until and unless officials here and abroad forswear extending new safety net coverages without first making sure that: (1) they can track and respond to the safety net implications of changes in their country's contracting environment, and (2) the tools and norms of their regulatory culture allow them to monitor and control the implicit safety net expansion that, going forward, regulation-induced innovations in financial instruments are bound to generate. Section 4 explains how, in difficult informational environments, introducing extended liability for bank stock can assist authorities in these tasks. But the unlikely politics of accomplishing even such a simple reform suggest that things will have to get a lot worse before they can get better.

1. Regulatory Culture and the Contracting Environment

Modern finance theory emphasizes that an institution's creditors and counterparties must worry about controlling incentives for opportunistic behavior by the institution's managers, owners, and borrowers (Jensen and Meckling, 1976; Diamond, 1984; La Porta *et al.*, 1998). Opportunistic managers exploit three intertwined "muniments" (i.e., protections from punishment):

(1) *Monitoring Costs*: difficulties a depositor or other counterparty faces in obtaining reliable information about unfavorable developments and adverse actions by financial institution managers, including recklessness, negligence, incompetence, fraud, and self-dealing;

(2) *Policing Costs*: difficulties an individual counterparty faces in adequately analyzing and responding to whatever information its monitoring activity turns up;

(3) *Coordination Costs*: difficulties counterparties face in coordinating collective action.

In most informational and contracting environments, government guarantees transfer these costs from private parties and concentrate them in government hands.

To control the value of safety net guarantees, a government must establish a centralized framework of tangible safeguards, monitoring activity, and deterrent response. Centralizing these functions seeks to increase confidence in institutional contract performance by solving three coordination problems — avoiding redundant monitoring expense; standardizing contracting protocols; and timing and calibrating disciplinary action. In principle, a centralized monitor-enforcer could make it unprofitable for banks to misrepresent their economic condition and to pursue profit-making opportunities that might exploit counterparties' informational disadvantage. In practice, the supervision of multinational firms is not centralized, and the Fed's propensity for rescue makes U.S. taxpayers serve as the *de facto* guarantors of last resort. Governmental fears of destructive creditor runs and sectoral meltdowns lead individual–country regulators both to give distressed institutions the benefit of the doubt, and to tolerate disclosure regimes that increase the level of that doubt by making it hard for outsiders (including themselves) to observe adverse information in a timely manner. Typically, by the time regulators can benchmark the depth of a developing financial crisis, firming up implicit safety net guarantees and minimizing creditor haircuts seems the least-humiliating path to follow.

1.1. Dimensions of regulatory culture

Financial regulation and supervision are cooperative endeavors. Anyone can propose rules, but to command compliance requires legitimacy — a mutual understanding that (regulatory capture aside), the rules are conceived and enforced to increase social welfare.

To win and sustain a legitimate right to wield coercive force, regulators must accept and respect appropriate checks on their authority. An "appropriate" check is one that is consistent with the country's political culture and its citizens' understanding of the country's past regulatory experience.

A culture is defined as customs, ideas, and attitudes that members share and transmit from generation to generation by systems of subtle and unsubtle rewards and punishments. Carnell (1993) and Kane (2003) assign every regulatory culture an espoused mission of defining, authenticating, and promoting the financial common good. However, individual–country regulatory cultures may differ from one another in any or all of six tangible dimensions:

(1) in the character of the statutory grant of authority and the reporting responsibilities a regulatory enterprise receives;
(2) in the specific rules the enterprise formulates and how it develops and promulgates them;
(3) in the methods the enterprise uses to monitor for violations;
(4) in the penalties it can and does impose on clients when it finds material violations;
(5) in the nature and extent of due-process restrictions (including specific burdens of proof and consultation) that protect regulated institutions from unfair administrative procedures;

(6) in the extent of insured institutions' rights to appeal regulatory decisions to a higher authority.

To be viable, the taboos and traditions incorporated into the espoused missions and tangible features of a regulatory culture must embody community standards of fair play and proper use of government power. However, as Schein (2010) emphasizes, all cultures share deeply imbedded norms and assumptions about how to behave in difficult circumstances. These unspoken and uncodified norms and beliefs often conflict with regulators' espoused goals, especially in crisis environments.

1.2. Transparency and deterrency

Regulators' tools of safety net control are rulemaking and enforcement. To understand the economic role these tools play, it is helpful to imagine a world in which counterparties' monitoring and policing costs would be uniformly zero. In this world, every financial contract would be self-enforcing and coordination costs would be irrelevant. Establishing a team of centralized monitors and enforcers to thwart risk-shifting and misconduct by financial institution insiders would offer no incremental benefit either to institutions or to their counterparties. In such a world, changes in an institution's condition and risk exposure would be transparent to all counterparties, and all counterparties would possess sufficient expertise and sanctions to deter bank insiders from trying to take advantage of them. *Maximal transparency* (MT) describes a framework of disclosure that would perfectly and costlessly inform counterparties about changes in a firm's performance and risk-taking activities. To provide a pair of parallel rhyming words, we use *maximal deterrency* (MD) to describe a situation in which counterparties would immediately and perfectly understand the implications of information flows, and would be able to protect themselves completely and costlessly from whatever threat to their wealth this information might reveal.

The more closely an economy comes to offering counterparties maximal transparency and maximal deterrency, the less *ex ante* value that financiers and safety net managers can create for institutional stakeholders. In an MTMD economy, cash in advance and credit could substitute perfectly for each other in every payment context. Similarly, direct and indirect finance would provide equally economical ways of mobilizing savings, of choosing which real investment projects savers ought to support, and of deciding how to price project risk. As envisaged in the Capital Asset Pricing Model, corporate and government securities could be offered in denominations small enough to allow virtually every individual saver to invest directly in a diversified portfolio of stocks, bonds, and derivative securities.

The MTMD thought experiment clarifies that safety nets owe their existence to difficulties of contract enforcement — blockages in information flows; differences in monitoring costs; variation in financial transaction costs; delays in appreciating and processing relevant information; and the costliness and inadequacy of the deterrent remedies that individual counterparties have available to them. It also clarifies that a safety net can be modeled effectively as a seven-party contract. The net imposes mutual rights and duties on financiers, borrowers, creditors, stockholders, credit-rating organizations, safety net managers, and suppliers of safety net capital (principally, assessable healthy institutions and taxpayers). The ethical touchstone by which to judge the performance of safety net managers is the fairness with which they treat each of their various counterparties and the efficiency with which they manage the diverse social costs of coping with divergences from MT and MD conditions.

It is not enough for safety net managers to aim at blocking corrupt and unwise flows of institutional credit and avoiding institutional runs. They must seek also to minimize the social damage caused by bouts of temporary illiquidity and insolvency. In administering lender-of-last-resort facilities, safety net managers are expected to perform the financial *triage* function of shielding solvent, but illiquid institutions from having to sell assets into momentarily disorderly markets.

1.3. Accountability for implicit coverages as an ideal feature of safety net design

Taxpayers' stake in the safety net can be measured by the value of the contingent tax liability they accept in explicitly and implicitly backing up the net's guarantees. In the absence of taxpayer back-up, private and government deposit-insurance managers would have to expend additional resources to convince contractual counterparties that the enterprise can be relied upon to fulfill its contractual commitments (Merton and Perold, 1993). The capitalized value of the protection-induced annual saving in enterprise expense may be defined as "equity capital" that taxpayers contribute to financial institutions though the safety net. Unless taxpayer-contributed risk capital generates a fair return in the form of dividends and safety net benefits to society, deposit-insurance and other bailout schemes unwisely subsidize bank risk-taking.

In managing safety net capital, regulators are pulled in contrary directions. On the one hand, they are expected to minimize the risk of a banking disaster. For this reason, regulators who show mercy to a troubled bank garner public praise for themselves and their agency. On the other hand, regulators are also expected to minimize the cost of bailing out troubled banks and to subject all banks to market-mimicking discipline. However, regulators who strongly and transparently discipline a weak bank fear that they will be accused of aggravating the bank's problems.

Suppressing evidence of banking weakness and relaxing capital requirements is a rational — albeit unhealthy — way to resolve this tension, especially if safety net officials expect to hold office briefly and can derive bureaucratic, reputational, and revolving-door benefits from currying industry support. This incentive conflict is not easily resolved. Unless regulatory decisions take place in a MTMD environment for taxpayers, safety net managers cannot be made fully accountable in a timely manner for managing taxpayers' economic stake in the safety net. Though helpful, efforts to privatize the loss exposure can never be complete, because even a privately managed and privately funded guarantee scheme enjoys implicit catastrophic taxpayer back-up. The taxpayer remains a silent partner whose investment in the net is both unfunded, undercompensated, and unlikely to be formally acknowledged by net managers.

To the extent that the informational environment allows, it is important to make specific officials responsible for tracking and publicizing the aggregate losses to which the safety net exposes taxpayers and for pricing and managing this exposure appropriately. However, the difficulty of implementing this principle in environments where information is unreliable and corruption is rampant implies that introducing explicit guarantees may end up substituting corrupt government supervision for value-preserving private discipline.

To guard against this unhappy result and to forestall safety net expansion, political independence for safety net officials is not enough. In low-accountability environments, safety net designers must incorporate features that can generate strong private discipline on safety net managers and bankers alike. A good starting point is for authorities to make risk more visible to outsiders at the individual-institution level. In particular, a positive obligation might be placed on every insured bank's top officers, not just to certify personally the material accuracy of marked-to-market estimates of bank net worth, but to prepare frequent estimates of the intangible capitalized value of the safety net benefits the bank enjoys and to report promptly all substantial changes in risk exposures and net worth to regulators. As mark-to-market estimates are especially hard to verify for complex institutions, complex firms should be asked to post proportionately higher levels of accounting capital, and their officers should be subject to particularly severe penalties for failing to disclose material adverse information.

As better information on bank capital and loss exposure becomes available, government regulators everywhere can be assigned two further specific tasks: (1) to calculate in a reproducible statistical manner interval estimates of the opportunity-cost value of safety net risk exposures in insured banks, and (2) to tailor insurance premiums and regulatory intervention to control the risk each bank passes through to the net. Accountability for these activities could be established by having regulators' calculations closely audited by a multinational private accounting firm, and by offering top regulators in each country a fund of deferred compensation that they would have to forfeit if statistical analysis of available data and subsequent events could prove that the agency's risk calculations were fudged.

For regulation and supervision to establish incentives for financial institutions and regulators that are compatible with the interests of all other parties, net design must be environment-specific. One issue is how transparent information systems and supervisory technology for monitoring financial institution capital and risk exposures are, especially to outside experts or to the financial press. A second issue is the extent to which regulator incentives lead to patterns of discipline that reinforce or displace market safeguards.

In practice, a safety net manager must assemble a staff that can wield six categories of regulatory instruments fairly and efficiently:

(1) record-keeping and disclosure requirements;
(2) activity limitations;
(3) capital, loss-reserving, and other position limits;
(4) takeover rights and other enforcement powers;
(5) lines of credit; and
(6) performance guarantees.

The first four categories delimit the net managers' authority to regulate financial firms. Along with regulatees' rights to challenge and appeal adverse actions, the last two categories provide credible ways for regulators to bond themselves to exercise their supervisory authority in the joint interests of institutions and their various counterparties. To complete the web of social contract enforcement, the suppliers of regulatory risk capital — explicitly insured institutions and taxpayers — must be able to observe and discipline the economic value of their stake in the rulemaking and enforcement activities that regulators undertake. Ideally, taxpayers must impose reporting requirements and establish deterrent rights sufficient to persuade net managers to deploy their examination, supervisory, and lending powers at reasonable economic cost to society as a whole. These costs must be defined realistically and comprehensively. They include costs of operating the net and costs of managing and repairing its occasional breakdown. Taxpayer–regulator contracting is the weak link in the chain. The practical politics of financial regulation and the exercise of consultation and appeal rights by regulated institutions tend to make regulatory personnel overly responsive to the concerns of the financial industry.

1.4. *Weaknesses in informational transparency*

Creditors and investors want to be sure that they are fairly compensated for the risk exposures that financial institutions, loans, and investments pass through to them. The "information" needed to benchmark their compensation consists of valid facts and projections that would help a skilled financial analyst to calculate the market value of financial institution net worth as the difference between the present discounted values of its assets and liabilities.

When a nation's financial markets inaccurately identify and price risks, they misdirect savings and investment. Such misdirection misallocates resources and undermines a nation's economic stability and well-being. It is helpful to think of financial institution disclosures as "ore" and information as a mineral that depositors and regulators can, only imperfectly and with effort, extract from this "ore". Extraction is imperfect for two reasons — because institutions have a legitimate interest in reserving proprietary information for their own use, and because they may want to conceal potentially damaging information from other parties.

Government regulators are supposed to identify material misinformation and correct it promptly. The less effectively the ethical norm of "fair dealing" constrains the business dealings of corporate and government officials in a given country, the more thoroughly safety net managers ought to double-check data provided by and to institutions within their purview. However, as a practical matter, strong incentives push regulators in the reverse direction. The less effectively ethical norms and investigative journalism constrain government officials, the more likely it becomes that safety net managers may be enlisted to use their instruments to help opportunistic institutions and at least some of their counterparties to exploit taxpayers.

In financially sophisticated environments, the reliability of disclosures about financial institution values is tested and disciplined — albeit imperfectly — by an array of outside parties. Rules governing financial institution disclosures come both from statutory and administrative law. Statutes are shaped in legislatures. Regulations governing how to value and itemize sources and uses of funds are established by administrative agencies and self-regulatory organizations. Enforcement by rulemaking entities is subject to due process and constitutional review by a nation's judiciary system.

Dishonest corporate and government reporting is additionally deterred by the knowledge that information flows will also be reviewed informally by private "watchdog institutions" — professional accountants, credit bureaus, credit-rating organizations, an independent financial press, investment analysts and advisors, and even academic researchers. However, even in high-income countries, the information-verification mission of individual watchdogs often conflicts with their other economic interests.

Elsewhere, inter-institutional competition is usually weak, reporting standards relatively uninformative, and validity checks on bank and borrower disclosures allow many informational impurities to survive the data-testing process.

Recapping the discussion, the quality of regulation varies across countries with informational quality or transparency [T]. In turn, [T] varies with accounting integrity [AI], integrity-promoting ethical norms [EN], press freedom [PF], and the quality and credibility of compensating restraints regulators place on financial transactors [R]. In symbols:

$$T = T [AI, EN, PF; R]. \tag{1}$$

Several research institutions rate in different ways the quality of the governance and information environments for depositors and taxpayers in different countries and across time. The quality of relevant information varies greatly across countries, but indexes for [T] and its determinants are positively correlated with the level of a country's per capita income (Kane, 2009).

The pattern of correlations suggests not that the level of development determines the level of informational transparency and accountability or vice versa, but that both variables are simultaneously determined by unobservable latent variables. I find it helpful to interpret these latent variables as a culture's shared beliefs about what is tolerable and intolerable deal-making behavior. Adopting this ethical perspective frames the level of economic and financial development as an imperfect control for slowly evolving social and cultural attitudes that strengthen the enforceability of financial contracts.

For a safety net to operate fairly and efficiently in environments where informational and ethical integrity are low, the policymaking process of selecting design features and resisting expansion must be open enough to establish accountability between regulators and taxpayers. Political accountability increases with the freedom accorded a nation's press, and with the political and economic freedoms it grants its citizens to challenge government policies. However, even in otherwise favorable political environments, accountability is lessened by the extent and frequency with which top regulators are drawn from — or retire into — positions in the financial industry.

1.5. Weaknesses in counterparties' deterrent capacity

Given a country's level of informational transparency, an individual depositor's ability to protect itself from looming bank or borrower defaults is limited by the deterrent rights and enforcement powers conveyed to contracting parties by its country's legal system. Modern finance portrays a bank's creditors as holding a contingent claim on the stock of their bank. Similarly, a portfolio of options written on borrowers' assets is imbedded in the value of the bank's loans. These options limit the losses creditors experience when banks and their borrowers choose to default.

All defects in counterparty rights, in their enforceability, or in judicial and bureaucratic efficiency leave financial markets less complete and banks and bank creditors more vulnerable to default. Besides [T], deterrency [D] depends on a country's systems for policing corporate and public governance [G]:

$$D = D[G, T] \qquad (2)$$

Weaknesses in [D] disadvantage three groups with stakes in the safety net — institutions as lenders; counterparties as financial institution creditors; and all suppliers of safety net capital. In low-deterrency environments, a rational saver will be reluctant to trust its funds to unrelated parties, unless the borrower bonds its repayment capacity in a credible way. Table 7.1 ranks 215 countries according to the 2014 level of a World Bank index of their government's "regulatory quality." Two other measures of deterrent protections taken from the World Bank website represent the ability to control corruption and the relevance of "voice and accountability" proved highly correlated with each other and with this index. As with transparency, the level of deterrency tends to increase on average as per capita income rises. This pervasive collinearity reinforces the hypothesis that unmeasured sociocultural norms and freedoms explain differences in transparency and deterrency. This encouraged Demirgüç-Kunt, Kane, and Laeven (2008) to investigate how differences in the quality of a country's corruption control and level of development affect safety net design.

A climate of corruption makes it harder for creditors to monitor insolvent institutions, and harder for taxpayers and solvent institutions to monitor regulators. Conceived as a proxy for informational transparency, strong corruption control implies that increases in informational reliability would lessen the scope of the safety net. However, viewed as a proxy for deterrency and public accountability, enhancements in corruption control could have the opposite effect. This is because, in seemingly lessening financial institution fragility, effective corruption control simultaneously reduces not just the costs, but also the incremental benefits of safety net protection.

The table does not precisely document cross-country differences in top officials' accountability for safety net performance. However, evidence of the expansion in safety coverages during the Great Financial Crisis is consistent with a hypothesis of accountability to financial firms. Demirgüç-Kunt *et al.* (2015) show that across the 189 countries for which they were able to compile comprehensive data, the Great Financial Crisis led a majority of governments to provide new forms of credit support to banks and their customers. The most common response was for authorities to ramp up explicit coverage in countries that already had deposit-insurance [DI] schemes and to install explicit insurance in countries where previously deposit insurance was merely implicit. Figure 7.1 shows both that reliance on explicit DI rises with per capita income, and that such reliance increased during the crisis across all income levels. Figure 7.2 shows that almost all European countries now offer explicit deposit insurance. Although the European Union formally committed itself to haircutting creditors in future crises, adherence to such a procedure would be contradictory to what Kane (2016) calls U.S. and European central banks' deeply imbedded culture of rescue. Incidence increased sharply in Asia and the Middle East, but remained notably lower in Africa than in other regions.

Figure 7.3 shows that most DI schemes are administered publicly and that other forms of administration are rare in both lower-income categories. Figure 7.4 shows that in all income classes, funds to support the system are collected in whole or in part by charges (usually *under*charges) levied on insured banks.

Figure 7.5 shows that, by 2013, between 25% and 40% of DI systems enjoyed formal backup from their government, with the percentage rising on average with country income. Figure 7.6 shows that, since 2003 and measured as a percentage of current-year per-capita GDP, coverage limits seem to have increased permanently in all income classes.

I believe that the evidence presented in Figure 7.7 offers considerable insight into how political·pressure and a perceived regulatory duty of rescue expand government safety nets during a crisis. Coinsurance is a form of creditor bail-in that, before the crisis, was in force in 16 high- and upper-middle income countries. Far from exercising their contractual right to haircut depositors by enforcing coverage limits and coinsurance rights, governments that held these rights tended to renounce them under crisis pressures. Moreover, even some countries that avoided an outright crisis raised coverage limits and renounced their coinsurance rights as a prophylactic measure.

2. Likelihood of Further Safety Net Expansion

In the absence of MT and MD, depositors must watch for harm from two directions:

(1) from *past* losses that bank insiders have managed (possibly with regulatory connivance) to conceal from public view;
(2) from hidden exposures to *future* losses from illiquidity, bad luck, incompetence, negligence, fraud, corruption, or zombieness.

For the safety net to protect counterparties fully from these dangers, governments must design their net to counter the particular shortfalls in transparency and deterrency that characterize financial affairs in their country.

The most important feature is whether the guarantees provided to depositors and institutional counterparties are made partially explicit or left completely implicit. Guarantees are explicit when they are embodied in enforceable obligations that depositors are entitled to collect from the insurer's assets as a matter of law. In many countries, one or more banks are state-owned. For such banks and for private institutions that seem too large or too complex to fail, creditor protection is widely perceived to be absolute.

Although implicit guarantees are by nature unfunded, they exist always and everywhere. This is partly because every financial institution is formally licensed as such by a specific government. Implicit government guarantees depend for their enforceability on public confidence in the strength of political incentives for a country's leaders to rescue stakeholders in particular institutions when they become economically insolvent. Even in an explicit system, a degree of implicit insurance comes from the discretion authorities have to treat stakeholders in troubled institutions compassionately. An incipient financial crisis creates political incentives for incumbent officials in any government with an explicit system to extend regulatory forbearances, subsidized loans, and unfunded *de facto* guarantees or coverages that exceed the formal limits specified in the nation's laws and regulations. This is illustrated in Figures 7.7 and 7.8 by the safety net expansion that occurred around the world during and before the crisis.

To measure the generosity of country deposit insurance schemes and the extent of government guarantees on bank assets and liabilities, Demirgüç-Kunt *et al.* (2015) developed an index of safety net generosity. Their safety net index is computed using principal component analysis of standardized design feature variables that each are increasing in moral hazard. Specifically, the index incorporates the following design features — coverage limit/GDP per capita and dummy variables for unlimited government guarantees in place, coverage of foreign currency deposits, coverage of interbank deposits, no co-insurance, payouts to depositors [per deposit account=2; per depositor per institution=1; per depositor=0], no risk-adjusted premiums, *ex ante* fund, funded by government, backstop from government, no losses imposed on uninsured deposits, government guarantees on bank deposits (limited or full), government guarantees on non-deposit liabilities since 2008, and government guarantees on bank assets since 2008. Each of these variables is constructed such that higher values denote more generosity or greater government support and encouarge more moral hazard. This index adds to the set of deposit insurance variables used by Demirgüç-Kunt and Detragiache (2002) and information on government guarantees in other parts of the financial sector. As such, the index captures moral hazard generated by the financial safety net at large. The safety net index [SNI] is the sum of the first six principal components for which the eigenvalues are found to exceed unity.

Figure 7.8 reports extreme values of this SNI index for 2013, with higher values denoting more generosity, and consequently, the likelihood of greater moral hazard. We observe much country variation in the SNI index. It ranges from lows of −11.9 in Argentina and −10.5 in Iceland (both of which have imposed losses on insured depositors), to highs of 4.6 in Ireland and the U.S. (which issued temporary guarantees on deposits and non-deposit liabilities during the recent crisis), and 4.5 in Turkmenistan and 7.8 in Uzbekistan (which have blanket guarantees). Some high-SNI countries will be able to fund their generous safety net promises, but the fairness and efficiency of imposing such a burden on households and non-financial firms is questionable. This chapter stresses that the moral hazard generous schemes are apt to generate can, in a crisis, easily put burdens on U.S. taxpayers if the Federal Reserve moves to make good the guarantees that other governments cannot cover.

Hovakimian, Kane, and Laeven (2003) show econometrically that, when explicit guarantees are adopted, unfavorable country characteristics adversely influence deposit-insurance design. For explicit deposit insurance to improve social welfare, the operative country and cross-country regulatory cultures must be healthy enough to generate more or less as much supervisory discipline as the private discipline that deposit insurance displaces.

It is unfortunate that the surge in adoption among countries with weak regulatory systems was distorted by pressure from multinational organizations. For example, Eastern European countries were eager to meet criteria for membership in the European Union and these criteria included explicit deposit insurance. Also, throughout the 1990s, IMF personnel encouraged countries in Latin America and Asia that experienced banking crises to craft explicit deposit insurance systems as a way to unwind unlimited guarantees installed in the heat of crisis.

2.1. Dangers of introducing explicit guarantees in difficult circumstances

In downturns and crises, the safety net tends to block the exit of insolvent institutions. Far from assisting the prompt exit of crippled or unprofitable firms, political forces urge regulators to clog the industry's "exit drainpipe." The blockage is strongest when politicians are eager to preserve troubled institutions' contributions to politically inspired credit-allocation programs, such as those that have perennially promoted homeownership in the U.S. Allowing unprofitable financial institutions to issue guaranteed debt can artificially prolong their lives at levels of net worth that would otherwise be too low to sustain their existence. Active, but insolvent, firms may be likened to "zombies," in that they are kept alive by the black magic of government guarantees. Zombie competitors are dangerous to society because they can bid down industry profit margins to levels so low that even healthy and well-managed banks can no longer turn a profit.

When safety nets retard the exit of poorly performing financial institutions, not only is new entry discouraged, but healthy competitors and taxpayers (as suppliers of safety net capital) are forced to back up high-risk gambles by the crippled firms. Bailing out zombie institutions distorts the stock of real capital by encouraging loans to high-risk enterprises, and assigns taxpayers an unbalanced option on industry profits. Taxpayers are required to pay off future losses, but receive little opportunity to participate in potential future gains. The most that taxpayers can receive from a recovered institution is temporary relief from the need to continue to fund bailout arrangements.

The root problem is governmental short-termism. In a crisis, the immediate benefits of rescue permanently expand the net because the long-run control of supervisory and industry risk-taking incentives loses urgency. Whenever a country's financial system experiences large losses, stakeholders lobby for a massive infusion of state resources and against rolling back the assistance when crisis pressures relent. Government guarantees can rescue a deeply troubled financial system without immediately requiring economic policymakers either to recognize the size of industry losses or to impose new taxes. Introducing explicit deposit insurance or other guarantees provides a convenient way for bank stakeholders to mask the size of the subsidies they extract. As the legacy of crisis-driven credit support further reduces counterparty concern for transparency and deterrency, post-crisis rounds of unsound and corrupt financial practices must be expected.

3. Will Crisis Management Better Protect Taxpayers in the Next Crisis?

In principle, careful safety net design can constrain banks' ability to exploit weaknesses in transparency, deterrency, and accountability. Market discipline can be generated by increasing the number of nonshareholder parties that are responsible for absorbing a "first-loss share" of the losses financial institution insolvencies entail. In practice, private loss bearers are either creditors (including very large depositors), bonding companies, or subordinated debtholders. The value to society of putting private parties in a first-loss position turns on the credibility of two expectations: (1) that government officials will force private parties to live up to their contractual responsibilities, and (2) that loss-sharing private parties will not stand by if governmental forbearance exposes them to increasing risks.

Several ways exist to expand first-loss exposures. One is to make private parties underwrite and manage some of the loss exposures inherent in the deposit-insurance system. For example, clearing members of stock and commodities exchanges operate a private safety net in which they promise in various ways to absorb losses traders suffer due to failures in settlement. Another is to issue debt instruments that convert into common stock under prespecified terms when emerging losses drive bank capital below safe levels (von Furstenberg, 2015).

A third way to enlist private parties in constraining bank risk shifting is to use exclusions and coverage limits to render insurance coverage incomplete. Most countries formally specify an upper limit to the size of deposit balance they protect. Relatively few countries cover interbank deposits, but it is fairly common to insure accounts denominated in foreign currency. A contractual device for controlling moral hazard similar to exclusions and coverage limits that private insurance companies use is coinsurance (Calomiris, 1998; Kane, 1995). Coinsurance requires that the insured party bear a specified share of the value that is destroyed when a loss-causing event occurs.

Post-crisis reforms adopted in Europe and the U.S. seek mainly to ramp up failed strategies of prompt insolvency prevention and resolution that have failed in the past. These reforms entail closer and more forward-looking supervision (stress tests), higher capital, and liquidity requirements, and procedures to "bail in" various investors and creditors to avert or resolve the insolvency of a distressed financial firm.

The idea of lifting losses that threaten to exhaust a bank's true net worth out of the bank's underwater balance sheet and bailing them into the "boats" of the bank's uninsured creditors seems in the abstract to be an act of simple justice. After all, the affected creditors previously volunteered to take on the loss exposures that menace them now. However, in the midst of a crisis, politicians and regulators are encouraged to see creditor losses differently — as cruel acts of fate visited disproportionately on parties that authorities have a duty to treat mercifully.

Post-crisis financial reforms adopted in the U.S. and Europe remind me of strategies used by so-called "helicopter parents" to deal with a wayward child. Although Mom and Dad promise to deliver "tough love" for their children as an abstract strategy for curtailing future bad behavior, they are moved by their children's expressions of remorse and a purpose of amendment to rescue them from the full consequences of each concrete instance of bad behavior. Such parents back into an endless cycle of tolerating bad behavior and accepting the child's insincere promise to avoid bad behavior going forward.

During the Great Financial Crisis, "helicopter" politicians and central bankers proved themselves similarly reluctant to enforce coverage limits and coinsurance provisions. Although the insolvency of many banks was resolved, officials were daunted by the prospect of showing tough love to complex giant financial organizations. Authorities *could* have followed tougher and fairer loss-distribution policies, but they were afraid to. When one looks at this experience squarely, it is hard to regard the new policy mix with more than an optimistically tinged form of policy pessimism. Post-crisis reforms have indeed opened a number of new *options* for showing tough love in the next crisis, but emotional, cultural, and political appeals by stakeholders for rescue and relief from deserved haircuts will remain as strong as ever. To my mind, the fact that the financial industry has succeeded in painting sponsors of no-haircut policies (such as Paulson, Geithner, and Bernanke) as national heroes cements a cultural precedent for the kind of institution-friendly accounting and crisis management policies that the agencies have followed for years.

4. Matching Safety Net Design Features with Individual-Country Characteristics

Contracting theory emphasizes that counterparties face strong incentives to minimize the costs of agency. Black, Miller, and Posner (1978) conceive of a country's deposit insurers as "stepping into the shoes of individual depositors." This conception clarifies that, absent outside pressure from international institutions, *conscientious* officials in individual countries would design their portion of the safety net to cope with the particular deficiencies in transparency and deterrency that depositors face in their country's financial and economic environment.

However, officials' conscientiousness varies with cross-country differences in transparency, deterrency, and accountability. Hovakimian, Kane, and Laeven (2008) show that, in weak institutional environments, authorities are unlikely to adopt a mix of loss-sharing rules, risk-sensitive premiums, and coverage limits strong enough to control moral hazard. This implies that in recommending changes in the structure of a country's safety net European Union, IMF, and World Bank personnel should look for measures that would improve some subset of transparency, deterrency, and accountability.

It is also possible to lessen incentive conflicts and safety net expansion by directly curtailing the benefits that stockholders of insolvent institutions can extract by go-for-broke risk-taking. In practice, the profitability of endgame plays can be blunted by extending stockholder liability for liquidation losses beyond the level of the capital actually paid-in at the corporate level. Several now-industrialized countries (including the U.K., the U.S., and Canada) imposed extended liability on bank shares when their contacting environments were more rudimentary.

Extended liability has the advantage of increasing transparency, deterrency, and accountability at the same time. It increases transparency by transforming movements in the stock price of publicly traded banks into a clearer signal of institutional strength or weakness. Extended liability means that the insurer's right to liquidate an insolvent commercial or investment bank carries with it a right to collect additional funds from the *personal* assets of every stockholder. As compared to limited-liability shareholding, deterrency is enhanced by stockholders' duty to pony up additional funds if (but only if) managers and regulators allow the bank to become so insolvent that it passes into liquidation. Stock markets would imbed the value of this contingency into the price of each bank's shares. The value of the contingency would be negligible for institutions that were performing well and adequately supporting their risk with paid-in capital. However, the insurer's right would become increasingly valuable whenever a bank began to take poorly supported risks or to slide into serious trouble. By increasing the sensitivity of bank stock prices to changes in bank earning power and earnings volatility, extended liability would encourage information-revealing *stockholder doubt* about troubled institutions in advance of their falling into complete economic insolvency. As they would be gradual, these "runs" would be far less catastrophic than the sudden meltdowns that Bear Stearns, Lehman, and AIG experienced in 2008.

This kind of stock sell-off would increase regulatory deterrency by helping safety net managers to identify institutions that deserve increased supervisory attention long before the enterprise-contributed capital of these institutions could be exhausted. Moreover, in contracting environments where the chance that stockholders might overreact to bad news is strong, the deterrent effect of extended liability would be particularly forceful.

Extended liability would raise the informational value of news to outside stockholders and taxpayers, which would in turn encourage the financial press to report on the distributional consequences of regulatory actions. This would increase regulatory accountability because adverse movements in bank stock prices would put pressure on regulators to investigate, devise remedial action, and publicly explain the actions they take.

To make sure that extended-liability assessments can be collected promptly from failed-bank stockholders, it would be reasonable for authorities to require each stockholder to bond its extended-liability obligation by depositing earning assets in a collateral account at the central bank.[1] Stockholders could be free to move individual assets into and out of the collateral account over time, as long as the aggregate market value of the collateral account remains sufficient and the value of all posted assets can be continuously verified. Just as in an ordinary margin

---

[1] Where appropriate, this account might be required to include some kind of currency hedge and could be held in safekeeping at the central bank or even the protected institution.

account, rules should specify that, if the total value of pledged assets were to fall below a specified threshold value, the account should be promptly replenished. When a bank fails to accomplish this, safety net managers need to be able to force managers to issue sufficient amounts of new stock.

For the many economies for which Table 7.1 shows gaps in political accountability and regulatory quality or that rank low in other unspecified measures of informational and ethical integrity, extended liability provides an elegant economic solution to the problem of narrowing incentives for bank risk-shifting. Adopting extended liability in information-poor venues would improve global and national private and public contracting environments by insinuating an observable, market-driven wedge between the economic interests of ethical and unethical bankers and regulators in the very regions where such a wedge could do the most good. Of course, this is precisely why it is politically difficult to build an effective constituency for such a reform. One must expect managers and stockholders that feel themselves adversely affected to resist any effort to constrain their risk-shifting capacity. One must also expect regulators and politicians in many of these countries to defend limited liability and the kickbacks that cross-country subsidies to tail risk generate. Still, for conscientious officials in the U.S., lobbying low-income countries to install extended liability represents a workable alternative to more-intrusive U.S. interventions into foreign bank activity that would work little harm on institutions whose managers prefer to operate in a safe and sound manner in any case.

4.1. *Desirability of rehearsing crisis management procedures*

When a safety net fails in a circus, managers face a multidimensional disaster — at least one dead or badly broken acrobat, a shocked and grieving staff, a panicked crowd of traumatized spectators, and a mess that needs to be contained and cleaned up before it can escalate into a catastrophe. Unless staff members have been drilled in containing and cleaning up a crisis, they are unlikely to prioritize and coordinate their activities in the best interests of the circus or the audience.

When a country's financial safety net breaks down or threatens to break down, similar problems of priority and coordination arise. Although the first line of crisis management is an unstinting program of preventive inspection, testing, and prompt repair, it must be recognized that troubled institutions have strong incentives to circumvent the prevention system. Whenever prevention fails to contain circumvention, a number of institutions may be expected to go splat (Laeven and Valencia, 2012). The second line of crisis management is resolving the insolvency of damaged firms. Insolvency resolution determines who loses what amounts when the net worth of many institutions is wiped out at the same time. For authorities to allocate losses efficiently, they must establish defensible policy priorities in advance and commit themselves to pursuing these priorities in the event. The first priorities are rescue and triage. Dead and injured institutions must be sorted out immediately and cared for appropriately. The second priority is crowd control. Evidence that triage is being handled efficiently should help to curtail panicky audience exits, but specific staff members must take up the task of helping creditors who want to extract their funds to do so in an informed and orderly manner. The third priority is to clean up the mess so that the show may resume without an undue delay.

4.1.1. *Cleanup*

In developing countries, financial crises are the deep downside of banks' efforts to lend to parties whose ability to repay can only very loosely be assessed in advance. A panic occurs when profound weaknesses in customer repayment capacities surface so suddenly that large losses need to be assigned not just to financial institution stockholders, but also to creditors and guarantors. To clean up the red ink that has been spilled, authorities must be careful not (as at least some U.S. officials did in 2008) to panic themselves. At least, some of the decline in asset values must be passed through to stakeholders whose claims constitute the liability side of financial institution balance sheets. To produce a crisis-management plan that the public can get behind, long-run costs of mitigating the transfer of an institution's losses to its creditors must be prudently traded off against the benefits of bringing the crisis to a quicker end.

Although it is deeply ingrained in U.S. and European regulatory cultures, it is unreasonable to suppose that keeping stockholders and managers in mega-institutions from paying for their mistakes is a desirable public policy, either nationally or globally. When mistakes in managing an institution's resources destroy its ownership capital, the loss of capital should unleash market forces or kick-start government resolution or disciplinary processes seeking to transfer the valuable parts of insolvent banks' franchises into better-capitalized and potentially more-skillful hands. It is false to claim that closing an institution that cannot recapitalize itself, or assigning its business to new managers or new ownership, is a cruel or unfair thing to do. The slow pace of recovery from the Great Financial Crisis should teach us that, unless creditors and investors expect loss-causing managers and undercapitalized firms to be promptly and appropriately disciplined, the incentives that govern the evaluation and selection of risky investment projects is bound to break down. On average, the more fairly the losses of an insolvent financial system can be allocated according to pre-existing contracts, the sooner socially desirable patterns of lending can resume. The more efficiently and fairly the process of loss resolution proceeds, the smaller the long-run cost in resource misallocation and social demoralization the citizenry must pay to make their country's financial system whole again.

5. Summary

This chapter seeks to explain that many DI systems were inadequately designed to stem the buildup of risk in their country's banks either by fostering market discipline or by pricing the risks being transferred to them. Co-insurance, a way to introduce market discipline, was largely phased out by most countries. DI procedures did not focus appropriately on tail risk. This effectively subsidized ruinous risk-taking by banks. In the U.S., about 97% of banks were being charged a zero percent explicit DI premium during the run-up to the crisis.

Safety net design must address differences in transparency, deterrency, and accountability that develop across time and across countries. The weaker is a country's informational, ethical, and corporate governance environment, the greater the danger that a wholly governmental system of explicit and implicit financial institution guarantees will undermine bank safety and stability and that every crisis it experiences will expand the size and scope of its safety net.

Barth, Caprio, and Levine (2005) and updates of their work that appear on the World Bank's website provide snapshots of the ways that banking and regulatory environments differ across countries. The analysis presented here stresses that the design features incorporated into a country's net ought to evolve over time with changes in private and government regulators' capacity for valuing banking institutions, for monitoring and disciplining risk-taking, for resolving insolvencies promptly, and for being held accountable for how well they perform these tasks.

A number of insights can be gained from the crisis experience. Together with monetary easing, deposit insurance schemes contributed to preventing open runs on country banking *systems* by household depositors. In particular, extensive liquidity support to the world's largest banks from the Federal Reserve and the temporary extension of FDIC insurance to money market funds stopped massive outflows from the most distressed institutions (mainly into U.S. banks). In Europe, despite diverging macroeconomic fundamentals between core and periphery eurozone countries, insured bank deposits remained stable in most countries.[2]

However, runs on *un*insured deposits and non-deposit liabilities were widespread. For example, there were significant runs on wholesale deposits and a repo run on broker dealers in the U.S. These runs stressed funding markets that relied on short-term wholesale funding. Such spillovers of risk underscore the dangers of insuring wholesale deposits and deposit-like instruments, and extending the perimeter of the financial safety net to non-banks.

To maintain public confidence in the banking system during the crisis, many countries raised deposit insurance coverage and introduced government guarantees on additional bank assets and liabilities. These measures had the intended beneficial short-run effect, but without massive credit support of foreign banks by the Fed, it is likely that some governments would not have been able to honor their expanding obligations. Even within the E.U., growing uncertainty about the ability of peripheral countries to roll over sovereign debt undermined confidence in their DI systems, triggering some deposit flight to banks with stronger sovereigns, such as Germany.

---

[2]Exceptions are a few isolated bank runs [Northern Rock in the UK and DSB Bank in the Netherlands] that were quickly contained, a slow moving "run" on deposits in Greece due to growing fears of a euro breakup, and a generalized run in Cyprus where authorities declared that a tax on insured deposits could be imposed [although this tax never did materialize].

Going forward, the issue is much broader than that faced during the crisis by a few troubled economies. Many DI systems appear underfunded, especially in countries with large financial systems. Demirgüç-Kunt *et al.* (2015) highlight imbalances between a country's ability to pay and potential liabilities imbedded in deposit insurance. It is hard to resist the hypothesis that, without the demonstrated willingness of Fed officials to support large foreign banks, weaker DI systems would have been tested more severely and some (if not many) would have failed the test. Unresolved imbalances in the strength of European banks and DI systems are bound to test the Fed's willingness and political ability to continue its support into the indefinite future.

References

Barth, JR, G Caprio and RE Levine (2005). *Rethinking Bank Regulation: Until Angels Govern.* (Cambridge, MA: Cambridge University Press).

Black, F, M Miller and R Posner (1978). An approach to the regulation of bank holding companies. *Journal of Business,* 51 (3), pp. 379–412.

Bradley, K and P Kuntz (2011). Wall Street Aristocracy Got $1.2 Trillion in Secret Loans. *Bloomberg News,* 22 August.

Calomiris, CW (1997). *The Postmodern Safety Net: Lessons from Developed and Developing Economies.* (Washington, D.C.: American Enterprise Institute).

Calomiris, CW (1999). Building an incentive-compatible safety net. *Journal of Banking Finance,* 23 (10), pp. 1,499–1,519.

Carnell, R (1993). The Culture of Ad Hoc Discretion, 113–121. In. G Kaufman and R Litan (Eds.), *Assessing Bank Reform: FDICIA One Year Later* (pp. 113–121). Washington D.C.: Brookings Institution.

Demirgüç-Kunt, A and E Detragiache (1998). The Determinants of Banking Crises: Evidence from Developing and Developed Countries. *IMF Staff Papers,* No. 45 (1), pp. 81–109, March.

Demirgüç-Kunt, A and E Detragiache (1999). Financial Liberalization and Financial Fragility. *Proc. Annual World Bank Conference on Development Economics,* pp. 303–331.

Demirgüç-Kunt, A and E Detragiache (2002). Does deposit insurance increase banking system stability?: An empirical investigation. *Journal of Monetary Economics,* 49 (7), pp. 1,373–1,406.

Demirgüç-Kunt, A and E Kane (2002). Deposit insurance around the world around the globe: Where does it work? *Journal of Economic Perspectives,* 16 (2), pp. 175–195.

Demirgüç-Kunt, A and E Kane (2008). *Deposit Insurance around the World: Issues of Design and Implementation,* Ed. L Laeven. Cambridge, MA: MIT Press.

Demirgüç-Kunt, A and E Kane (2015). Deposit insurance around the world: A comprehensive analysis and database, Ed. L Laeven. *Journal of Financial Stability,* 20 (C), pp. 155–183.

Diamond, D (1984). Financial intermediation and delegated monitoring. *Review of Economic Studies*, 51 (3), pp. 343–414.

Diamond, D and P Dybvig (1983). Bank runs, deposit insurance, and liquidity. *Journal of Political Economy*, 91 (3), pp. 401–419.

Garcia, GGH (1999). Deposit Insurance: A Survey of Actual and Best Practices. *IMF Working Paper*, No. 99/54, April.

Goldstein, M and P Turner (1996). *Banking Crises in Emerging Economies: Origins and Policy Options*. Basel: Bank for International Settlements.

Hovakimian, A, E Kane and L Laeven (2003). How country and safety net characteristics affect bank's risk-shifting. *Journal of Financial Service Research*, 23 (2), pp. 177–204.

Jensen, MC and M Meckling (1976). Theory of the firm: Managerial behavior, agency costs, and ownership structure. *Journal of Financial Economics*, 3 (4), pp. 305–360.

Kane, EJ (1995). Three paradigms for the role of capitalization requirements in insured financial institutions. *Journal of Banking Finance*, 19 (3–4), pp. 431–459.

Kane, EJ (2003). What kind of multinational deposit-insurance arrangements might best enhance world welfare? *Pacific-Basin Finance Journal*, 11 (4), pp. 413–428.

Kane, EJ (2009). Financial Safety Nets: Why Do They Keep Expanding? In *Research in Finance*, Chen, AH (ed.), pp. 1–43. Bingley, UK: Emerald Press.

Laeven, L and F Valencia (2012). *Systemic Banking Crises Database: An Update*, IMF *Working Paper*, No. 12/163, June.

La Porta, R, F Lopez-de-Silanes and A Shleifer (1999). *Government Ownership of Commercial Banks* [manuscript], Harvard University.

La Porta, R, F Lopez-de-Silanes, A Shleifer and R Vishny (1998). Law and finance. *Journal of Political Economy*, 106 (6), pp. 1,113–1,155.

Lindgren, C, G Garcia and M Saal (1996). *Bank Soundness and Macroeconomic Policy*. International Monetary Fund, Washington, D.C.

Merton, RC and AF Perold (1993). Theory of risk capital in financial firms. *Journal of Applied Corporate Finance*, 6 (3), pp. 16–32.

Miller, GP (1997). Deposit insurance for economies in transition. *Yearbook of International Finance Economic Law*, Kluwer Law International, pp. 103–138.

Talley, SH and I Mas (1990). Deposit Insurance in Developing Countries. *World Bank Policy, Research, and External Affairs Working Paper Series*, No. 548, November.

von Furstenberg, G (2015). *Contingent Convertibles (CoCos): A Potent Instrument for Reform*. Singapore: World Scientific Publishing Co.

Appendix

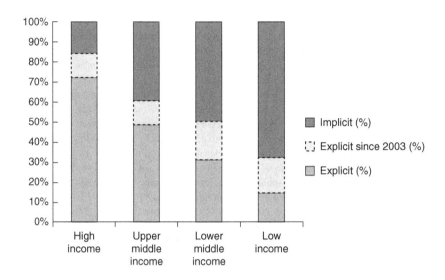

Fig. 7.1.   Explicit Deposit Insurance by Income Group, 2013.

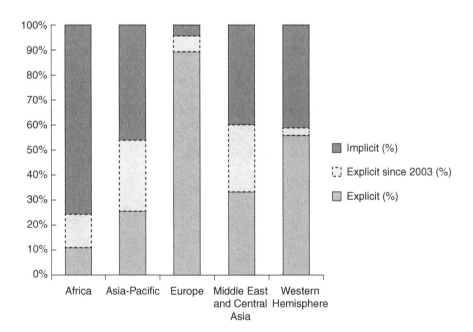

Fig. 7.2.   Explicit Deposit Insurance by Region, 2013.

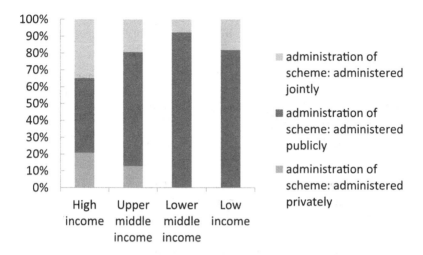

Fig. 7.3.   Administration of the DI Scheme, 2013.

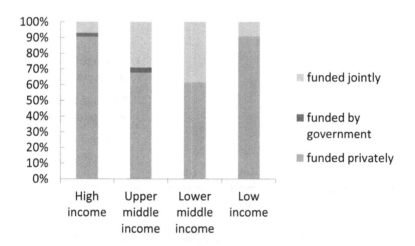

Fig. 7.4.   Funding of the DI Scheme, 2013.

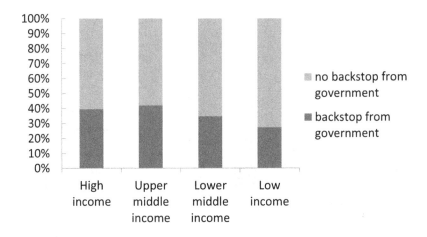

Fig. 7.5.   Government Support of the DI Schemes, 2013.

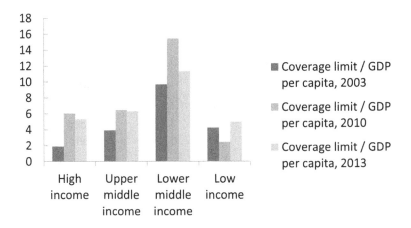

Fig. 7.6.   Coverage Increased During Crisis and Remains above Pre-Crisis Levels.

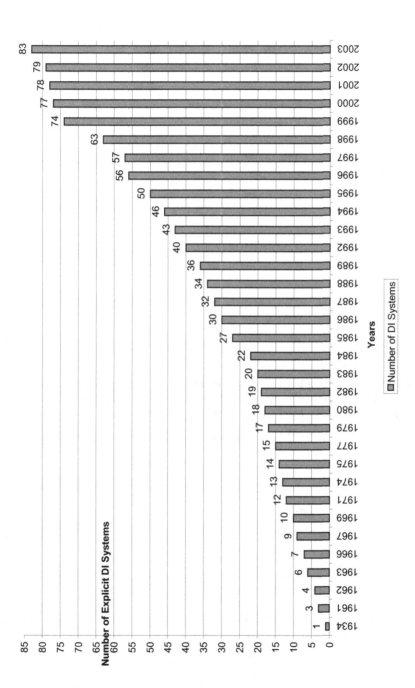

Fig. 7.7. Long-Term Trend in the Adoption of Explicit Deposit Insurance.

Source: Demirgüç-Kunt, Kane, and Laeven (2008). At least 14 more countries installed explicit deposit insurance between 2008 and 2013.

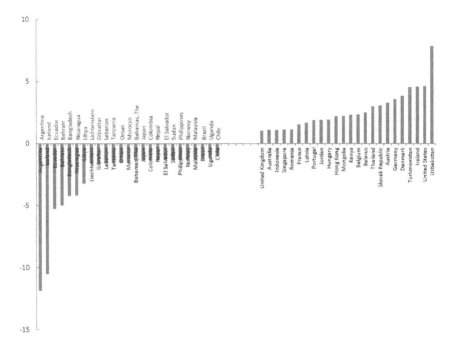

Fig. 7.8.   Safety Net Index, 2013.

Notes: The safety net index is a principal components index of DI design and other safety net features that is increasing in the generosity of the safety net, 1/Countries with safety net index (SNI) values between −1 and +1 are excluded from the chart.

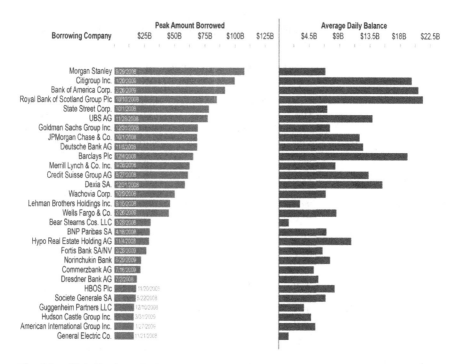

Fig. 7.9. Globalization of US Net Occurred *de facto* During 2007–2010 Crisis: The Fed, used its Last-Resort Lending Powers Creatively to Provide Subsidized Funding to Many Of the Largest Banks in the World [Fed Loans 8/2007–4/2010].

Source: Keoun and Kuntz (2011).

Table 7.1: A Rank of 215 Countries According to the 2014 Wolrd Bank Index Level of Governments' "Regulatory Quality"

Country	Year	REGULATORY QUALITY		CONTROL OF CORRUPTION		VOICE AND ACCOUNTABILITY	
		Min. Percentile Rank	Number of Surveys Sourced	Min. Percentile Rank	Number of Surveys Sourced	Min. Percentile Rank	Number of Surveys Sourced
Singapore	2014	100	9	97.1	10	45.3	10
Hong Kong SAR, China	2014	99.5	8	92.3	9	65	9
New Zealand	2014	99	8	100	9	97.5	10
Finland	2014	98.6	8	98.1	9	98	9
Australia	2014	98.1	8	95.2	10	93.6	9
Canada	2014	97.6	8	93.8	10	95.6	10
United Kingdom	2014	97.1	8	92.8	9	92.1	10
Switzerland	2014	96.6	7	98.6	8	99	8
Sweden	2014	96.2	8	97.6	8	99.5	10
Netherlands	2014	95.7	8	95.7	8	98.5	9
Ireland	2014	95.2	7	91.8	7	92.6	8
Denmark	2014	94.7	8	99.5	9	97	9
Germany	2014	94.2	8	94.7	8	96.1	10
Macao SAR, China	2014	93.8	3	78.4	3	36	1
Estonia	2014	93.3	11	87.5	12	85.2	10
Luxembourg	2014	92.8	6	96.6	6	96.6	7
Norway	2014	92.3	8	99	9	100	10
Chile	2014	91.8	10	90.9	12	80.3	12
Austria	2014	91.3	8	90.4	8	95.1	9
French Guiana	2014	90.9	2	81.3	2	91.1	1
Liechtenstein	2014	90.4	3	96.2	2	93.1	3
Greenland	2014	89.9	1	83.7	1	91.1	1
Aruba	2014	89.4	2	81.3	2	91.1	1
Taiwan, China	2014	88.9	8	77.4	10	72.9	9
United States	2014	88.5	8	89.4	11	79.8	11
Iceland	2014	88	7	94.2	7	94.1	8
Israel	2014	87.5	7	76.4	8	70.4	8
Lithuania	2014	87	10	68.8	11	74.9	9
Martinique	2014	86.5	1	87	1		
Réunion	2014	86.5	1	74	1		
Jersey, Channel Islands	2014	85.6	1	83.7	1	91.1	1
Belgium	2014	85.1	8	91.3	9	94.6	9

(Continued)

Table 7.1: (*Continued*)

Country	Year	REGULATORY QUALITY		CONTROL OF CORRUPTION		VOICE AND ACCOUNTABILITY	
		Min. Percentile Rank	Number of Surveys Sourced	Min. Percentile Rank	Number of Surveys Sourced	Min. Percentile Rank	Number of Surveys Sourced
Latvia	2014	84.6	10	66.3	11	71.9	9
Japan	2014	84.1	8	93.3	10	79.3	9
Korea, Rep.	2014	83.7	10	69.7	12	69	11
Malta	2014	83.2	6	78.8	6	85.7	7
Cyprus	2014	82.7	7	82.2	7	78.8	7
France	2014	82.2	8	88	8	89.2	10
Poland	2014	81.7	12	70.7	12	81.8	11
Czech Republic	2014	81.3	10	65.4	12	77.8	11
Mauritius	2014	80.8	9	67.8	11	73.4	11
United Arab Emirates	2014	80.3	9	84.1	8	19.2	9
Brunei Darussalam	2014	79.8	4	71.6	3	28.6	4
Georgia	2014	79.3	12	75.5	13	55.7	11
Slovak Republic	2014	78.8	10	60.1	11	75.4	10
Cayman Islands	2014	78.4	2	81.3	2	62.1	1
Puerto Rico	2014	77.9	3	69.2	4	71.4	4
Andorra	2014	77.4	1	87	1	86.7	2
Anguilla	2014	77.4	1	87	1		
Bermuda	2014	77.4	1	87	1		
Malaysia	2014	76	10	68.3	12	36.9	11
Spain	2014	75.5	8	70.2	9	77.3	10
Portugal	2014	75	8	79.3	9	83.3	10
Hungary	2014	74.5	11	60.6	12	67	10
Bahrain	2014	74	7	64.4	7	11.3	7
Oman	2014	73.6	7	63	6	19.7	7
Slovenia	2014	73.1	11	74.5	12	74.4	11
Italy	2014	72.6	8	55.3	9	75.9	10
Botswana	2014	72.1	10	76	12	61.6	13
Romania	2014	71.6	12	53.4	13	60.1	12
Bulgaria	2014	71.2	12	48.6	13	59.6	12
Qatar	2014	70.7	8	82.7	8	22.2	10
Costa Rica	2014	70.2	9	75	10	83.7	12
Uruguay	2014	69.7	10	89.9	13	82.8	12

(*Continued*)

Table 7.1: (*Continued*)

Country	Year	REGULATORY QUALITY		CONTROL OF CORRUPTION		VOICE AND ACCOUNTABILITY	
		Min. Percentile Rank	Number of Surveys Sourced	Min. Percentile Rank	Number of Surveys Sourced	Min. Percentile Rank	Number of Surveys Sourced
Peru	2014	69.2	11	32.7	14	51.2	14
Antigua and Barbuda	2014	68.8	1	74	1	68	2
Virgin Islands [U.S.]	2014	68.8	1	74	1		
Colombia	2014	67.8	11	42.8	14	45.8	14
Macedonia, FYR	2014	67.3	9	59.1	10	44.3	9
Mexico	2014	66.8	11	26.4	14	47.8	14
Turkey	2014	66.3	13	53.8	13	37.9	12
Croatia	2014	65.9	12	62	13	63.5	12
Panama	2014	65.4	9	46.2	11	63.1	11
Greece	2014	64.9	8	51.4	9	67.5	9
El Salvador	2014	64.4	10	43.3	13	52.2	13
South Africa	2014	63.9	12	54.3	15	68.5	15
Barbados	2014	63.5	4	81.7	3	91.6	3
St. Vincent and the Grenadines	2014	63	3	72.6	2	87.7	1
West Bank and Gaza	2014	62.5	2	35.1	4	24.6	4
Thailand	2014	62	11	42.3	13	25.6	12
St. Lucia	2014	61.5	4	67.3	3	86.2	2
Dominica	2014	61.1	3	72.6	2	82.3	1
Albania	2014	60.6	11	35.6	11	54.7	11
Armenia	2014	60.1	12	40.4	13	30.5	10
Trinidad and Tobago	2014	59.6	7	33.7	7	62.6	9
Grenada	2014	59.1	2	63.9	2	73.9	1
Rwanda	2014	58.7	9	76.9	11	17.2	11
American Samoa	2014	58.2	1	87	1		
Guam	2014	58.2	1	87	1		
St. Kitts and Nevis	2014	57.2	2	63.9	2	84.7	1
Jamaica	2014	56.7	10	43.8	12	65.5	11
Serbia	2014	56.3	11	51.9	12	56.2	11
Montenegro	2014	55.8	8	57.2	8	55.2	7
Bahamas, The	2014	55.3	4	88.9	3	80.8	4
Jordan	2014	54.8	12	61.5	11	26.6	12

(*Continued*)

Table 7.1:   (*Continued*)

Country	Year	REGULATORY QUALITY		CONTROL OF CORRUPTION		VOICE AND ACCOUNTABILITY	
		Min. Percentile Rank	Number of Surveys Sourced	Min. Percentile Rank	Number of Surveys Sourced	Min. Percentile Rank	Number of Surveys Sourced
Namibia	2014	54.3	9	62.5	11	66.5	12
Moldova	2014	53.8	11	20.7	12	48.8	10
Saudi Arabia	2014	53.4	7	59.6	7	3.4	9
Cape Verde	2014	52.9	7	79.8	8	76.4	8
Morocco	2014	52.4	12	50.5	14	28.1	14
Philippines	2014	51.9	11	39.9	13	52.7	12
Dominican Republic	2014	51.4	9	23.1	11	53.7	12
Ghana	2014	51	11	51	14	64.5	14
Brazil	2014	50.5	11	44.2	12	60.6	14
Sri Lanka	2014	50	11	46.6	12	27.6	11
Bosnia and Herzegovina	2014	49.5	10	49	11	46.3	10
Indonesia	2014	49	11	34.1	13	53.2	12
Kuwait	2014	48.6	7	50	6	29.1	8
Kosovo	2014	48.1	7	39.4	8	40.4	6
Guatemala	2014	47.6	10	28.4	12	35	13
Samoa	2014	47.1	4	65.9	3	70	2
Lebanon	2014	46.6	10	13.5	10	34	12
Senegal	2014	46.2	11	57.7	14	57.6	14
Mongolia	2014	45.7	12	38.5	12	56.7	10
China	2014	45.2	11	47.1	11	5.4	11
Kazakhstan	2014	44.7	12	26	13	15.3	12
Paraguay	2014	44.2	9	13.9	12	42.9	11
Azerbaijan	2014	43.8	11	17.8	11	7.9	11
Seychelles	2014	43.3	7	66.8	7	49.3	7
Burkina Faso	2014	42.8	11	37	13	34.5	14
Kenya	2014	42.3	11	16.3	14	42.4	14
Papua New Guinea	2014	41.8	8	15.4	8	50.2	7
Tanzania	2014	41.3	11	22.6	14	41.9	14
Tunisia	2014	40.9	12	55.8	14	49.8	14
Vanuatu	2014	40.4	4	71.2	4	70.9	1
Maldives	2014	39.9	4	54.8	5	37.4	3
Uganda	2014	39.4	11	12	14	30	14
Honduras	2014	38.9	10	23.6	12	33.5	13
Nicaragua	2014	38.5	10	19.2	12	35.5	13
Mozambique	2014	38	10	27.9	13	40.9	14
Fiji	2014	37.5	4	56.7	3	46.8	5
Cambodia	2014	37	10	12.5	12	17.7	10

(*Continued*)

Table 7.1:   (*Continued*)

Country	Year	REGULATORY QUALITY		CONTROL OF CORRUPTION		VOICE AND ACCOUNTABILITY	
		Min. Percentile Rank	Number of Surveys Sourced	Min. Percentile Rank	Number of Surveys Sourced	Min. Percentile Rank	Number of Surveys Sourced
Russian Federation	2014	36.5	12	19.7	12	20.2	12
Kyrgyz Republic	2014	36.1	11	11.5	12	31	10
Lesotho	2014	35.6	8	61.1	10	51.7	10
Tonga	2014	35.1	4	48.1	3	69.5	2
India	2014	34.6	11	38.9	13	61.1	12
Swaziland	2014	34.1	7	45.7	9	14.3	9
Gambia, The	2014	33.7	8	28.8	8	13.3	8
Benin	2014	33.2	8	24	10	57.1	11
Belize	2014	32.7	5	52.4	6	66	6
Zambia	2014	32.2	11	41.3	13	43.3	14
Guyana	2014	31.7	7	26.9	8	54.2	8
Djibouti	2014	31.3	6	38	7	8.9	7
Mali	2014	30.8	10	27.4	12	41.4	13
Vietnam	2014	30.3	11	37.5	13	9.9	11
Suriname	2014	29.8	5	31.3	5	64	7
Côte d'Ivoire	2014	29.3	11	41.8	13	32	13
Ukraine	2014	28.8	12	14.9	13	47.3	12
Niger	2014	28.4	9	30.8	11	39.9	12
Pakistan	2014	27.9	11	21.6	12	27.1	11
Malawi	2014	27.4	10	25.5	12	44.8	13
Mauritania	2014	26.9	9	18.3	10	23.2	10
Madagascar	2014	26.4	11	22.1	14	31.5	13
Gabon	2014	26	8	30.3	9	23.6	9
São Tomé and Principe	2014	25.5	6	52.9	6	59.1	6
Egypt, Arab Rep.	2014	25	12	32.2	14	14.8	14
Burundi	2014	24.5	9	9.6	11	21.2	11
Sierra Leone	2014	24	11	15.9	14	38.4	14
Nigeria	2014	23.6	11	7.2	14	29.6	14
Togo	2014	23.1	9	16.8	11	26.1	11
Liberia	2014	22.6	10	24.5	13	38.9	13
Palau	2014	22.1	1	45.2	1	88.7	1
Yemen, Rep.	2014	21.6	8	1.9	9	10.3	9
Lao PDR	2014	21.2	9	25	9	4.4	8
Nepal	2014	20.7	10	36.1	11	33	10
Bolivia	2014	20.2	10	29.8	13	48.3	13

(*Continued*)

Table 7.1:   (*Continued*)

Country	Year	REGULATORY QUALITY		CONTROL OF CORRUPTION		VOICE AND ACCOUNTABILITY	
		Min. Percentile Rank	Number of Surveys Sourced	Min. Percentile Rank	Number of Surveys Sourced	Min. Percentile Rank	Number of Surveys Sourced
Timor-Leste	2014	19.7	7	29.3	6	50.7	6
Tuvalu	2014	19.2	3	58.2	3	81.3	1
Cameroon	2014	18.8	11	10.1	14	21.7	14
Bangladesh	2014	18.3	11	18.8	12	32.5	11
Marshall Islands	2014	17.8	2	56.3	2	87.7	1
Kiribati	2014	17.3	5	64.9	4	76.8	2
Angola	2014	16.8	10	3.4	11	16.7	12
Ethiopia	2014	16.3	11	40.9	13	12.8	12
Tajikistan	2014	15.9	10	14.4	10	7.4	9
Bhutan	2014	15.4	8	88.5	8	43.8	7
Ecuador	2014	14.9	9	21.2	11	39.4	12
Haiti	2014	14.4	9	7.7	10	25.1	10
Belarus	2014	13.9	10	47.6	10	6.9	9
Micronesia, Fed. Sts.	2014	13.5	4	77.9	3	84.2	1
Argentina	2014	13	11	33.2	14	58.6	14
Guinea	2014	12.5	10	13	12	24.1	12
Solomon Islands	2014	12	5	49.5	5	58.1	2
Afghanistan	2014	11.5	9	6.3	10	15.8	9
Comoros	2014	11.1	5	36.5	6	36.5	7
Chad	2014	10.6	9	8.2	10	10.8	11
Congo, Rep.	2014	10.1	9	9.1	10	18.2	10
Algeria	2014	9.6	9	31.7	12	22.7	12
Iraq	2014	9.1	7	5.8	9	13.8	9
Nauru	2014	8.7	1	45.2	1	72.4	1
Guinea-Bissau	2014	8.2	6	2.9	6	20.7	7
Congo, Dem. Rep.	2014	7.7	9	6.7	11	11.8	11
Cuba	2014	7.2	7	58.7	6	6.4	8
Sudan	2014	6.7	9	3.8	11	3.9	10
Myanmar	2014	6.3	11	17.3	11	9.4	10
Central African Republic	2014	5.8	8	10.6	9	8.4	9
Equatorial Guinea	2014	5.3	5	0	5	2	6
Iran, Islamic Rep.	2014	4.8	8	34.6	8	4.9	9

(*Continued*)

Table 7.1:   (*Continued*)

Country	Year	REGULATORY QUALITY Min. Percentile Rank	Number of Surveys Sourced	CONTROL OF CORRUPTION Min. Percentile Rank	Number of Surveys Sourced	VOICE AND ACCOUNTABILITY Min. Percentile Rank	Number of Surveys Sourced
South Sudan	2014	4.3	6	1	8	5.9	7
Syrian Arab Republic	2014	3.8	7	2.4	7	3	8
Uzbekistan	2014	3.4	11	11.1	11	2.5	9
Venezuela, RB	2014	2.9	11	4.8	14	18.7	14
Zimbabwe	2014	2.4	10	4.3	13	12.3	13
Turkmenistan	2014	1.9	7	8.7	6	0	6
Somalia	2014	1.4	6	0.5	7	0.5	8
Eritrea	2014	1	6	20.2	6	1.5	6
Libya	2014	0.5	8	1.4	10	16.3	10
Korea, Dem. Rep.	2014	0	5	5.3	4	1	5
Monaco	2014					78.3	1
San Marino	2014					88.2	1

Source: The Worldwide Governance (WGI) Project http://info.worldbank.org/governance/wgi/index.aspx#home

Chapter Eight

Housing and Other Price Bubbles: The Buildup, the Burst, and the Impact

George G. Kaufman*

Loyola University Chicago

A. G. Malliaris*

Loyola University Chicago

Richard W. Nelson*

RWNelson Economics

Abstract

This chapter argues that asset price bubbles need to be re-examined carefully because their adverse impact on an economy has often been very substantial. The bursting of the housing bubble in 2006 and its consequences on triggering the near global financial crisis is such example. After reviewing the general literature on asset bubbles on housing and stock markets bubbles and their impacts on an economy, we contribute to the literature by proposing a fundamental housing price model that allows us to estimate the magnitude of residential housing bubbles and their starting and ending dates. The duration and the magnitude of the U.S. housing bubble in the early 2000s are estimated under alternative assumptions about the nature of forces affecting the demand for housing and housing prices.

1. Introduction

This chapter revisits the apparent residential housing bubble that recently occurred in the first decade of the 21st century in the U.S. and many other

*Presented at the Annual Meetings of the Western Economic Association, Portland, Oregon, June 30, 2016. The authors are grateful to Ed Kane and Ellis Tallman for thoughtful comments that improved substantially this version of the paper.

countries. This bubble is of both interest and importance because there is wide agreement that the buildup and subsequent bursting of the bubble was the largest single factor causing the broader Global Financial Crisis of 2007–2009, and set in motion a series of adverse events that resulted in the Great Economic Recession that lasted from December 2007 to June 2009. Had the housing bubble not burst, the observed financial panic may not have materialized.

Yet, at the same time, much of the profession remains skeptical both about the very existence of bubbles and about the ability of the Federal Reserve to mitigate, if not eliminate altogether, bubbles in the pursuit of macro-financial stability with its present toolkit. Improved knowledge of the causes and sustainability of bubbles will aid in the development of the monetary and prudential tools necessary for the Federal Reserve and the potential to reduce the number of bubbles and the harm done by them.

Asset price bubbles (APBs), or more precisely, the bursting or implosion of price bubbles, have plagued almost all economies throughout the past century. Among others, Kindleberger and Aliber (2015) and Reinhart and Rogoff (2009) have documented in great detail famous financial bubbles of the last few centuries. APBs exist when the prices of individual assets or groups of assets differ significantly for some time from their prices determined by basic long-run economic forces or "fundamental" prices. As fundamental prices cannot be observed directly, they must be modelled. The difference between the observed actual prices and the modelled unobserved fundamental prices may be considered the "bubble gap."

APBs may be either positive or negative. In positive APBs, prices at which the designated assets actually trade overshoot fundamental prices. After a period of accumulation, for various reasons examined later in this chapter, the bubbles for some assets may suddenly burst with little or no widespread warning. When the bubbles burst, substantial downward pressure is suddenly released on the prices of the specified assets and actual prices decline closer to their fundamental levels. The bubble shrinks, may disappear totally, or may even turn negative. Negative APBs exist when actual asset prices are below their estimated fundamental prices. When negative bubbles burst, upward pressure is suddenly released on the prices of the assets, driving them to or above their fundamental prices.

The magnitude of bubble gaps as well as their direction matter. Small gaps built up over prolonged periods of time (slow bubble buildups) are unlikely to produce significant adverse impacts. However, even small gaps that build up slowly through time may, after sufficient time, do considerable damage when they burst. Likewise, burst large gaps may do little damage if anticipated. Thus, measures of bubble gaps are at times increased or reduced in size by adding or subtracting a constant term to the fundamental price. Changes in value smaller than the constant term are within the collar formed by the adjusted ceiling and floor, and may not do great damage to the economy and may thus not be considered bubbles.

The bursting of bubbles impacts both aggregate income and its composition. As income is likely to be redistributed when bubbles burst, there will be winners and losers. The former will likely cheer and the latter will likely cry. The changes in prices and quantities are likely to be sudden and large, relative to other shocks affecting the prices and quantities of these assets. The additional uncertainty and volatility generated is likely to ignite additional instability in both financial and non-financial sectors with adverse implications for economic welfare.

The magnitudes of the damages or benefits introduced by the bursting depends also on the absolute and relative magnitudes of the assets in question. Bursting of residential housing prices may be expected to impact most economies more than others such as, say, the bursting of the Dutch tulip bubble of 1634–1638 or of the U.S. Internet market in 2007–2010.

In the long-run, positive APBs will likely lead to overproduction of output and negative ABPs likely to underproduction. Almost all published analyses of bubbles have been for upward APBs, where before bursting actual observed prices exceed their fundamental prices. This chapter focuses on the characteristics and consequences of APBs not previously examined, in particular, differences between upward and downward bubbles. The resulting increase in our understanding should prove useful in designing, among other things, more effective private and public policy strategies to minimize or avoid altogether the damage caused by positive APBs.

We distinguish three stages of APB: (1) the buildup, (2) the bursting, and (3) the impact on economic activity. Bubbles for different assets or for the same asset over different time periods may be expected to have different characteristics that produce different estimates of damage and require different economic stabilization policies.

2. The Housing Bubble and the Global Financial Crisis of 2007–2009

The near-global major financial crisis of 2007–2009 started early in 2007 as a problem in the subprime home loan mortgage market in the U.S. and evolved into a broader financial crisis that seriously affected countries beyond the U.S and sectors beyond home mortgages and related financial securities. According to the U.S. the great recession associated with this financial crisis lasted some 18 months from December 2007 to June 2009. Ex-Federal Reserve Chairman Ben Bernanke (2013) describes this crisis in detail, and calls it the worst financial crisis in modern U.S. financial history. Evanoff, Kaufman, and Malliaris (2012) describe in detail numerous aspects of the recent financial crisis from the perspective of asset bubbles. The introductory sections of this paper rely heavily on material in Evanoff *et al.* (2012; 2017).

The causes of financial crisis are manifold and embrace the following broad categories, among others:

(1) Microeconomic factors, including excessive subprime lending, financial innovation, and increasingly complex and opaque derivative and structured securities, inadequate and inaccurate risk management strategies, poorly designed financial deregulation, inadequate credit evaluation by rating agencies and by credit originate-to-distribute models of banking, reduction in ethical standards, and greater reliance on psychological behavior (animal spirits).

(2) Macroeconomic factors, such as excessive housing credit availability at low interest rates, low down payments, and high leverage. Economists such as Jorda, Schularick, and Taylor (2015) describe bubbles caused by such factors as leveraged bubbles. Among other macroeconomic factors, monetary policy influenced asset pricing and the housing boom.

(3) The shadow financial sector, including financial intermediaries that like banks facilitate the creation and allocation of credit, but whose activities are not regulated by regulators with necessarily the same objectives and tools as bank regulators. Examples of such financial

entities or activities include hedge funds, special purpose entities, mutual funds, insurance firms, asset management, and structured investment vehicles, among others. The two large investment banks Bear Stearns and Lehman Brothers that failed in 2008 belong in this category. They were financing much of their long-term less-liquid real estate investments with short-term and more liquid funding through selling commercial paper. Due to its large size, not only did the Lehman Brothers commercial paper market dry up, but nearly the entire commercial paper markets valued at approximately $500 billion dried up. Finally, global factors, such as the international saving glut, use of fixed exchange rates by some large countries, such as China, and free global capital mobility contributed to producing an economic and financial environment susceptible to instability.

Distinguishing the three stages of the housing bubble — the buildup, the bust and the aftermath — allows us to quantify empirically both the macroeconomic benefits gained during the formation periods of bubbles in terms of additions to employment, income, consumption and investment, and the harm inflicted during the impact period to evaluate the net benefits and answer the basic question whether some, all, or more than all of the benefits gained during the long buildup of the housing bubbles were lost again during its rapid collapse.

In this section, we review the fundamental and behavioral characteristics as well as the stylized facts of past asset bubbles for housing and equities. With this general background, Section 4 develops two broad explanations of the recent housing bubble. In Section 5, we propose a general model for fundamental measures in general and for housing in particular. Section 5 also describes the technical challenges encountered in the econometric modeling of the duration and magnitude of the housing bubble.

Having estimated the size and duration of the housing bubble, we compute the build-up, bursting and economic impact components of this bubble in Section 6. Our main conclusions are summarized in Section 7.

3. Conceptual Issues and Stylized Facts

What is an asset price bubble? Why do they exist in financial markets? Why do they burst? A bubble is said to exist if an asset price exceeds its price as determined by "fundamentals" — i.e., the present value of its expected future cash flows — by a significant amount that persists for some time. If the price of an asset exceeds its fundamentals only by a very small amount, the differential may only represent noise instead of a meaningful bubble. If the deviation from fundamentals lasts for only a short trading interval, this may represent only temporary mispricing. However, the popular market efficiency paradigm developed in the 1960s argued that prices in financial markets reflect all publicly available information regarding the fundamental factors that drive asset prices. Therefore, since observed market prices equal fundamental values in these models, price bubbles cannot exist.

Due to the difficulties in measurement, some economists define a bubble as simply any substantial upward price movement over an extended range that suddenly implodes. These bubbles form initially because the purchase of an asset is made in anticipation that the asset can be resold to a "greater fool" at an even higher price. Behavioral economists argue that a key factor explaining the formation of bubbles and their eventual bursting is the feedback mechanism. A price increase for an asset leads to investor enthusiasm for that asset, which further causes increased demand and additional price increases, and so on. The high demand is supported by the select memories of investors of high past returns and optimism that this asset will generate high future earnings. Different bubbles have different positive feedback mechanisms. However, since price increases driven by factors other than the asset's fundamentals cannot be sustained indefinitely, a negative feedback pattern will eventually replace the positive one — i.e., the bubble will eventually burst. As the initial price increases are generally slow it, generally takes a long time for the bubble to grow. In contrast, bubble crashes tend to take place quite quickly.

The current state of knowledge about asset price bubbles is rather disappointing. There is not even a universally accepted definition of what bubbles are or even how to identify their characteristics, for instance when they begin or end. There is also disagreement as to what causes them to grow and at what speed. Most of the empirical literature focuses only on the significant costs of bubbles bursting. We will examine both the positive benefits of the housing bubble as it grew as well as the substantial costs during its bursting. In contrast to the many challenges in deriving

Table 8.1:   Equity and Housing Price Bear Markets in Industrial Countries, 1959–2002.

[median overall episodes]

	Real Equity Prices		Real Housing Prices	
	Contraction[a] [%]	Duration[b] [quarters]	Contraction[a] [%]	Duration[b] [quarters]
Bear Markets[c]	−24	5	−6	5
Busts[d]	−46	10	−27	16
1960s	−41	11	—	—
1970s	−50	10	−27	19
1980s	−48	10	−29	16
1973[e]	−60	10	—	—
2000[f]	−44	10	—	—

Source: International Monetary Fund, 2003: Table 2.1.
[a]Contraction from peak to trough in real equity and housing price, respectively
[b]Time from peak to trough [excluding the peak quarters]
[c]All bear markets, including busts
[d]All bear markets in the bottom quartile
[e]Busts beginning during 1972–1974
[f]Busts beginning at the peaks recorded in 2000 and ending in 2002: Q3 (end of sample)

a theoretical description of a financial asset bubble ex-ante, numerous bubbles have been identified *ex post* both in terms of frequency and economic costs.

To give some quantitative evidence of past stock market and housing bubbles, we describe three stylized sets of facts produced in a study by IMF economists in 2003 and summarized in Table 8.1. The study analyzed quarterly equity prices over the 1959–2002 period for 19 industrialized countries, and residential housing prices for 14 countries during 1970–2002.

This IMF (2003) study shows a number of things. First, between 1959: Q1 and 2002: Q2, there were 52 equity market busts in 19 countries. A bust is defined by the IMF as a peak to trough price change that is in the most negative quartile of price decreases in the sample. For equity markets, this required at least 37% correction from peak to trough. The average magnitude of a crash for this sample was 45%. Half of the crashes were recorded during the 1970s, and were associated with the breakdown of Bretton Woods and the oil shock that resulted in an average equity price decline of 60% over a period of about 10 quarters.

Second, only one-fourth of all booms or bubbles ended in busts. A boom or bubble is defined as a trough to peak price change that is in the top quartile of prices increases.

Third, housing price busts were less frequent than equity price crashes.[1] In the sample period, 20 housing crashes were recorded and the average decline was about 30% and deflated over a four-year period. Housing market crashes resulted in price declines of about 30% compared to equity price declines of 45%. Additionally, the equity market crashes take about 1.5 years longer to unfold.

This evidence documents that equity and housing bubbles are not "black swan" events occurring, say once every hundred years. Rather, they occur relatively often; equity crashes occurred on average every decade and housing crashes once every 20 years. When stock market and housing bubbles burst at the same time their impact is more severe. Consider the concurrent crashes of the stock and real estate bubbles in Japan and the U.S. They both generated serious real effects in the form of the "lost decade" in Japan and the "Great Recession" in the U.S. that were considerably deeper and longer than the average post-WWII recessions. As measured by the NBER, the U.S. Great Recession lasted 18 months, from December 2007 to June 2009, and witnessed significant declines in real GDP, increases in unemployment from 4.7% in late 2007 to above 10% in 2009, and, after several years from the recession trough, real GDP growth remains subpar. Bubble crashes often destabilize financial markets, but need not destabilize the macroeconomy — a classic example being the October 1987 U.S. stock market crash. Similarly, the bursting of the internet bubble in 2001, despite an almost 75% drop in the NASDAQ, had only a relatively small impact on the real economy in the form of a short, mild recession.

4.   What Caused the Housing Bubble of 2004–2007?

Economists have long debated the role of monetary policy towards the housing bubble. The Greenspan (2004) Fed used discretion in its "risk-management approach" to monetary policy and argued that it is unwise to use Fed funds to regulate the housing market. The story told by several

---

[1] Given our definition of a bust, house (equity) prices had to decline a minimum of 14% (37%) over the sample periods.

economists, such as Taylor (2007), is that the bursting of the internet bubble in 2001 destabilized financial markets and wiped out about 30% of the S&P 500 stock market capitalization representing substantial losses in household wealth. They claim that the Fed had initiated significant decreases in Fed Funds rates and kept them low for too long. Taylor (2007) argues that the easy monetary policy followed by the Fed during 2000–2004 to offset the bursting of the internet bubble contributed to lower fed funds rates and lower longer-term rates that increased the demand for housing. In turn, this increased demand for housing caused prices to increase significantly during 2002–2006 in the U.S. Similar policies in several other countries, such as the U.K., Ireland, and Spain, fueled a global real estate boom.

Had the Greenspan Fed used the Taylor rule as a tool to set fed funds rates from early 2002 to the end of 2005, these rates would have been higher and would have leaned against the emerging real estate bubble. Taylor (2007) further claims that the housing bubble may have been deflated gradually and the enormous costs associated with its bursting may have been mitigated or avoided.

This story however is not acceptable to all. Bernanke (2010) provides detailed evidence that Federal Reserve Fed Funds policies are not responsible for the housing bubble. His central argument is the global character of the housing bubble. Put differently, if housing prices increased across many different countries which pursued dissimilar monetary policies, Taylor's arguments fail to explain the determinants of the bubble. In addition, Bernanke argues that the housing market is driven by long-term mortgage interest rates and the Fed does not have any influence on such rates. In particular, Fed Funds and long-term interest rates have complex nonlinear dynamic relationships and one cannot argue that low Fed Funds imply low mortgage rates.[2] Rather, Bernanke proposes that it was the global saving glut as the more likely factor that powered the global housing boom. Recently, Bernanke (2015) has revisited these issues in a blog arguing more that Taylor's mechanistic approach cannot replace the extensive deliberations of the FOMC. Recently, Jorda *et al.* (2015) have

---

[2]In this vein, Greenspan has argued that long term interest rates became decoupled from short-term interest rates in 2002. He offers "a surge in growth in China and a large number of other emerging market economies that led to an excess of global intended savings relative to intended capital investment" as the explanation. See Alan Greenspan (2009).

emphasized the role of leveraged bubbles to explain the housing bubble, and also to argue that although housing bubbles on average deflate by 30% in comparison to stock market crashes that often drop by over 50%, the real economy during the 2007–2009 financial crisis suffered significantly more from the housing bubble bursting than the stock market crash. To shed additional light on the determinants of the housing bubble, we model asset bubbles with special emphasis on the housing bubble.

5. Modelling Simple Asset Price Bubbles

The preceding analysis has argued that asset price bubbles can be identified with high probability only after they burst. For example, if equity prices drop by 20% in one day as in October 19, 1987, it is very unlikely that real fundamentals have changed so drastically and so rapidly to justify such an infrequent large drop. In other words, such a large drop in such a short period of time allows one to postulate the presence of a bubble. However, if the bursting of the bubble denotes its end, how can we identify its beginning date? This may be done by constructing a model describing the fundamentals of the particular asset market. For example, let P_n = Price of an asset in period n,

$$P_n = f[i_n, EP_n Y_n, W_n] + \mu_n$$

Where, i_n = interest rate in period n, EP_n = Expected [predicted] prices, Y_n = Income, W_n = Wealth and μ = Error. This is a fundamental equation that prices an asset under investigation. However, economists have not successfully identified such a fundamental equation with great precision either theoretically and/or econometrically. In this chapter, we develop a fundamental equation for the pricing of housing.

6. Modelling the Housing Bubble

We next proceed to apply the general theory of bubbles developed above to recent home prices. The preceding analysis of bubbles leads us to assume their existence, particularly *ex post* once they have collapsed. It also challenges us to develop a general econometric approach to identifying bubbles and defining their characteristics prior to their bursting and to measuring their characteristics and effects on the economy. Since each bubble is expected to have at least some of its own market characteristics, the goal of the present analysis of home prices is limited to developing an initial approach which we then can further expand and test in future work.

A number of different indices of home prices are available. In this section, we use the Case-Shiller indices of home prices over the 1987–2015 period, as computed by Core Logic and released by the Standard and Poor's Corporation.[3] First, this allows us to examine the course of housing prices between 1987 and 2015. Next, we estimate an equation which can explain the fundamental price of housing and identify the housing bubble and its characteristics.

6.1. Home Prices between 1987 and 2015

Chart 8.1 shows movements in the Case Shiller index for the U.S. as a whole, in nominal and in real terms.

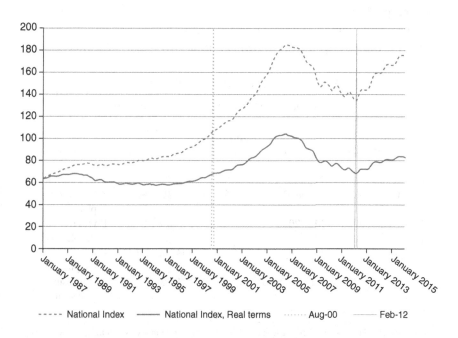

Chart 8.1.   U.S. National Home Price Index Nominal and Real.

---

[3] http://us.spindices.com/index-family/real-estate/sp-corelogic-case-shiller.

The nominal index rose slowly through early 1997, but began a period of acceleration after that point. The annual rate of increase increased from 4.0% in 1997 to a high of 13.5% in both 2004 and 2005, before falling sharply again through 2012. The index has risen since 2012 and, by 2016, was close to its previous peak level.

In real terms, housing prices actually declined between January 1987 and February 1996.[4] Subsequently, real home prices increased at a 3.8% rate through August 2000, and then accelerated to a 7.6% annual rate through May 2006. At its peak in 2004 and 2005, the annual rate of increase was over 11%. In all, the index rose by 53% between August 2000 and May 2006, the period of most rapid growth, before declining again by 35% between May 2006 and February 2012, back to the August 2000 level. The August 2000 level thus proved to be a plateau below which prices never subsequently declined. Since February 2012, growth has resumed at a 5.1% annual pace but the level of prices remained 20% below its previous peak as of early 2016.

The evolution of real home prices during this period may be broken into five, distinct stages, as shown in Table 8.2. Stage 3 shows several

Table 8.2:   Real Housing Price Behavior in Select Periods 1987–2016.

National Index Deflated by the Consumer Price Index

Stage	Begin	End	Duration [months]	Price change Total	Annual	Characterization
1	January 1987	February 1996	109	−9.7%	−1.1%	Prices decline
2	February 1996	August 2000	54	+18.4%	+3.8%	Prices rise to a plateau
3	August 2000	May 2006	69	+52.8%	+7.6%	Prices rise above the plateau
4	May 2006	February 2012	69	−34.5%	−7.1%	Prices return to the plateau
5	February 2012	January 2016	47	+21.7%	+5.1%	Prices resume increasing

[4]We deflate the Case-Shiller National Index by the consumer price index excluding food and energy, using January 1987 as the base. Source: US. Bureau of Labor Statistics, Consumer Price Index for All Urban Consumers: All items less food and energy [CUUS0000SA0L1E], retrieved from FRED, Federal Reserve Bank of St. Louis; https://fred.stlouisfed.org/series/CUUS0000SA0L1E August 29, 2016.

characteristics — duration and magnitude of the upswing and the eventual burst — commonly ascribed to bubbles.[5]

6.2. Modeling fundamental housing prices

Although the descriptive analysis above is highly suggestive of a bubble, Kindleberger's definition of a bubble also requires a deviation in the price of an asset which cannot be explained by the fundamentals. Consequently, it would be desirable to have a more formal approach to identify the level of prices consistent with economic fundamentals (the "fundamental" price level). Unfortunately, there is no generally agreed-upon method of identifying the fundamental level of real home prices. Indeed, Shiller, after a review of real home price data back to 1890, concludes that "there is no hope of explaining (real) home prices in the United States solely in terms of building costs, population, or interest rates".[6]

We construct a simple supply/demand framework to develop our model. We assume a downward sloping demand curve, in both the short run and the longer run. The longer term relationship would be expected to be more price elastic since over the longer run homebuyers are more likely to move to areas with lower home prices. In the very short term, the supply of new homes is effectively inelastic, while in the longer run, it is likely to be perfectly elastic at the cost of production plus the cost of new land.[7] The supply curve may be a postively sloping function of quantity if resource constraints, such as land availability, are effective. The model is summarized in the chart below.

At any time, the price of homes observed is determined by the intersection of the short term supply and demand functions. Point A shows an initial equilibrium, with a price of 20 which also is a long-term

---

[5]For example, consider Kindleberger's definition of a bubble: (1) "any deviation in the price of an asset or a security or a commodity that cannot be explained in terms of the 'fundamentals'", and, *more practically* (2) *"an upward price movement over an extended period of fifteen to forty months that then implodes"* and that (3) "Someone with 'perfect foresight' should have foreseen that the process was not sustainable and that an implosion was inevitable". See Kindleberger and Aliber (2015).
[6]Shiller, 2015: 22.
[7]An alternative approach might model the supply and demand of new homes on the market rather than total homes existing. This approach might suggest more elasticity in supply in the short run as higher prices would be expected to encourage existing homeowners to put their houses on the market and either rent or move to less costly geographic areas.

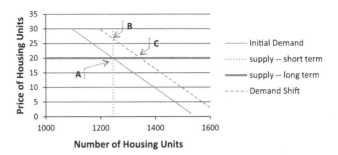

Chart 8.2.   Supply and Demand for Homes.

equilibrium. Point B shows that the initial effect of an upward shift in demand is an increase in prices, to 26. However, as the short-term supply shifts outward (not shown), Point C is eventually established as the long-term equilibrium, at the same price as Point A.

If we can identify the long-term supply price, 20 in the chart, we can then measure the difference between the current price and the supply price, equal to 6 or about 25% of the long-term price at Point B in the chart. We define this difference as the supply gap. This gap can be positive or negative. We expect a positive supply gap to be associated with increased building activity, and a negative gap to be associated with diminished building activity.

A supply gap may result from traditional housing cycle factors, for instance a shift in demand associated with changes in demographics, income, wealth, or interest rates. Such a shift in demand would be expected to cause home prices to rise above or fall below the supply price, but the gap is likely to be self-correcting over a relatively short period of time as production or demand adjusts to longer run states of nature.[8] Changes in demographics occur very slowly and tend to move in the same direction for years and, as a result, are unlikely to create the pattern of upward and downward price movements that characterizes a bubble.

---

[8]The time required for such a correction would be determined by the length of time required to construct a new home, but also by the time required to obtain permits and, in some cases, changes in zoning requirements. This suggests adjustments which may vary by market and require several years. Some increase is demand, however, may be anticipated by builders, in which case no adjustment may be necessary.

Further, builders can be expected to attempt to anticipate demographic shifts and to meet the increased demand without an increase in prices. Changes in income, wealth, and interest rates are likely to be associated with the economic cycle and less likely to be anticipated by builders and, as a result, are likely to be associated with increases or decreases in housing prices. However, economic cycles are not regularly associated with housing bubbles.

The situation is materially different when a change in expectations occurs. Importantly, depending on dynamics of the expectations process, such a supply gap may not be subject to a self-correcting adjustment process or alternatively involve a much more lengthy adjustment process. As a result, the supply gap and the resulting change in prices may be expected to be maintained over longer periods, to rise to greater magnitudes, and to be corrected only with a change in the expectational environment. Thus changes in expectations are very likely to result in a "bubble."

We can identify and measure bubbles in a number of ways within the framework of this model. One approach would be to identify a full supply/demand model. Such a model was estimated by Case (1986) in his attempt to determine whether the increase in home prices in Boston during the 1980s constituted a bubble.[9] Case estimated a supply function with housing starts as the dependent variable and price, construction cost, the interest rate, and regional dummies as independent variables. His demand function included price, employment, income, interest, utilities, and taxes as dependent variables. Without expectational demand variables, the price implied by such a model might be considered the "fundamental" price and any divergence from that price considered a "bubble". Including expectational factors in such a model would permit an explicit identification of bubbles.

As supply/demand models are difficult to specify and estimate, we adopt an alternative and simpler approach by focusing on the supply gap. The supply gap can be estimated empirically by modeling the supply price without the complexities of a full supply demand model provided that

---

[9] See Case (1986).

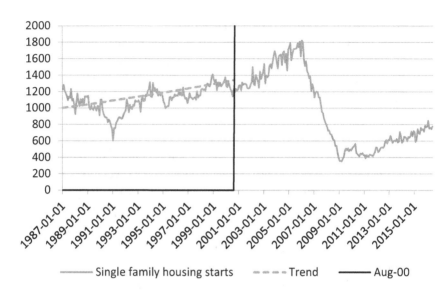

——— Single family housing starts   – – – – Trend   ——— Aug-00

Chart 8.3.   Single Family Housing Starts,1987–2016.

Source: U.S. Bureau of the Census.[10]

we can find a period in which the market is in or close to long-term equilibrium. We believe that January 1987 and August 2000 is such a period. After August 2000, housing prices moved above the "plateau" identified previously, with significant increases after that date. Housing starts also increased from their trend after that time, an indicator of an increased supply gap (see Chart 8.3). In contrast, between January 1987 and August 2002, housing starts increased fairly steadily, at a trend rate of 2.2% per year. Conditions during the 1987–2002 period are consistent with a market at or close to longer run equilibrium when price on average equaled the long-term supply price.

The principal factors affecting the long-run supply price are thought to be real building costs and the price of land. The basic form of the supply function is assumed to be:

$$P_t = aC_t^b L_t^c u_t$$

---

[10]Source: US. Bureau of the Census, Privately Owned Housing Starts: 1-Unit Structures [HOUST1F], retrieved from FRED, Federal Reserve Bank of St. Louis; https://fred.stlouisfed.org/series/HOUST1F, August 6, 2016.

Where 'P' represents the real supply price, 'C' represents real construction cost, and 'L' represents the real cost of land. The equation can be rewritten in logarithmic form as:

$$\ln P_t = \bar{a} + b \ln C_t + c \ln L_t + \ln u_t$$

We derive 'P' and 'C' from the notional Case-Shiller national index of home prices and the building cost index, both as presented by Shiller.[11] 'L' is an index of residential land prices taken from Davis and Heathcote (2007).[12]

We estimate this equation monthly from January 1987 through August 2000. The results of the estimation are provided in Table 8.3.

Table 8.3:   Regression Results.

	Coefficient	t Stat
Intercept	−2.57	−8.41
ln[land price]	0.24	13.64
ln[building cost]	1.55	22.06
Observations	164	
Standard Error	0.03	
Adjusted R Square	76%	

The model explains 76% of the variation in home prices over the 1979–2000 period. The coefficients all have the expected signs and are statistically significant at a high level of confidence. As expected, both building costs and land costs have a positive effect on housing prices.

6.3.   Was there a "bubble" in housing prices?

We now apply our model to estimate the real supply price of homes over the 1987–2016 period, and compare it with actual prices to evaluate the presence and dimensions of bubbles. Inputs in this calculation are the

---

[11] Shiller (2015). As Shiller's data on building costs is reported annually, we interpolate the data to produce a monthly series consistent with our home price data.
[12] See Davis and Heathcote (2007).

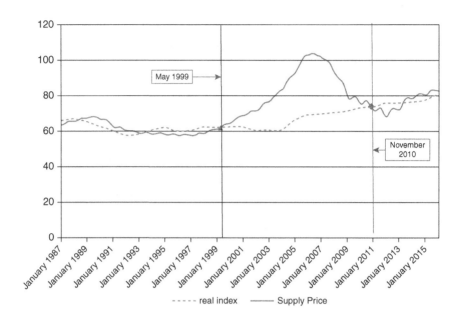

Chart 8.4.   National Home Price Index: Actual vs. Predicted Supply Prices.

price of land and the level of construction costs. The price of land merits further inspection. As the estimates of land prices that we are using are calculated as a residual by subtracting construction costs from the sales price of homes, they will be artificially increased during bubble periods. Whether or not actual land prices increase in this manner, we want to use a longer term estimate of the supply price in our measurements. We accomplish this by projecting the rate of growth of land prices over the 1987 to 2000 period to the post 2000 period, and using those projections in our calculation of the supply price of housing. The results are shown in Charts 8.4 and 8.5.

The movement of the actual price above the supply price signals either the beginning of a normal housing cycle or a bubble, depending on its magnitude and possibly its duration. The increase in housing prices above their supply price between 1988 and 1993 provides a calibration of the threshold that separates normal housing cycles from bubbles. The 1988–1993 period was not widely perceived as a bubble, and the supply gap never exceeded 10% during that period. This suggests that

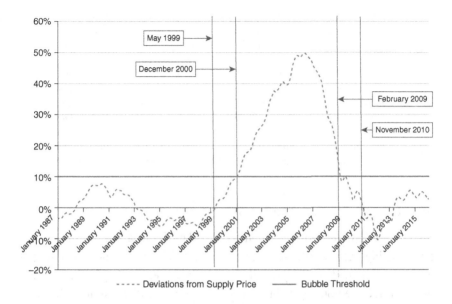

Chart 8.5.   Actual Real Home Price Index Deviation from Supply Price.

the deviations from our estimated supply price are consistent with a "normal" housing cycle. Consequently, we use 10% as the threshhold of a bubble.[13]

Housing prices again moved above the supply price in May 1999, but this time, the increase was more rapid, and by December 2000, the deviation had exceeded the 10% threshold. The supply gap then continued to increase until it peaked at 50% in May 2006, and then fell sharply to 10% in February 2009 and to zero in November 2010. This pattern strongly suggests a bubble beginning in either 1999 or 2000. The gap increased relatively slowly during the early bubble period when the gap less than 10% and also through 2002, when it started accelerating. The bubble broke in May 2006 and returned to normal in November 2010. The timing of the bubble is summarized in Table 8.4.

---

[13] Since this conclusion is based on one observation, it should be regarded as a lower bound of the threshold. Extension of the analysis to previous time periods other countries, or other asset commodities will provide additional information in this regard.

Table 8.4: Periods Defining the Housing Bubble and its Context.

	Beginning	End	Supply Gap	Description
1	January 1987	April 1999	−10% to +10%	Pre Bubble
2	May 1999	December 2000	0 to +10%	Early bubble
3	January 2001	October 2005	>10% increasing	Bubble Up
4	November 2005	January 2009	>10% decreasing	Bubble Down
5	February 2009	November 2010	0 to +10%	Late bubble
6	December 2010	July 2015	−10% to +10%	Post Bubble

6.4. Causes of the housing bubble

So far, we have proposed a method for identifying a bubble in housing prices using supply-side variables, specificly the emergence of a supply gap greater than 10%. Supply-side factors, however do not give insight into what caused the housing bubble. Thus, we turn to a discussion of demand-side factors. We consider the following demand variables. The growth in households reflects the number of potential buyers. Employment growth, unemployment, personal income, and interest rates are economic factors which affect buyers' ability and willingness to pay. Finally, expectations of future price increases, also are expected to increase individuals willingness to finance housing. As suggested earlier, household growth and economic factors are often thought to be associated with normal housing cycles, whereas expectations are more likely to cause bubbles. These variables are summarized in Table 8.5.

We review these factors over the six subperiods between 1987 and 2016 previously defined in Table 8.4. The first subperiod is that prior to the housing bubble that we have identified. The second is the early part of the bubble, when the supply gap was greater than zero but less than the 10% threshold that we used to identify a bubble. Were it not for the eventual rise in the supply gap to a level greater than 10%, this period would not have been identified as a bubble. Although it might be excluded from the definition of bubble based on this criteria, it was the period in which the initial price increases occurred and would likely be a crucial period in the formation of expectations during later stages of the bubble. The third and fourth periods are the main bubble, separating the period of rising prices and the period of falling prices after the burst. In the fifth subperiod, the

Table 8.5: Factors Affecting the Demand for Housing.

Variable	Source	Relationship	Expected sign
Household growth	U.S. Census.[14]	Number of buyers	+
Payroll employment growth	BLS[15]	Willingness to Pay	+
Unemployment	BLS[16]	Willingness to pay	−
Federal funds rate	Federal Reserve[17]	Willingness to pay	−
Mortgage rate	Federal Reserve[18]	Willingness to pay	−
Expectations of Future Housing Price Increases	calculated	Willingness to pay	+

supply gap had dropped below 10% but had still not returned to zero. The sixth is the post-bubble period.

During Period 1, prior to the bubble, annual household growth[19] varied between 1% and slightly over 2%, but the pattern was relatively stable over the period (see Chart 8.6a). This was a period of mixed economic growth, including the recession of March 1990 to March 1991. Unemployment declined and annual payroll employment growth rose to slightly over 2% after the recession (see Chart 8.6b). Personal income fluctuated but generally was greater than 3% per year and rose higher toward the end of the period (see Chart 8.6c). The Federal funds rate rose to around 3% after the recession, while the mortgage rate declined over the period, presumably reflecting declining inflation expectations (see Chart 8.6d).

---

[14]We use households headed by an individual aged 30 to 64 to measure household growth. Source: Table HH-3 from the current population survey, as reported by the U.S. Bureau of the Census, http://www.census.gov/cps

[15]US. Bureau of Labor Statistics, All Employees: Total Nonfarm Payrolls [PAYNSA], retrieved from FRED, Federal Reserve Bank of St. Louis; https://fred.stlouisfed.org/series/PAYNSA, August 28, 2016.

[16]UNRATE: US. Bureau of Labor Statistics, Civilian Unemployment Rate [UNRATE], retrieved from FRED, Federal Reserve Bank of St. Louis https://research.stlouisfed.org/fred2/series/UNRATE, June 14, 2016.

[17]FEDFUNDS: Board of Governors of the Federal Reserve System (US.), Effective Federal Funds Rate (FEDFUNDS), retrieved from FRED, Federal Reserve Bank of St. Louis https://research.stlouisfed.org/fred2/series/FEDFUNDS, June 14, 2016.

[18]MORTG: Board of Governors of the Federal Reserve System (US.), 30-Year Conventional Mortgage Rate© (MORTG), retrieved from FRED, Federal Reserve Bank of St. Louis https://research.stlouisfed.org/fred2/series/MORTG, June 15, 2016.

[19]We use households headed by an individual aged 30 to 64 to measure household growth. Data is from Table HH-3 from the current population survey, as reported by the U.S. Bureau of the Census, http://www.census.gov/cps.

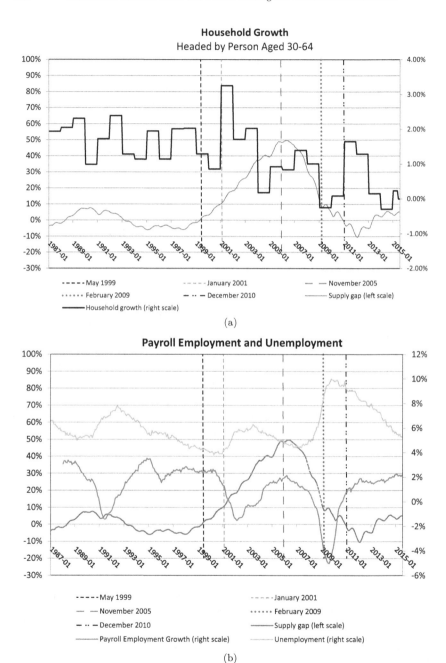

Chart 8.6.   Factors Affecting Demand for Housing.

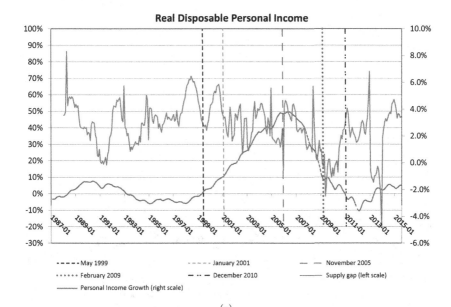

(c)

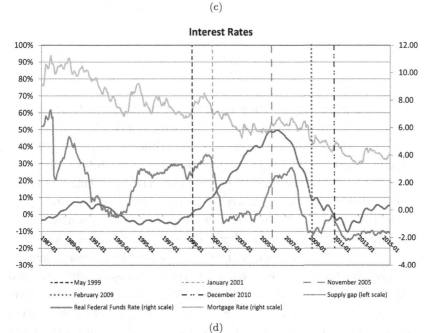

(d)

Chart 8.6.   (*Continued*)

(e)

Chart 8.6. (*Continued*)

Housing prices began rising toward the end of Period 1, but from a negative supply gap to a level in equilibrium with supply. This increase thus can be interpreted as a normal adjustment in the housing market to previous economic conditions, although stronger economic growth toward the end of the period and declining mortgage rates may have contributed. Housing prices continued to increase during the early bubble, Period 2, from May 1999 to January 2001, but this time with an increasing, positive supply gap. Demand factors were mixed during the early bubble period. Household growth was relative weak compared with the pre-bubble. Economic activity weakened slightly toward the end of the period, but generally continued the strong trend of the pre-bubble period. Interest rates, both short-term and long, increased. Thus, the rise in housing prices during this period appears more of a continuation from Period 1, perhaps an overshooting of equilibrium and perhaps driven by trends in employment and income.

A different set of demand factors appeared to emerge in Period 3, between January 2001 and November 2005, when housing prices rose to bubble levels. Household growth strengthened at the beginning of this period but then slowed below the pre-bubble and early bubble periods. The recession of March 2001 through November 2001 brought weaker payroll employment growth and higher unemployment. All of these factors would normally be expected to reduce housing demand and thus not cause the bubble. However, their impact may have been indirect, through their effect on monetary policy, as countercycle monetary policy brought the real Federal funds rate close to zero during the bubble-up period and mortgage rates continued falling, to around 6%. Monetary policy thus is the factor most likely to have increased demand during the up bubble period.

The bubble burst and moved into Period 4, the down bubble. Household growth remainded at the weaker levels late in the up-bubble period. Economic activity weakened, reducing housing demand, but this began after burst and and does not appear to be a precipitating factor. In contrast, interest rates began to rise in late-2004, rising significantly prior to the burst, and consequently may have been the determining factor, albeit with a significant lag.

The role of expectations as a factor affecting demand also warrants further consideration. We do not have an explicit measure of price expectations, but it is reasonable to believe that they are a function of actual past changes in housing prices and their duration. We analyze the average increase in housing prices over the previous five years as a factor likely to be important in the formation of expectations.[20] This expectational variable, in fact, almost perfectly mimics the actual price of housing prices over all five periods reviewed (see Chart 8.6e). Importantly, expectations of future price increases are likely to have begun rising at the end of the pre-bubble period and then continued rising through the early bubble and bubble-up periods, before leveling off and then declining at the peak in housing prices. Since expectations are likely to be based on actual past price increases, they cannot by themselves explain an upward trend in prices. Rather, something

---

[20]Developing an explicit, expectation construct for bubbles in general is an objective that we hope to pursue in subsequent research.

else needs to initiate the process. However, it is likely that expectations did play a significant role in the housing bubble. If monetary policy and the resulting low interest rates early in the bubble-up period provided the initial impulse for the continued rise in housing prices, it may well be that expectations eventually took over, and even ensured continued increases even after monetary policy eventually tightened. Thus, expectations provide a plausible explanation for both the magnitude and duration of the bubble, as well as for the lag in the burst following the eventual tightening of monetary policy as the bubble proceeded.

7. Conclusions

This paper argues that asset price bubbles need to be examined carefully because their adverse impacts on an economy have been often very substantial and promise to remain so in the future. The introductory sections review the basic ideas about asset bubbles and describe how the economics profession has slowly moved towards the realization that asset price bubbles are no longer uncommon economic events that occur in isolated markets such as the Dutch tulip bubble. Although basic conceptual issues about defining an asset bubble, identifying its causes, and anticipating its sudden burst are not settled intellectually, the empirical evidence demonstrates that stock market and housing bubbles occur quite often. Also, the evidence from the last 50 years shows that the average correction in a stock market bubble crash is a decrease in price of about 50% while the typical housing price decline is about 30%.

After reviewing the general literature on asset bubbles for housing and stock markets and their impact on an economy, we estimate a fundamental housing price model that allows us to distinguish among the buildup, the bursting, and the impact in its aftermath. Our proposed econometric methodology estimates the magnitude of the housing bubble and its starting and ending dates and duration. We first discuss both the macroeconomic environment that may have contributed to the housing bubble with an emphasis on the role of monetary policy and credit expansion, and then focus on the challenging issues of identifying factors affecting the demand and supply for housing. The particular determinants of the demand for housing that we explore are household growth, employment, income, price expectations, and mortgage interest rates; on the supply side, we focus on building costs and the supply of land. Our analysis allows us to identify the housing bubble and describe the various chronological steps in its evolution. The goal of our future work is to extend our current work and investigate further the development of dynamic econometric models.

References

Bernanke, B (2010). *Monetary Policy and the Housing Market* [Speech]. Annual Meeting of the American Economic Association, Atlanta, GA, 3 January.

Bernanke, B (2013). *The Federal Reserve and the Financial Crisis*. Princeton, NJ: Princeton University Press.

Bernanke, B (2015). *The Taylor Rule: A Benchmark for Monetary Policy?* Brookings Institution, 28 April.

Bernanke, B and M Gertler (1999). Monetary Policy and Asset Prices Volatility, *Economic Review*, Federal Reserve Bank of Kansas City, 84, pp. 17–51.

Bernanke, B and M Gertler (2001). Should central banks respond to movements in asset prices? *American Economic Review*, 91(2), pp. 253–257.

Case, KE (1986). The market for single-family homes in the Boston area. *New England Economic Review*, May/June, pp. 38–48.

Davis, MA and J Heathcote (2007). The price and quantity of residential land in the United States. *Journal of Monetary Economics,* 54(8), pp. 2,595–2,620.

Evanoff, D, G Kaufman and A. G. Malliaris (Eds.) (2012). *New Perspectives on Asset Price Bubbles*. New York: Oxford University Press.

Evanoff, D and AG Malliaris (2017). Asset Price Bubbles and Public Policy in Evanoff, D, G Kaufman and A.G. Malliaris (Eds.) (2017). *Public Policy and Financial Economics: In Honor of Professor George Kaufman for his Lifelong Contributions*, Hackensack, NJ: World Scientific Publishers, forthcoming.

Greenspan, A (2004). Risk and uncertainty in monetary policy. *American Economic Review*, 94(2), pp. 33–40.

Greenspan, A, (2009). The Fed Didn't Cause the Housing Bubble. *Wall Street Journal*, March 11.

International Monetary Fund (2003). When Bubbles Burst. *IMF World Economic and Financial Surveys*, pp. 61–94.

Jorda, O, M Schularick and A Taylor (2015). Leveraged Bubbles. *Working Paper*, Federal Reserve Bank of San Francisco, No. 2015-10.

Jorda, O, M Schularick and A Taylor (2016). Bubbles, Credit, and Their Consequences. *Economic Letter*, Federal Reserve Bank of San Francisco, September.

Kindleberger, CP and R Aliber (2015). *Manias, Panics, and Crashes: A History of Financial Crises* (7th ed.) Hoboken, NJ: John Wiley & Sons.

Reinhart, C and K Rogoff (2009). *This Time is Different: Eight Centuries of Financial Folly*. Princeton, NJ: Princeton University Press.

Shiller, RJ (2015). *Irrational Exuberance* (3rd ed.) Princeton, NJ: Princeton University Press.

Taylor, JB (1993). Discretion versus Policy Rules in Practice. *Carnegie-Rochester Conference Series on Public Policy*, 39, pp. 195–214.

Taylor, JB (2007). Housing and Monetary Policy. *NBER Working Paper*, No. 13682, December.

Tarullo, DK (2014). *Monetary Policy and Financial Stability* [Speech]. 30th Annual National Association for Business Economics Economic Policy Conference, Arlington, VA., 25 February.

Chapter Nine

What Caused the Great Recession
in the Eurozone?

Robert L. Hetzel*

Federal Reserve Bank of Richmond

Abstract

Since 2008, the Eurozone has undergone two recessions, which together constitute the "Great Recession." The combination of a decline in output and disinflation as well as a persistent decline in inflation suggests that contractionary monetary policy was one factor. This chapter makes two methodological points. First, in analyzing the causes of the Great Recession, it is important to distinguish between credit and monetary policy. Second, a multiplicity of estimated models can "explain" the Great Recession. In practice, economists choose between models through an associated narrative that adds additional information about causation.

The Great Recession, which encompassed back-to-back recessions in the Eurozone, has reinvigorated debate over the causes of recession. Given the prominence of disruptions to financial markets, it has also generated controversy about the desirability of central bank "inflation targeting," especially the question of whether central banks should add a measure of financial stability to their traditional objectives for output and inflation (Curdia and Woodford, 2009;

---

*The author is Senior Economist and Research Advisor at the Federal Reserve Bank of Richmond. He gratefully acknowledges helpful criticism of an earlier version (Hetzel, 2013) from Ernst Baltensperger, Mark Bills, Yongsung Chang, Douglas Diamond, Michael Dotsey, Marvin Goodfriend, Joshua Hendrickson, Andreas Hornstein, Peter Ireland, Thomas Lubik, Christian Matthes, Alberto Musso, Edward Nelson, Andrew Owen, Ricardo Reis, Kurt Schuler, Felipe Schwartzman, Peter Welz, and Alexander Wolman, as well as participants in seminars at the Bundesbank, European Central Bank, Swiss National Bank, and the Banca D'Italia without implicating any of these individuals in the exposition. Miki Doan, Samuel Marshall, Raymond Wong, and Steven Sabol provided invaluable research assistance. The views in this paper are the author's not the Federal Reserve Bank of Richmond's or the Federal Reserve System's.

Woodford, 2012).[1] Answers are complicated if the origin of the Great Recession lay in a combination of contractionary monetary policy and disruption to financial intermediation. The discussion here of recession in the Eurozone suggests this possibility and makes two methodological points.

First, it is essential to distinguish monetary policy from credit policy. "Monetary policy," considered as the central bank reaction function for setting its policy rate, exercises its influence on the nominal expenditure of the public through its influence on the term-structure of the risk-free interest rate. The "stance" of monetary policy, the central bank's impact on stabilizing or changing growth in nominal expenditure, derives from the interaction of this risk-free term structure with the "natural" term structure. The latter is derived under the assumption of perfectly flexible prices and reflects the way in which the real rate of interest reconciles the desire of households to smooth consumption with unevenness in the expected availability of the consumption good. "Credit policy" concerns how the central bank influences financial intermediation. In terms of the models discussed below, credit policies affect the external finance premium that firms face.[2]

Second, narrative complements model. While identification of the shocks that produce a recession requires a model, all models are abstractions and incorrect in significant ways. Moreover, a multiplicity of models exists, capable of fitting any given time series. In practice, economists use a model in conjunction with a (often implicit) narrative. The narrative brings in information from outside the model that renders plausible the association of a model's shocks, which are unobservable, with observable time series. The narrative here suggests that the monetary policy of the European Central Bank (ECB) was contractionary at times even though its credit policies were stimulative. At the same time, the reader should keep in mind that both monetary disorder and financial-market disruption work through financial markets and are therefore inherently difficult to separate.

---

[1] Riva and Perez-Quiros (2015: 557) are critical of incorporating macroprudential policy:

> The comparison of the forecast performance of models that include credit with other global models shows that there is no significant gain from introducing credit.... [O]ur results indicate that the role of credit in the identification of the economic cycle... is very limited.... [C]redit can describe the past but not infer the future.

[2] The analytical distinction made here is not common among policymakers. The more common practice is to characterize monetary policy in terms of the level of the policy rate and to characterize credit policies as "liquidity" enhancing programs that facilitate the "transmission" of monetary policy. In the U.S., it is natural to think about how the Federal Reserve's reaction function shapes the behavior of the risk-free term structure of interest rates because there is a term structure for government securities. In the Eurozone, in contrast, with the absence of a supranational risk-free Euro bond, the focus of attention is more naturally on the disparate banking systems of each member of the Eurozone. Credit-market interventions appear attractive as a way of facilitating the "transmission" of monetary policy and appear less abstract than monetary policy. The arguments here, however, point to the importance of a clear distinction between monetary and credit policy and to the importance of getting monetary policy right as the foundation.

Aoki (2001) serves here as the basic New Keynesian (NK) framework. As Aoki (2001) contains a flexible-price and a sticky-price sector, it is useful for discussing the effects of the commodity-price shock that unfurled from summer 2004 through summer 2008 and again in 2010 and 2011. With the Aoki model as background, one can then discuss how alternative estimated NK DSGE models with financial frictions add to an understanding of the Great Recession.

Section 1 discusses how the basic NK model can make explicit long-standing monetarist criticisms of a monetary policy that creates negative output gaps in order to control inflation. Section 2 asks how expansion of the basic NK model to include financial frictions modifies these implications. Section 3 provides one narrative of the Great Recession. It highlights how, in 2008 and 2011, the ECB effectively attempted to lower headline inflation by creating a negative output gap. Section 4 discusses the credit policies of the ECB. Section 5 puts the decline in output associated with the decline in inflation in the Great Recession into the perspective of estimates of the "sacrifice ratio." Section 6 offers concluding comments.

1. Monetarism and the Basic NK Model

In *A Program for Monetary Stability*, Milton Friedman (1960) criticized policies of aggregate-demand management. His critique is pertinent to the current debate over the desirability of "inflation targeting," especially because he stated it in the context of criticism of a simple feedback rule for eliminating misses in the price level from target. In practice, given the "long and variable" lags between changes in the policy instrument and in inflation, such a rule effectively entails manipulation of an output gap as an intermediate target for eliminating misses of an inflation target.[3] Later, Friedman (1968; 1969) developed his argument further in a critique of attempts by the central to exploit Phillips curve trade-offs between inflation and an output gap.

Although monetarists focused their criticisms on the procyclical behavior of money, they attributed that behavior to the cyclical inertia introduced by central banks into the setting of their interest-rate targets (Friedman, 1984: 27; Poole, 1978: 105). In the stop-go era, after cyclical troughs and during economic recovery, the Federal Reserve postponed

---

[3]Friedman (1960, 88) wrote: "[M]onetary changes have their effect only after a considerable lag and over a long period and that lag is rather variable... Under these circumstances, the price level... could be an effective guide only if it were possible to predict, first, the effects of non-monetary factors on the price level for a considerable period of time in the future, second, the length of time it will take in each particular instance for monetary actions to have their effect... "

raising the funds rate in order to speed a decline in the negative output gap. Similarly, the Fed was slow to lower the funds rate as the economy weakened prior to and after cyclical peaks, in order to create a negative output gap that would lower inflation (Hetzel, 2008: Chaps. 23–25; 2012: Chap. 8).

Friedman (1960) proposed that the central bank make money grow at a low, stable rate. The underlying hypothesis was that as long as the central bank provides a stable nominal anchor in terms of the domestic price level, the price system works well to ameliorate cyclical fluctuations. Alternatively, major cyclical fluctuations derive from central bank interference with the price system. His *k*-percent money rule would have provided that nominal anchor while letting the price system determine real variables. The basic NK model explains how central banks controlled inflation after the disinflations of the early 1980s in this spirit, albeit without money targets.

That is, they abandoned recourse to Phillips curve trade-offs and instead relied on the way in which a credible rule shapes the behavior of forward-looking agents. In the 1980s, central banks moved to the control of trend inflation through creation of an environment of nominal expectational stability that conditioned the way in which firms set nominal prices for multiple periods. They conditioned that nominal price setting through aligning the expectation of inflation of firms in the sticky-price sector (core inflation) with their inflation targets.

In the absence of markup shocks, if the central bank maintains price stability in the sticky-price sector so that actual and expected inflation equal zero, it also maintains the aggregate output gap equal to zero (Aoki, 2001: Eq. 33). Blanchard and Gali (2007) characterized this combination of price stability and a zero-output gap as "divine coincidence," a model characteristic noted in Goodfriend and King (1997). With divine coincidence, in order to maintain price stability in the sticky-price sector and the output gap equal to zero, the central bank should maintain the real rate of interest equal to the natural rate of interest, which is the real interest rate with price flexibility (Aoki, 2001: Eq. 50). That is, it should let the price system work freely to determine real variables.

As high headline (aggregate) inflation in the Eurozone in 2008 and 2011 reflected a commodity-price shock emanating from the influence of internationally-determined prices on inflation in the flexible-price sector, the ECB should have accommodated it. Aoki (2001: 57, 75) stated this implication of the NK model:

> [T]here is a trade-off between stabilizing the aggregate output gap and aggregate inflation, but... there is no trade-off between stabilizing [the] aggregate output gap and stabilizing core inflation... [S]uppose there is an increase in the price of food and energy... putting an upward pressure on aggregate inflation... The central bank could respond with a sharp contractionary policy and reduce aggregate demand by a large amount so as to decrease prices in the sticky-price sector... However, our model shows that such a policy is not optimal. The optimal policy is to stabilize core inflation.

2. Adding Frictions in Financial Intermediation to the Basic NK Model

In the context of the basic NK model with no financial frictions, consider first shocks that create a wedge between the household's intertemporal rate of substitution in consumption and the risk-free real rate of interest. To this end, Smets and Wouters (2007: Eq. 2) adds a shock to the Euler equation. The Board of Governors EDO model adds a wedge in the budget constraint between the policy rate and the return on bonds held by households (Chung *et al.*, 2010: Eq. 12). In Aoki (2001: Eq. 1), the shock enters directly in the household utility function. For example, an intertemporal preference shock that causes households to value future consumption relatively more highly than current consumption lowers the natural rate of interest.

The way in which one interprets this variety of shock, termed here a "demand shock," depends upon the narrative adopted. In Aoki (2001), it is natural to interpret it as a savings shock. That is, with a positive savings shock, at the existing interest rate, households want to transfer additional consumption from the present to the future.[4] Regardless of the interpretation of the shock, the implications for monetary policy remain the same. Consider a positive savings shock, which manifests itself as an increased demand for the risk-free asset.

---

[4]Although practitioners use the shock as a portmanteau variable for capturing an increase in risk, the implicit financial frictions are not modeled in the basic NK model. It is also hard to talk about risk in a linear model because risk concerns tail outcomes captured by higher order moments of the correlation between expected rates of return and consumption.

The central bank can neutralize the impact on the economy by lowering its policy rate in line with the natural rate. In doing so, it satisfies the increased demand for the risk-free asset. The real-world counterpart is that with an interest rate target, the increased demand by households for insured deposits is met by an increased supply of deposits. It is plausible that the Lehman bankruptcy on September 15, 2008 produced a sharp decline in the natural rate of interest.[5] However, if the central bank puts inertia into declines in the policy rate relative to the natural rate as occurs with an inertial Taylor rule, nominal rigidities require that real income decline in order to offset the incipient increased demand for the risk-free asset.[6] As documented in Section 3, the ECB was slow to lower its policy rate after the increase in summer 2008 because of its focus on headline inflation.[7]

An NK model like Smets-Wouters (2007), SW, uses a representative household with no financial intermediation. Christiano, Motto, and Rostagno (2010; 2013), CMR, allow for financial intermediation and thus for financial frictions. Their model includes savers and investors whose rates of intertemporal substitution differ in a time-varying way due to a financial friction. An external finance premium that moves negatively with the net worth of firms creates a financial-accelerator mechanism that amplifies the effect of macroeconomic shocks on economic fluctuations. A "credit-risk" shock in the form of a positive exogenous shock to the external finance premium caused by the belief that the productivity of firms has become more dispersed exacerbates default risk and captures the idea of a financial crisis.

---

[5] To the best of the author's knowledge, none of the papers estimating NK models for the Eurozone includes estimates of the natural rate of interest. One paper contains a measure of the "unconditional flexible-price output gap" for the period 1999:Q1 through 2010:Q1 (Vetlov *et al.*, 2011: Fig. 2.2). This measure declined by about 7 percentage points from 2008:Q1 through 2009:Q1 (10 percentage points through 2010:Q1). For the U.S., also using a DSGE model and for the comparable period 2008:Q1 through 2009:Q1, Gali *et al.* (2012) estimated a decline of about 6 percentage points for the output gap and 12.5 percentage points for the natural rate of interest. Numbers kindly supplied by Rafael Wouters.

[6] Fève *et al.* (2009: 13) repeat for Europe the monetarist critique contained in the above references to Friedman (1984) and Poole (1978): "[T]he form of monetary policy, namely monetary policy inertia, has played an important role in the large and persistent increase of the real interest rate and the sizeable output losses that have followed from disinflation policies of the eighties."

[7] An additional way in which financial disruption and monetary disorder can be mutually reinforcing is through disinflation, which increases the real value of debt in an unanticipated way.

In the basic NK large-scale DSGE model without financial frictions, a demand shock like a positive savings shock would by itself raise investment by lowering consumption.[8] Similarly, in a model with financial frictions, a credit-risk shock that depresses investment increases consumption (see, for example, Kollmann *et al.*, 2016: Fig. 3e). Models that include financial frictions then also include demand shocks. As noted, with demand shocks, the central bank can neutralize the impact on the real economy by following the change in the natural rate with the policy rate. At the same time, adding a friction in addition to sticky prices creates one more objective in the central bank's objective function. The central bank should go beyond the divine coincidence that entails tracking the natural rate and trade off among objectives (Carlstrom *et al.*, 2010). Optimal policy in a financial crisis would require missing the inflation and output objectives on the upside, however, not the downside as occurred in the Great Recession.

It is instructive to review the results of DSGE estimation for the Great Recession in the Eurozone keeping in mind that demand shocks, which affect the household's intertemporal preferences for consumption, possess consequences for the real economy only if the central bank does not neutralize them by allowing its policy rate to vary in line with the natural rate of interest. Smets *et al.* (2010: Figs. 3 and 4) includes a decomposition of real GDP that extends through 2009:Q2 for two models. One is the New Area-Wide Model (NAWM) based on SW (*see* Christoffel *et al.*, 2008) and the other is the CMR model. For the recession quarters 2008:Q3 through 2009:Q2, the NAWM model shows demand, policy, and international shocks as the major determinants of the decline in GDP. For these same quarters, the CMR model shows demand, technology, and financial shocks as all significant contributors to the decline in GDP. Christiano *et al.* (2010: Fig. 18a) basically repeat these results for the CMR model with a somewhat different grouping of individual shocks into more inclusive combinations. Over the interval of 2008:Q3 through 2009:Q2, the most significant shocks are demand shocks, capital formation shocks, which create a wedge between the risk-free rate and the cost of external finance to firms, and technology

---

[8]In order to generate the simultaneous decline in consumption and investment characteristic of recession, one can include a marginal efficiency of investment (MEI) shock that increases the relative price of investment in terms of the consumption good.

and markup shocks. In 2009:Q1 and 2009:Q2, the first two of these shocks dominated.[9]

Neither the basic NK model nor the NK model with financial frictions can reconcile for the Great Recession an assumption of optimal monetary policy with the observed combination of a decline in output below trend and inflation below target as well as the persistent shortfalls of inflation from target.[10] The monetarist and NK DSGE approaches both suggest cyclical inertia in the central bank's policy rate as a source of monetary shocks (Hetzel, 2012: Chaps. 7, 12; 2008: Chaps. 23–24). Nevertheless, empirical estimation of the NK model reveals how hard it is to distinguish between shocks that reflect disruption to financial intermediation and shocks that reflect monetary disorder, that is, central bank interference with the operation of the price system. Neither shock is directly observable while both manifest themselves through increased uncertainty in financial markets.

3. A Narrative Account of the Great Recession

Figure 9.1 shows cyclical peaks in 2008:Q1 and 2011:Q1 for real GDP growth. Figure 9.2 shows real GDP growth for the core countries of the Eurozone and the main peripherals. In Figure 9.2, for the first recession, the basic coincidence of the series indicates a common shock among Eurozone countries. In the second recession, the near coincidence of peaks also suggests a common shock but the severity of the downturn for the peripheral countries indicates the severity of the capital flight they experienced (Hetzel, 2014).[11]

---

[9]The CMR model shows "policy" shocks making a small positive contribution to GDP. However, such shocks measure the policy rate relative to the Taylor rule benchmark not relative to the natural rate of interest.

[10]Fève *et al.* (2010) make this point for the countries of the Eurozone for an earlier period: "Using euro area data and structural vector autoregressions (SVARs), we identify disinflation shocks as the only shocks that drive nominal variables to a lower long-run level. We find that in the immediate aftermath of a disinflation shock, the euro area enters a persistent recession."

[11]One common explanation for the Great Recession points to a collapse of speculative excess in the peripherals characterized as a "boom-bust cycle... not unlike the subprime bubble" (Honkapohja, 2014: 261–262). This explanation suggests counterfactually that for the first recession the initial decline in output should have started in the peripheral countries and spread subsequently to the core countries and that the decline in output should have been significantly more pronounced in the latter.

Figure 9.3 shows the real (inflation-adjusted) one-year Euribor rate constructed by subtracting forecasted inflation using the ECB's Survey of Professional Forecasters from the Euribor rate. Use of the one-year Euribor rate accounts for the forecast by financial markets of the near-term path of the ECB's MRO (main refinancing operations) rate. With each recession, the real interest rate declines significantly only well after the cyclical peak. The Eurozone economy weakened after 2001:Q1 but, in contrast, the real rate of interest had already begun a steady decline after 2000:Q3.

Figure 9.4 shows that prior to 2008 the ECB had moved its policy rate in a "lean-against-the-wind" way without imparting significant inertia to it. Figure 9.4 plots changes in the ECB's MRO rate as a bar chart. As a measure of economic activity, it plots the growth rate in real retail sales.[12] The two periods of increases in the MRO rate (2/2000 to 10/2000 and 12/2005 to 6/2007) correspond to growth measured by retail sales strong enough to lower the unemployment rate (see Figure 9.5). The two periods of decreases in the MRO rate (5/2001 to 11/2001, and 12/2002 and 6/2003) correspond to growth weak enough to raise the unemployment rate.

Econometric evidence is consistent with the hypothesis that the ECB's control of inflation occurred mainly through the way in which a credible rule conditioned price-setting in the sticky-price sector rather than through manipulation of an output gap. Based on estimation of a Taylor rule, as an average over the first decade of the ECB's operation, Aastrup and Jensen (2010) concluded:

> We show that the ECB's interest rate changes during 1999–2010 have been mainly driven by changes in economic activity in the Euro area. Changes in actual or expected future HICP inflation play a minor, if any, role.

Goldman Sachs (2016a) highlighted the departure in the 2008 period by estimating a Taylor rule using real-time data with a rolling coefficient on core inflation. The coefficients on the inflation term fluctuate around '0' until 2008, when they jump to '2' and only decline to '0' at the end of 2012. That is, in 2008 when the ECB became concerned about headline inflation well above its target, it began to respond directly to inflation and as a result to create a negative output gap.

---

[12] The Markit purchasing manager's index, PMI, and industrial production yield similar graphs.

In 2008, both core inflation and expected inflation remained close to the objective of 2% or somewhat less with the latter declining only after mid-2013 (see Figures 9.6 and 9.7). As shown in Figure 9.8, which graphs the Euro price of oil and the CRB Commodity Spot Price Index, the price of oil began to rise in 2004 followed by commodity prices in 2006.[13] Starting in late 2007, this commodity price inflation passed into headline inflation (see Figure 9.6).[14]

The jump in commodity price inflation reduced household real income. Figure 9.9 shows the cessation in 2007:Q3 of the prior steady increase in real disposable income. Growth in real consumption declined after 2007:Q3.[15] The smoothed, year-over-year percentage change in real retail sales was 2.8% in April 2007 (see Figure 9.4). It then declined steadily, became negative in April 2008, and was −1.6 in August 2008. Consumer confidence (Economic Sentiment Indicator) peaked in May 2007 and then fell rapidly.[16] The resulting pessimism of households about their future income prospects required a lower real interest rate.[17]

Despite a weakening economy after mid-2007, the ECB failed to lower its policy rate. Instead, in July 2008, it raised the MRO rate from 4.0% to 4.25% (see Figure 9.4). Moreover, the ECB's communications caused markets to anticipate further increases in rates. Figure 9.10, which plots

---

[13] In early 2004, the price of oil was €25 per barrel. It rose to €85 per barrel in June 2008. The growth of emerging-market economies, especially, China, India, and Brazil accounted for the increase in the relative price of commodities. For example, in 2000, China accounted for 12% of global consumption of copper. In 2012, the number had grown to 42% (*Financial Times*, 6/3/2013).

[14] Initially, the commodity-price shock did not pass through to headline inflation presumably because of an offsetting appreciation of the euro. From 2002 until mid-2008, the euro appreciated from less than 0.9 dollars/euro to almost 1.6 dollars/euro.

[15] Over the interval 2004:Q4 through 2007:Q3, real personal consumption expenditures (PCE) grew at an annualized rate of 2%. Annualized real PCE growth then declined as follows: 1.6% (2007:Q4), 0.2% (2008:Q1), −0.6% (2008:Q2), and −1.9% (2008:Q3).

[16] Data from Economic and Financial Affairs page of the European Commission website.

[17] As shown in Figure 9.9, the persistent decline in real income after 2007Q3 is consistent with households forecasting a persistent decline in their income and consequently a reduction in the natural rate of interest. Blanchard and Gali (2007: 36) noted, "The effects of changes in factors such as the price of oil... appear through their effects on natural output." The persistence of the commodity price shock first from 2004 through summer 2008 and then from 2009 through 2011 suggests a reduction in the natural rate of interest through pessimism about growth in natural output. It is also plausible that the risk of a disastrous outcome due to the possible breakup of the Eurozone in 2011 and 2012 exacerbated pessimism about future growth. For a discussion of how left-tail risk can lower the natural rate of interest, see Rietz (1988) and Guvenen *et al.* (2014).

the difference between 12-month and one-month Euribor rates, suggests that from the beginning of 2008 until Fall 2008 markets expected a significant increase in rates.[18] The ECB lowered rates only when headline inflation fell (see Figure 9.11). The decline in 2009 in both core inflation and in real output is consistent with contractionary monetary policy (see Figures 9.1 and 9.6).

The ECB explained its actions in 2008 by a concern that high headline inflation would exacerbate wage demands of French and German unions.[19] Wage inflation (year-over-year in the business sector) had increased from 3.2% over the interval 2003:Q1 through 2007:Q4 to 4.1% in the first three quarters of 2008. In terms of the model, one can interpret ECB actions as reflecting the belief that a positive mark-up shock would increase inflation in the sticky-price sector. The ECB then created a negative output gap in order to keep headline inflation at 2%. It did so by raising rather than lowering its policy rate when economy went into recession.

When the world economy began to recover in 2009, commodity-price inflation rose once more (see Figure 9.8). Starting in early 2011, turmoil in the Middle East also caused oil prices to rise. Headline inflation, which had fallen to −0.5% in 2009, rose to 3% by end-2011, although core inflation remained well below target (see Figure 9.6). The second commodity-price shock intensified the ongoing decline in real disposable income after 2010:Q4. Consumption, which had been recovering slowly, again began to decline after 2010:Q4 (see Figure 9.9). Real retail sales peaked in September 2010 (see Figure 9.4). Growth in real GDP peaked in 2011:Q1 (see Figure 9.1). Given its focus on headline inflation, the ECB raised its policy rate twice in 2011, from 1% to 1.25% in April and to 1.5% in July.

---

[18] The policy rate in the NK model can be thought of as the level of the one-year Euribor rate, which depends upon the MRO rate and the ECB's communication about its future path. Some of the upward slope in the term structure is likely due to increased uncertainty raising the term premium.

[19] See *Financial Times* (6/5/2013: 8). Lucas Papademos (2013: 510), vice president of the ECB, explained, "For more than a year after the outbreak of the global financial crisis, the ECB did not ease monetary policy, as determined by its key interest rates, mainly because it was concerned about the materialization of second-round effects of supply shocks on wage- and price-setting and the potential unanchoring of inflation expectations." The ECB (European Central Bank July, 2008a: 6) noted: "This worrying level of inflation rates results largely from sharp increases in energy and food prices at the global level... There is a... very strong concern that price and wage-setting behaviour could add to inflationary pressures via broadly based second-round effects."

Monetary-contraction as an explanation has the advantage of simplicity in that it offers a common explanation of each recession. First, monetary contraction is consistent with the observed decline in core inflation and in output in both recessions.[20] Second, the ECB responded to the commodity-price shock in the same way in each recession. Moreover, repeated monetary contraction can explain why in contrast to past experience a strong recovery did not follow a deep recession.

If the central bank follows a rule that keeps the real rate of interest equal to the natural rate, given the accommodation of money supply to money demand implied by an interest rate target, nominal money grows at a rate consistent with the central bank's inflation target. Money then offers no information about the evolution of the economy. However, if the central bank creates a difference between the natural and real rates of interest, the behavior of money becomes informative.

The monetary aggregate M1 offers a better measure of transactions demand than M3, which includes a significant amount of debt.[21] Banks issue debt to finance loan growth when loan demand is high. As shown in Figure 9.12, apart from 2002–2003 and 2012–2013 when banks made up for weak loan demand by holding more government securities, M3 growth and loan growth move together. For this reason, it is hard to disentangle causation between growth in M3 and in the economy. M3 is then a contemporaneous indicator of the economy.

M1 growth slowed starting in mid-2006 and slowed sharply at the end of 2007 (see Figure 9.13).[22] Real GDP growth then declined from an annualized rate of 2.2% in 2008:Q1 to −1.2% in 2008:Q2. After falling to near '0' in 2008:Q3, M1 growth revived. Real GDP growth then reached a

---

[20]Fève *et al.* (2010: 200) "find that in the immediate aftermath of a disinflation shock, the euro area enters in a persistent recession."

[21]M1 includes currency in circulation and overnight deposits. M3 includes M1 plus time deposits with maturity up to two years, deposits redeemable given notification up to three months, repurchase agreements, money market fund shares, and debt instruments with maturity up to two years.

[22]In May 2003, the ECB demoted the behavior of money (M3) to a "cross-check" from one of its two "pillars," the other pillar being the behavior of the economy (Deutsche Bank, 2013). For example, the *Editorial* in the July 2010 ECB *Monthly Bulletin* (European Central Bank, 2010a: 6) noted, "[T]he annual growth rate of M3 was unchanged at −0.2% in May 2010... [T]hese data continue to support the assessment that the underlying pace of monetary expansion is moderate and that inflationary pressures over the medium term are contained." The ECB Governing Council left its policy rate unchanged.

trough in 2009:Q1 with annualized growth of −11.3%. M1 growth fell sharply starting in 2010:Q3. Real GDP growth then declined from an annualized growth rate of 3.4% in 2011:Q1 to −1.3% in 2011:Q4.

Despite possessing some predictive value, the signal to noise ratio is low for M1. In a time of financial turmoil when market participants desire liquidity, they transfer out of the illiquid debt instruments in the non-M1 part of M3 into the liquid demand deposits of M1 thus inflating M1 growth. One is on firmer ground using M1 growth as a measure of the stance of monetary policy in the first half of 2008 when growth in M1 and M3 both declined and after May 2010 through early 2012 when M1 growth declined while M3 growth remained low (see Figure 9.13).

4. The Interaction of Financial Crisis and Contractionary Monetary Policy

In the Great Recession, following its "separation principle," the ECB focused monetary policy on headline inflation and focused credit (liquidity) policy on maintaining financial intermediation.[23] As noted by Cour-Thimann and Winkler (2013: 2):

> The ECB's approach to date appears to stand out among central banks: its non-standard measures have been aimed not at providing additional direct monetary stimulus to the economy but [rather its] non-standard measures are a complement to rather than a substitute for standard interest rate policy.

Cahn *et al.* (2014: 3) made a similar point:[24]

> In response to the 2008–2009 crisis, central banks in most advanced countries embarked in large-scale asset purchase programs. In the euro area… instead, the bulk of non-standard interventions took the form of long-term refinancing operations (LTRO's)… Through these operations, the ECB aimed at increasing the average maturity of outstanding liquidity, from approximately 20 days before the crisis to more than 200 days in the second half of 2009.

While financial-market disruption must have impacted economic activity adversely in the Great Recession, the two cycle peaks preceded

---

[23] For an overview of the latter, see (European Central Bank, 2010b; and Gonzalez-Páremo, 2013).

[24] The authors use a DSGE model in which credit policies are stimulative by reducing the interest-rate wedge imposed by banks on financial intermediation. Cahn *et al.*, (2014: 2) find that the LTROs "can have large macroeconomic effects… when the separation principle is breached… that is to say when we force monetary policy not to react to the stimulative effects of LTROs."

the episodes of the most severe disruption. The first cycle peak occurred in 2008:Q1. Real GDP fell at annualized rates of −1.3% and −2.2% in 2008:Q2 and 2008:Q3, respectively. Industrial production including construction peaked in February 2008. In 2008:Q1, stresses in financial markets were still contained, however.

In August 2007, when cash investors ceased buying the commercial paper that financed the holding of subprime mortgages in U.S. banks' off-balance-sheet entities, banks moved them onto their own balance sheets. European banks held many of these illiquid mortgages (Hetzel, 2012: 179, 242). Uncertainty over the extent to which individual European banks held them lessened the willingness of European banks to lend to each other in the interbank market. Instead of relying on interbank loans to meet liquidity needs, they began to hold additional excess reserves (Heider *et al.*, 2009). The ECB accommodated that increased demand. In August 2007, it introduced fixed rate/full allotment tenders and in October 2008 made them standard. The EONIA rate (the euro equivalent of the funds rate) remained fixed at the ECB's MRO rate.

The Federal Reserve and the ECB cooperated in order to relieve funding pressures on European banks with dollar liabilities. With the term auction facility, the Fed auctioned dollars to the U.S. branches of European banks. Through swap lines, the Fed provided dollars to the ECB, which it relent to European banks to replace the dollar funding no longer supplied by money market mutual funds (Hetzel, 2012: 244, 267). Only with the Lehman bankruptcy in September 2008, however, did the amounts outstanding in this facility jump significantly.[25]

Loan growth remained healthy until after the economy entered recession in 2008:Q1. Bank loans to the private sector (MFIs) averaged 10.7% year-over-year from May 2006 through May 2008 (see Figure 9.12). Only in June 2008, did growth fall below 10%.[26] By these measures, funding pressures were manageable through the cycle peak.[27] After the

---

[25] Before Lehman, swap amounts outstanding averaged about $50 billion (Goldberg *et al.*, 2010).

[26] In recession, it is hard to separate disruption to financial intermediation as a causal factor from reduced demand due to a weakening economic outlook. The July 2008 "Euro Area Bank Lending Survey" (European Central Bank, 2008b) reported:

> The most important factor in the net tightening continued to be a deterioration in expectations about the economic outlook... Banks reported that net demand for loans to enterprises and households continued to be negative in the second quarter of 2008.

[27] Significant disruption did occur with the Lehman Brothers bankruptcy on September 15, 2008. It precipitated a run of cash investors who ceased funding financial institutions with long-term, illiquid

recovery took hold in 2009:Q3, loan growth recovered steadily until peaking in 2011:Q3. Economic recovery, however, aborted earlier. Growth in real GDP fell from 3.4% in 2011:Q1 to zero in 2011:Q2 and 2011:Q3 and to −1.3% in 2011:Q4.

From mid-Summer 2011 to mid-Summer 2012, investors fled the sovereign debt markets of the peripheral countries, most noticeably because of their size, Italy and Spain, out of fear that they would exit the Eurozone. Sovereign credit default swap spreads for Italy and Spain started their climb to alarming levels in mid-2011. In early July 2011, the spread of two-year yields on Italian over German debt climbed above 2%, and reached 7% in late November 2011. However, the Eurozone economy had already begun to weaken after 2011:Q1 (see Figure 9.1). The timing suggests causation going from the economic weakness to a debt crisis rather than the reverse.

The spread in the interest rates on loans made to corporations in Germany and France, compared to Italy and Spain, only began to widen in July 2011 along with, not prior to, the end of recovery from the first recession (see Figure 9.14). In 2011, the unemployment rate rose sharply in Italy and was already above 20% in Spain. Plausibly, this interest rate spread reflected a normal risk premium and was therefore not indicative of a failure of financial intermediation.

The year 2011 illustrates the difference between monetary and credit policy. In the last half of 2011, ECB lending to banks in the peripheral countries jumped. Consider ECB lending to Spanish banks, which replaced loans previously made by German banks. German banks placed the reserves gained from calling in their loans in the ECB's deposit facility. In effect, the ECB became the conduit for lending by German banks to Spanish banks. The increase in the size of the ECB's balance sheet indicated a stimulative credit policy, that is, a supportive effect on financial intermediation. The ECB's credit policies were largely successful in limiting increases in money-market spreads like Euribor-OIS (Goldman Sachs, 2016b).[28]

---

mortgage assets. They transferred their funds to the too-big-to-fail banks, to conservatively managed institutions, and into government debt. The underlying shock was a retraction of the financial safety net to a new, more limited but ambiguous line (Hetzel, 2012a: Chap. 13).

[28] De Andoain *et al.* (2014) sought instances of "fragmentation:" episodes in which banks in some Eurozone countries paid a premium to borrow in the interbank market. The most significant occurred at yearend 2011 before the introduction of LTROs (long-term refinancing operations)

Also in 2011, in April and July, the ECB tightened monetary policy by raising its policy rate. As late as the April 2012 *Editorial* in the ECB *Monthly Bulletin* (April 2012: 5), the ECB Governing Council retained hawkish language on inflation: "Inflation rates are likely to stay above 2% in 2012, with upside risks prevailing." Only in July 2012 did the Governing Council guide the EONIA rate toward zero by cutting the MRO rate from 1% to 0.75%, and the deposit rate to zero. As late as May 2012, the ECB had still ruled out forward guidance, the essence of which is pre-commitment. In response to a question, Mario Draghi (5/3/2012: 4) responded, "[A]s we always say, we never pre-commit."[29] As implied by indexed swap markets, in mid-2011, the expected time for inflation to return to 2% was almost nine years. After falling briefly, in mid-2012, it returned to that value but then rose to 20 years after Summer 2014 (Goldman Sachs, 4/2/15: 3).

5. The Quantitative Impact of a Monetary Shock

Even if one believes that contractionary monetary policy contributed to the Great Recession, there remains the issue of magnitude. One way to arrive at an estimate is to draw on the sacrifice-ratio literature, which measures the cost in terms of lost output produced by a reduction in inflation. The first thing to note is that estimated Phillips curves have become "flat," a fact that implies a high sacrifice ratio. Atkeson and Ohanian (2001) noted that lagged inflation does a better job of predicting inflation than do Phillips curves, which include resource slack as an explanatory variable. With expected inflation the dominant determinant of trend inflation, contractionary monetary policy in an environment of central bank credibility implies a high sacrifice ratio. In reference to the

---

on December 8, 2011 providing three-year financing to banks by the ECB. They concluded, that "Overall, the evidence suggests that non-standard measures such as long-term liquidity operations were broadly effective in dampening market tensions" (De Andoain *et al.*, 2014: 11).

[29] Kang *et al.*, (2015) documented that equity markets responded positively to the Fed's interest rate cuts but negatively on average to the EC's rate cuts. They attributed the difference to the belief by markets that the cuts by the Fed manifested its commitment to restore full employment while the cuts by the ECB simply conveyed pessimism about the economy. Kang *et al.* (2015: 45) used ECB communication to argue that "When commodity prices were pushing inflation up, the ECB sought to nip it in the bud; but when commodity prices pushed inflation down, the ECB preferred to wait in anticipation of a return to more normal inflation rates." In contrast, after the 2009 cycle trough, the FOMC sought to anchor expected inflation while using forward guidance to stimulate the economy.

FRB/US model of the staff of the Board of Governors, Kiley *et al.*, (2006) noted:

> [A]gents' beliefs about the FOMC's long-run inflation objective respond only slowly to changes in actual inflation, in a manner consistent with survey evidence on expectations formation. Moreover, inflation is only modestly responsive in the short run to changes in resource utilization. Together these effects cause the long-run sacrifice ratio in FRB/US to be relatively large: Permanently reducing the inflation rate in FRB/US by 1 percentage point requires keeping the unemployment rate above the NAIRU by roughly a full percentage point for six years.

How well does this sacrifice ratio of '6' do in explaining Eurozone experience? For the first recession, from 2008:Q1 through 2010:Q2, the unemployment rate rose 3 percentage points from 7.3% to 10.3%, while the inflation rate in the services sector (sticky-price sector) fell 1.3 percentage points from 2.6% to 1.3% (see Figures 9.5 and 9.15). With 7.3% as NAIRU and average unemployment over this period of 8.8%, unemployment averaged 1.5 percentage points above NAIRU for 2.25 years. Roughly, the sacrifice ratio would be 2.6. For the second recession, from 2011:Q1 through 2013:Q2, the unemployment rate rose 2.1 percentage points from 10.0% to 12.1%, while the inflation rate in the services sector fell 0.2 percentage points from 1.6% to 1.4%. With 10.0% as the NAIRU and average unemployment over this period of 11.1%, unemployment averaged 1.05 percentage points over NAIRU for 2.25 years. Roughly, the sacrifice ratio would be about '12'.

The estimated sacrifice ratio for the first recession appears consistent with historical experience while the estimated sacrifice ratio for the second recession appears implausibly high (see also, Ball and Mazumder, 2015). For the second recession, it thus seems likely that the increase in the unemployment rate originated to a significant extent in the disruption to financial intermediation associated with the capital flight crisis in 2011–2012 (Hetzel, 2014). At the same time, the decline in services sector inflation to 1.3% in 2016:Q1 is inconsistent with the expansionary monetary policy appropriate if the central bank's reaction function includes mitigation of financial frictions (Carlstrom *et al.*, 2010).

6. Concluding Comment

In 2008, and again in 2011, the Eurozone experienced a commodity-price shock, which raised inflation in the flexible-price sector. Rather than concentrating on core inflation (inflation in the sticky-price sector), the ECB created a negative output gap in order to keep headline inflation at its 2% inflation target. Optimal policy would have entailed concentrating on core inflation and lowering the policy rate in order to maintain a zero-output gap in the sticky-price sector. In both episodes, disruptions to financial intermediation would have called for expansionary monetary policy. If the pessimism from the financial crisis in Fall 2008 and again after mid-2011 lowered the natural rate of interest, then the credit policies of the ECB would have been insufficient to stem recession without more aggressive reductions in the policy rate combined with forward guidance.

Two different responses to the Great Recession are possible. Central banks could add the mitigation of financial frictions to their reaction function by adding a response to variations in credit spreads, to the degree of leverage in the financial system, or to the cyclical behavior of credit. Alternatively, they could concentrate on the design of an optimal reaction function assuming no credit frictions and then use credit-market interventions in an *ad hoc* way in order to deal with disruptions to financial-market intermediation. With either choice, it is important for policymakers to maintain a clear distinction between monetary policy and credit policy.

References

Aastrup, M and H Jensen (2010). *What Drives the European Central Bank's Interest-Rate Changes?* University of Copenhagen.

Aoki, K (2001). Optimal monetary policy responses to relative-price changes. *Journal of Monetary Economics,* 48(1), pp. 55–80.

Atkeson, A and LE Ohanian (2001). Are Phillips Curves Useful for Forecasting Inflation? *Quarterly Review,* Federal Reserve Bank of Minneapolis, pp. 2–11.

Ball, L and S Mazumder (2015). A Phillips Curve with Anchored Expectations and Short-Term Unemployment. *IMF Working Paper,* No. 15/39.

Blanchard, O and J Gali (2007). Real wage rigidities and the new Keynesian model. *Journal of Money, Credit and Banking,* 39(s1), pp. 35–65.

Cahn, C, J Matheron, and J Sahuc (2014). Assessing the Macroeconomic Effects of LTROS. *Banque de France Document de Travail,* No. 528.

Carlstrom, CT, TS Fuerst and M Paustian (2010). Optimal monetary policy in a model with agency costs. *Journal of Money, Credit and Banking* (Supplement), 42(6), pp. 37–70.

Christiano, L, R Motto and M Rostagno (2010). Financial Factors in Economic Fluctuations. *ECB Working Paper,* No. 1192.

Christiano, L, R Motto and M Rostagno (2013). Risk Shocks. *NBER Working Paper,* No. 18682.

Christoffel, K, G Coenen and A Warne (2008). The New Area-wide Model of the Euro Area. *ECB Working Paper*, No. 944.

Chung, HT, MT Kiley and J Laforte (2010). Documentation of the Estimated, Dynamic, Optimization-based (EDO) Model of the U.S. Economy: 2010 Version. *Finance and Economics Discussion*, Series 29.

Cour-Thimann, P and B Winkler (2013). The ECB's Non-Standard Monetary Policy Measures. *ECB Working Paper Series*, No. 1528.

Curdia, V and M Woodford (2009). Credit Spreads and Monetary Policy. *NBER Working Paper*, No. 15289.

De Andoain, CG, P Hoffmann and S Manganelli (2014). Fragmentation in the Euro Overnight Unsecured Money Market. *ECB Working Paper*, No. 1755.

Deutsche Bank Research. (2013). ECB reaction function(s). *Focus Europe*, 13 September.

Draghi, M (2012). *Introductory Statement to the Press Conference (with Q&A)*. Barcelona: European Central Bank, 3 May.

European Central Bank. (2008a). Editorial. *Monthly Bulletin*, pp. 5–8.

European Central Bank. (2008b). The Euro Area Bank Lending Survey. July.

European Central Bank. (2010). Editorial. *Monthly Bulletin*, pp. 5–8, pp. 59–74, July.

European Central Bank. (2011). Editorial. *Monthly Bulletin*, p. 5.

European Central Bank. (2012). Editorial. *Monthly Bulletin*, pp. 5–6, April.

Fève, P, J Matheron, and J Sahuc (2009). Inflation Target Shocks and Monetary Policy Inertia in the Euro Area. *Banque de France Document de Travail*, No. 243.

Fève, P, J Matheron and J Sahuc (2010). Disinflation shocks in the Eurozone: a DSGE perspective. *Journal of Money, Credit and Banking*, 42(2–3), pp. 289–323.

Financial Times. (2013a, 3 June). Beijing returns to global metals market. p. 15.

Financial Times. (2013b, 5 June). ECB's untimely change of mind. p. 8.

Friedman, M (1960). *A Program for Monetary Stability*. New York: Fordham University Press.

Friedman, M (1969). The Role of Monetary Policy (1968). In *The Optimum Quantity of Money*, Friedman, M (ed.), pp. 95–110. Chicago: Aldine.

Friedman, M (1984). *Monetary Policy for the 1980s*. In John. H. Moore (Ed.), *To Promote Prosperity: U.S. Domestic Policy in the mid-1980s* (pp. 23–60). Stanford: Hoover Institution Press.

Gali, J, F Smets and R Wouters (2012). Slow Recoveries: A Structural Interpretation. *NBER Working Paper*, No. 18085.

Goldberg, LS, C Kennedy and J Miu (2010). Central Bank Dollar Swap Lines and Overseas Dollar Funding Costs. *NBER Working Paper*, No. 15763.

Goldman Sachs (2015). European Economics Analyst: Euro Area Inflation Expectations and QE: Moments of Truth. *Economics Research*, April.

Goldman Sachs (2016a). European Economics Analyst: Explaining Time-Varying Rate Sensitivity to Inflation in the Euro area. *Economics Research*, May.

Goldman Sachs (2016b). European Economics Analyst: Unconventional Monetary Policy and Financial Stability. *Economics Research*, June.

Gonzalez-Páremo, JM (2013). Innovations in Lender of Last Resort Policy in Europe. In *Handbook of Safeguarding Global Financial Stability: Political, Social, Cultural, and Economic Theories and Models*, G Caprio, Jr. (ed.), pp. 435–442. London: Elsevier.

Goodfriend, M and RG King (1997). The New Neoclassical Synthesis. In *NBER Macroeconomics Annual*, Bernanke, BS and J Rotemberg (eds.), pp. 231–296. Cambridge, MA: National Bureau of Economic Research.

Guvenen, F, S Ozkan and J Song (2014). The nature of countercyclical income risk. *Journal of Political Economy*, 122(3), pp. 621–660.

Heider, F, M Hoerova and C Holthausen (2009). Liquidity Hoarding and Interbank Market Spreads: The Role of Counterparty Risk. *ECB Working Paper*, No. 1126.

Hetzel, RL (2008). *The Monetary Policy of the Federal Reserve: A History*. Cambridge: Cambridge University Press.

Hetzel, RL (2012). *The Great Recession: Market Failure or Policy Failure?* Cambridge: Cambridge University Press.

Hetzel, RL (2013). ECB Monetary Policy in the Great Recession: A New Keynesian (Old Monetarist) Critique. *Federal Reserve Bank of Richmond Working Paper*, No. 13-07R.

Hetzel, RL (2014). *Should Greece Remain in the Eurozone? Economic Quarterly 100*, Federal Reserve Bank of Richmond, pp. 241–278.

Honkapohja, S (2014). The Euro area crisis: a view from the north. *Journal of Macroeconomics*, 39(PB), pp. 260–271.

Kang, DW, N Ligthart and A Mody (2015). The European Central Bank: Building a Shelter in a Storm. *Griswold Center for Economic Policy Studies Working Paper*, No. 248.

Kiley, M, T Laubach and R Tetlow (2006). *Optimal-Control Policies*. Memo to Members of the Federal Open Market Committee, Board of Governors of the Federal Reserve System, 20 June.

Kollmann, R, B Pataracchia, R Raciborski, M Ratto, W Roeger, and L Vogel (2016). The Post-Crisis Slump in the Euro Area and the US: Evidence from an Estimated Three-Region DSGE Model. *Federal Reserve Bank of Dallas Globalization and Monetary Policy Institute Working Paper*, No. 269.

Pappademos, L (2013). The Great Inflation: Lessons for Central Banks. In, *The Great Inflation: The Rebirth of Modern Central Banking*, Bordo MD and A Orphanides (eds.). New York and London: The University of Chicago Press, pp. 503–511.

Poole, W (1978). *Money and the Economy: A Monetarist View*. Reading, MA: Addison-Wesley Publishing Company.

Rietz, TA (1988). The equity risk premium: a solution. *Journal of Monetary Economics*, 22(1), pp. 117–131.

Rivas, MDG and G Perez-Quiros (2015). The failure to predict the Great Recession — a view through the role of credit. *Journal of the European Economic Association*, 13(3), pp. 354–559.

Smets, F, K Christoffel, G Coenen, R Motto and M Rostagno (2010). DSGE models and their use at the ECB. *Journal of the Spanish Economic Association*, 1(1), pp. 51–65.

Smets, F and R Wouters (2007). Shocks and frictions in US business cycles: a Bayesian DSGE approach. *American Economic Review*, 97(3), pp. 586–606.

Vetlov, I, T Hlédik, M Jonsson, H Kucsera and M Pisani (2011). Potential Output in DSGE Models. *ECB Working Paper Series*, No. 1351.

Woodford, M (2012). Inflation Targeting and Financial Stability. *NBER Working Paper*, No. 17967.

Appendix

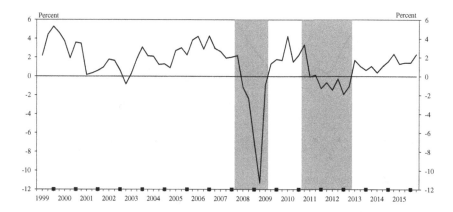

Fig. 9.1. Growth in Real GDP.

Notes: Quarterly observations of quarterly annualized percentage changes in real GDP. Shaded areas mark recessions with cycle peaks 2008:Q1 and 2011:Q1. Heavy tick marks indicate fourth quarter.
Source: Haver Analytics.

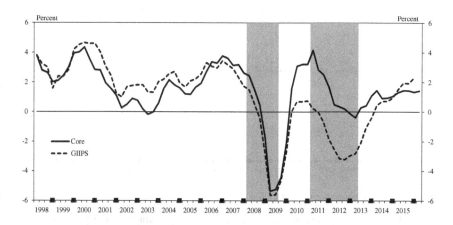

Fig. 9.2. Growth in Real GDP for Core and GIIPS Countries.

Notes: Four-quarter percentage change in real GDP for core countries (Austria, Belgium, Finland, France, Germany, and the Netherlands) and the GIIPS (Greece, Ireland, Italy, Portugal, and Spain). Heavy tick marks indicate fourth quarter.
Source: Haver Analytics.

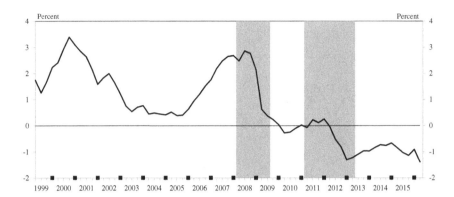

Fig. 9.3.   Real Euribor Interest Rate.

Note: Quarterly observations of real one-year Euribor interest rates constructed using one-year ahead inflation forecasts from ECB Survey of Professional Forecasters mean point estimates. Heavy tick marks indicate fourth quarter.
Source: ECB and Haver Analytics.

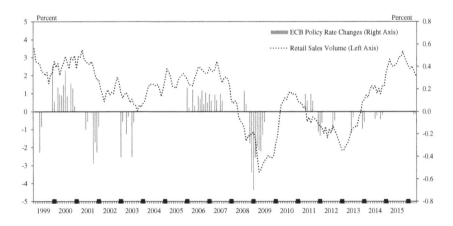

Fig. 9.4.   Retail Sales and ECB Policy Rate.

Notes: Retail Sales Volume is the three-month moving average of the year-over-year percentage change in the EA 17: Retail Sales Volume Index (SA/WDA, 2010=100). ECB Policy Rate is the Main Refinancing Operations (MRO) Rate. As changes in the MRO rate occur within the month and data are monthly, the changes are distributed over two months. Heavy tick marks indicate fourth quarter.
Source: Eurostat and Haver Analytics.

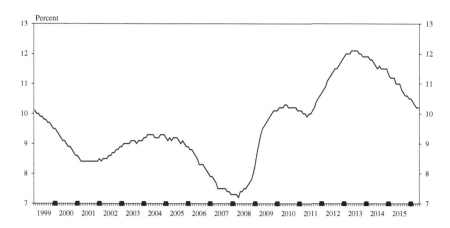

Fig. 9.5.   Unemployment Rate.

Notes: Unemployment rate for the Euro Area. Heavy tick marks indicate December.
Source: Eurostat and Haver Analytics.

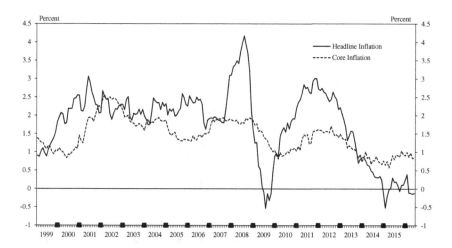

Fig. 9.6.   Headline and Core Inflation.

Notes: Monthly observations of 12-month percentage changes. Headline inflation is the
harmonized CPI. Core inflation excludes energy, food, alcohol and tobacco. Heavy tick
marks indicate December.
Source: ECB and Haver Analytics.

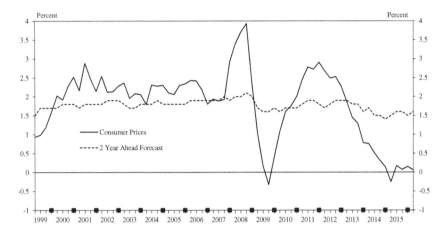

Fig. 9.7.   Expected and Realized Inflation.

Notes: Quarterly observations of four-quarter percentage changes in Harmonized Index of Consumer Prices. Inflation forecast is from ECB Survey of Professional Forecasters mean point estimates: two years ahead. Heavy tick marks indicate fourth quarter.
Source: ECB and Haver Analytics.

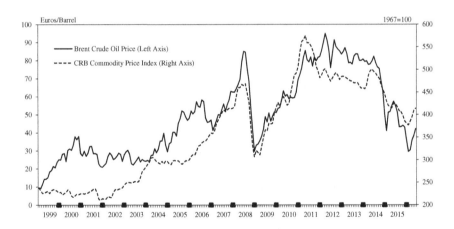

Fig. 9.8.   Brent Crude Oil Price in Euros and CRB Commodity Spot Price Index.

Notes: Brent crude oil price multiplied by the EUR/US$ spot exchange rate. CRB Spot Commodity Price Index: All Commodities (AVG, 1967=100). Heavy tick marks indicate December.
Source: Reuters-CRB Commodity Index Report and Haver Analytics.

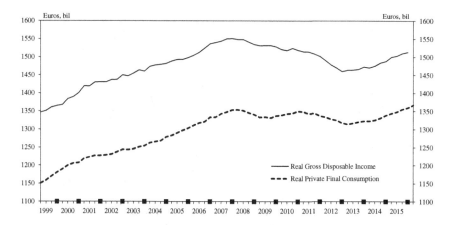

Fig. 9.9.   Real Gross Disposable Income and Private Consumption.

Notes: Real gross disposable income is gross disposable income divided by the harmonized consumer price index times 100. Heavy tick marks indicate fourth quarter.
Source: Eurostat and Haver Analytics.

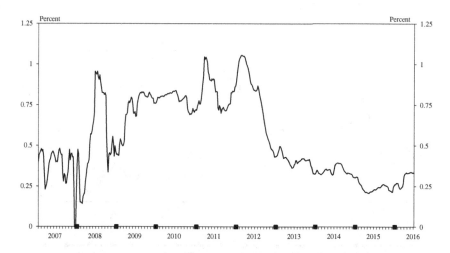

Fig. 9.10.   Euribor Term Structure.

Notes: Difference between 12-month and one-month Eurobor interest rates. Heavy tick marks indicate December.
Source: ECB and Haver Analytics.

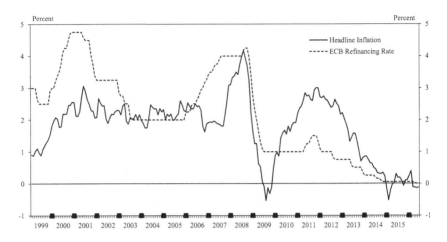

Fig. 9.11.   Inflation and ECB Policy Rate.

Notes: Monthly observations of 12-month percentage changes in Harmonized Index of Consumer Prices. ECB refinancing rate is the Main Refinancing Operations Rate. Heavy tick marks indicate December.

Source: ECB and Haver Analytics.

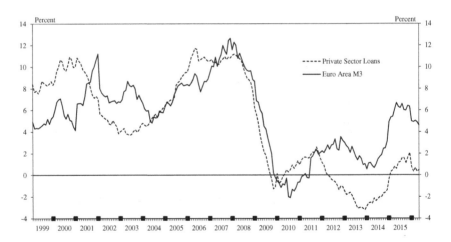

Fig. 9.12.   M3 and Private Loan Growth.

Notes: Monthly observations of 12-month percentage changes in M3 and loans to private sector by monetary financial institutions. Heavy tick marks indicate December.

Source: Eurostat and Haver Analytics.

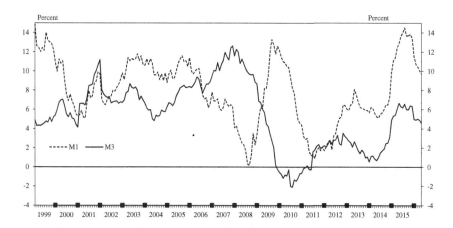

Fig. 9.13. Money Supply.

Notes: Monthly observations of 12-month percentage changes in M1 and M3. Heavy tick marks indicate December.

Source: Eurostat and Haver Analytics.

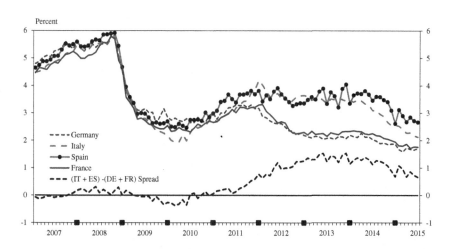

Fig. 9.14.   Average Interest On New Loans to Non-Financial Corporations.

Notes: Heavy tick marks indicate fourth quarter of year. Spread is between the average of Italy + Spain and Germany + France.

Source: ECB and Haver Analytics.

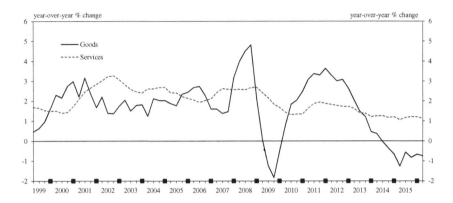

Fig. 9.15.   Goods and Services Inflation.

Notes: Quarterly observations of Harmonized CPI. Heavy tick marks indicate fourth quarter.
Source: Eurostat and Haver Analytics.

Chapter Ten

The Shadow Financial Regulatory Committee's Views on Systemic and Payments System Risks

Robert A. Eisenbeis

Cumberland Advisors

Abstract

This chapter reviews the evolution of the Shadow Financial Regulatory Committee's statements on payment system and systemic risk. Six major themes emerge. First, from the outset, the Committee has argued against forbearance and taxpayer bailouts and instead advocated early regulatory intervention and prompt corrective action to force recognizing losses and recapitalizing troubled institutions. Second, when taxpayer bailouts take place there is a pressing need to protect taxpayer interests. Third, the Committee favored regulatory simplicity over complexity when it comes to structuring capital requirements and macroprudential policies. Fourth, the committee favored market price mechanisms when it comes to structuring capital constraints. Fifth, market mechanisms and prices should also be relied upon to monitor risk. Finally, the Committee urged the Fed to modernize how it implements monetary policy and cease its reliance upon the primary dealer system as the main conduit for such policy.

1. Introduction

The Shadow Financial Regulatory Committee was formed in 1986. Its roots were in a study commissioned by the American Bankers Association, and focused on issues concerning banking regulation, deposit insurance, the geographical expansion of banking, and the role of government in the financial system.[1] The interesting thing about that study was that the

---

[1] See Benston, Eisenbeis, Horvitz, Kane, and Kaufman (1986); and Litan (2016).

authors were constrained to consider the issues, but were not to make policy recommendations. However, before the project was completed, recommendations were requested, and many of us admitted that we came to different conclusions than we might have otherwise if we had known we were preparing a policy document from the outset. That process and the interaction with representatives of the banking industry highlighted the need for independent and objective assessment of banking regulations and policy. That need resulted in the creation of the Shadow Financial Regulatory Committee.

The Committee held its first regular meeting and published two statements in February 1986. One dealt with the Reagan Administration's Baker Plan to encourage U.S. banks to extend loans to prop up debtors in some 15 countries, rather than let the debt resolution process run its course (Shadow Financial Regulatory Committee, 1986a; 1986b). The second statement opposed a plan by the Office of the Comptroller of the Currency (OCC) to prop up failing agricultural banks by permitting them to avoid recognizing losses and to permit the FDIC to provide direct assistance to those institutions. Those two statements help set the tone for the Committee over the next 30 years. Specifically, while the Committee has taken positions on a wide range of financial issues, it consistently has sought to avoid bailouts of failing institutions, to oppose schemes that avoid prompt recognition of losses, and to protect the interests of taxpayers when bailouts are proposed.

Many of the Shadow Committee's early statements during the 1980s focused on issues surrounding the S&L debacle, capital forbearance, deposit insurance reform, capital standards and the thrift crisis more generally. However, as time passed, emphasis turned to deposit insurance reform, capital adequacy and risk related capital standards, concepts in resolving troubled financial institutions, agency reform, securities market regulation, GSEs, and so on. A more detailed summary is provided in Table 10.1.

Consistent with that general theme, this chapter begins by summarizing the evolution and scope of the Committee's concerns and then tries to synthesize and characterize the evolution of the Shadow's views on payment systems and systemic risks. In the remaining sections, the issues are discussed and the Committee's stances on the issues are laid out.

Table 10.1:   Shadow Financial Regulatory Committee Themes.

1. Subsidization of Bad Lending Practices, Forbearance	1. Interest Rate Risk Measurement and Regulation
2. Disclosure — Financial Disclosure — Regulatory Disclosure and Transparency — To Shareholders — Use of soft dollars — Financial Rescue and Relief Programs	10. Fair Value Accounting
3. Capital Adequacy and Risk Related Capital and Leverage Requirements	9. Systemic Risk
4. Expansion of Powers and Geographic Scope	10. Payments System Risks
5. Deposit Insurance Reform [both banks and thrifts]	11. Securities Market Regulation — Agency Structure — Derivatives — National Market — Short Selling — Swaps
6. Prompt Corrective Action and Resolution of Failed and Failing Institutions	12. Executive Compensation
7. Regulatory and Regulatory Agency Reform	13. Unintended Consequences of Regulation
8. The Problems in GSEs, the Federal Home Loan Banks and Pensions	14. Interactions Between Foreign and Domestic Regulation of Institutions and Markets

2.   Shadow Views on Payment System and Systemic Risk

In the wake of the Great Recession, the major thrust of the regulatory agencies, be it the Financial Stability Oversight Council (FSOC), the Federal Reserve or other agencies, has been on macroprudential policies designed to address concerns about systemic risk. Major focus has been on the largest financial institutions designated systemically important financial institutions (SIFIs) and globally systemically important financial institutions (G-SIFIs). In particular, to ensure that they are resilient to financial stress, higher capital requirements have been imposed, liquidity requirements have been put in place and agency-designed stress tests have been required.[2]

In a similar vein, both prior, as well as subsequent, to the Great Recession, the Federal Reserve has undertaken efforts to strengthen the resilience of the payments system, and especially the electronic payments systems. This, in part, reflects the increased role of non-bank providers of payments services and their vulnerability to cyber-terrorism, breach of personal financial information, and issues raised by new technologies like Bitcoin and related private sector technologies.

In the remaining sections of this paper, the Committee's recommendations concerning payments system risks are considered first. This is followed by a discussion of the many statements concerning too-big-to-fail and efforts to address systemic risk.

2.1. *Payment system risk*

Two dimensions of payments system risks were addressed early on by the Shadow Committee. In 1989, the main issues centered on the large dollar payments system, Fedwire, and the risks that it exposed the Federal Reserve to due to the widespread volume of daylight overdrafts the Fed extended to participating institutions. The Committee commented on the Federal Reserve's proposal to reduce the volume of daylight overdrafts that arose because payments initiated over the system were guaranteed by the Fed as final to the receiving bank, even though actual settlement by the initiator of the transaction did not take place on the Fed's books until the end of the day, resulting in a daylight overdraft that amounted to free intraday credit provided by the Fed. The Committee estimated that the value of this subsidy was on the order of $750 million per year. The Fed proposed instituting a charge if daylight overdrafts exceeded a specific amount. The Committee argued that the proposed fee was insufficient to cover the credit risks inherent in the practice. Moreover, under provisions of the Monetary Control Act of 1980, the Fed was obligated to price its services reflecting the true and full underlying costs. The Committee went even further, as a precursor to payment of interest on reserves, and argued

---

[2]In part, while stress tests were already being employed, they were made a requirement by the Dodd–Frank Act.

that the Fed should also pay interest on intraday credit balances and also price its overdrafts according to risk (1989).

The Shadow Committee addressed the daylight overdraft issue again in an open letter to then-Chairman Bernanke in 2006. Although the Statement covered a wide range of topics, it again urged that the charges on daylight overdrafts be increased. Furthermore, the Committee also suggested that transfers should be restricted to good funds rather than providing overdrafts, and that full collateralization also be required. In this way, the Fed would not be exposed to risk nor providing subsidies to overdraft users (2006).

More recently, a different dimension of payments system risks emerged that involve non-bank retail payments systems with significant linkages to depository institutions. In particular, there have been almost a continuous series of data breaches at companies like Target, Nieman Marcus, and Home Depot, just three among many notable examples, that the Committee argued should be addressed by the FSOC and the Fed. In particular, as payments have evolved to increase dependence upon the Internet and electronics, ensuring the integrity of the nation's payment system, when retail and other businesses are interconnected with financial institutions, is of national concern. Critical issues include establishment of security protocols, formalization of loss-sharing arrangements between merchants and depository institutions, and rationalization of the legal treatment of credit card and debt transactions. The current treatment of liability for different payments are governed by 1960s laws geared to paper-based systems and depend to a great extent on coordination of both local and national law enforcement agencies with overlapping jurisdictions and need to be rationalized (2014a).

2.2. Bailouts and policies creating moral hazard and systemic risk

From its very inception, the Shadow Committee has been concerned with and warned against the negative effects that bailouts and forbearance might have on institutions' incentives to take risk and engage in behavior that would ultimately impose costs on taxpayers. As previously mentioned, in its very first meeting in February 1986, the Committee warned against a proposal by the OCC to prop up failing agricultural banks through deferred loss accounting and direct assistance from the Federal Deposit

Insurance Corporation (FDIC). It opposed the loss accounting proposals but did suggest that FDIC assistance might be appropriate if a turnabout were likely, provided that appropriate penalties were imposed upon stockholders, management, uninsured depositors, and other creditors. It further argued that if FDIC support were provided, the Corporation should receive an equity position that would allow it to recover its outlays through subsequent sale of that equity (1986b).

At its next meeting in June 1986, the Shadow Committee argued against an FDIC, Federal Reserve, and OCC proposal to not enforce a minimum capital requirement of 5.5% for a period of seven years for troubled agricultural and energy concentrated banks experiencing losses, provided their capital ratios remained above 4%. The Committee noted that the capital requirement was already too low and lowering it would only encourage "go-for-broke" strategies by management. Furthermore, it would reduce incentives on the part of shareholders to rebuild capital, and in any case, forbearance was unlikely to succeed. As an aside, the Committee also argued against a Financial Accounting Standards Board accounting proposal to forestall the recognition of loan losses if future payments were greater than the principal value of the loan. The Committee argued that it was much better to recognize current losses rather than gamble that future income would be realized (1986c).

In February 1990, the Committee again noted concern that New England banks experiencing financial difficulties were borrowing more than a billion dollars from the Federal Reserve Bank of Boston discount window at subsidized rates. As the Fed had a policy against lending to insolvent institutions, the Committee expressed the hope that such lending was not supporting insolvent institutions, and that those institutions with less than 3% capital would immediately be required to raise more equity. The Committee noted that past history suggested that open bank assistance often failed, and mainly provided time for uninsured creditors to remove their funds and ultimately shift losses to the FDIC and taxpayers (1990).

As early as September 1992, the Shadow commented on provisions of the FDIC Improvement Act (FDICIA) granting regulatory agencies broad discretion in determining least cost resolution to justify extending protections to other banks and institutions in cases of too-big-to-fail institutions. In implementing relevant sections of the Act, limits were imposed upon interbank exposures (1992a). However, the question is — what happened to those limits over time?

In 1993, the Clinton administration proposed programs to speed up the flow of credit to small businesses and farms by modifying criteria employed by examiners to evaluate credit. The policy involved especially lax treatment of loans with minimal documentation at well-capitalized banks. The procedures amounted to exempting such loans from examiner criticism. While the Committee recognized that examination standards could vary based upon credit quality and condition of the lending bank, it also voiced the belief that the proposals could subvert the examination process, impede the flow of information to examiners, and ultimately damage the FDIC. Furthermore, exempting certain loan programs from scrutiny might also lead to excessive risk-taking, lax internal controls, and losses. This prescient concern ultimately was realized in the subprime loan debacle that precipitated the Great Recession (1993).

2.3. *Primary dealers and systemic risk*

In 2009, the Shadow Committee turned its attention to issues of systemic risk that arose out of the Great Recession and associated financial crisis. In particular, the Committee commented on changes in the Federal Reserve's operating procedures that depended upon new tools, like interest payments on reserves and overnight repurchase transactions, and its dependence upon only a few designated primary dealers to act as counterparties. Indeed, the Fed expressed concern about the fact that because of financial difficulties and near and actual failures, there was a reduction in the effective number of counterparties. Furthermore, because the primary dealers were capital-constrained and in weakened condition, they had adversely affected the redistribution of liquidity the Fed had injected into the system to support credit extension by the nation's commercial banks. The Committee argued that the current system was outdated. Due to electronics and electronic bidding, the bidding and transaction process should be extended to all well-capitalized member banks, similar to the process employed by the European Central Bank. It argued that broadening access would increase the efficiency of the process, lower costs, reduce dependence upon a small group of counterparties that are viewed as 'too big to fail,' and "...enhance the monetary policy transmission process" (2009d).

Problems involving the primary dealer structure arose again in 2011, in the wake of the failure of the primary dealer, MF Global. The collapse, the Committee argued, exposed weaknesses in both the Commodity Futures Trading Commission's and Federal Reserve Bank of New York's processes for evaluating MF Global's risk-taking, and the exposures of its clients, creditors, and counterparties to those risks. The Shadow Committee noted that relevant information was available in a timely fashion in the firm's 10K SEC filings that should have enabled regulators to assess MF Global's exposure to European debt and its overall risk profile, but apparently, that information was not used.

Similar to its previous warnings, the Committee again noted that the stress and liquidity problems experienced by the primary dealers, and the Federal Reserve's emergency liquidity programs put in place to support them, only reinforced market perceptions that these institutions were special. At the same time, that reliance and the fact that subsequent rescue actions were necessary demonstrated the danger of relying on a small number of systemically important institutions for the implementation of monetary policy. The experience heightened the need to reevaluate the primary dealer system, and the Committee also went on to suggest that the Fed needed formal examination and perhaps supervisory authority over the dealers, regardless of whether they were also subject to SEC regulation. The second, and the Committee's preferred option, was to pursue the strategy it had recommended in 2009 to eliminate the primary dealer system and open the desk to bidding to all qualified commercial banks (2011c).

In late 2013, a movement began in Congress to try to address what was perceived to be undue influence of Wall Street on the policies and their supervision by the New York Fed. Proposals were made to make the president of the bank a presidential appointment, instead of being appointed by the Bank's Board of Directors. Similar to its previous positions, the Shadow Committee argued that part of the perceived close relationship between the large New York banks and investment banks was structural and likely due, in part, to their roles as primary dealers and in the transmission of open market policies. The Committee again recommended doing away with the primary dealer system, by opening the daily bidding process to qualified member banks. However, it also went two steps further. It recommended rotating the Open Market Desk responsibility for implementing monetary policy among the Reserve Banks, and removing the president of the New York Fed as permanent vice-chairman of the FOMC. That position too should be rotated among the Reserve Banks. This would diffuse reliance upon Wall Street firms, and have the added benefit of providing experienced backup capabilities in the event of another disaster like 9/11 that paralyzed the financial system for a short while in 2000 (2014c).[3]

2.4. Bailouts and systemic risk-the Great Recession and next level of concern

The onset of the Great Recession and efforts by the Fed to deal with the liquidity problems it perceived by creating a series of special programs and invoking its emergency lending powers under Section 13(3) of the Federal Reserve Act spawned a number of Shadow statements about those programs.

At its May 2008 meeting, the Shadow Committee commented on the Fed's extraordinary actions to stem financial turmoil and its brokering of the acquisition of Bear Stearns by JPMorgan Chase. The Committee observed that Bear would have been resolved differently if it had been a bank rather than a non-bank primary dealer. As a bank, it would have been subject to least-cost resolution, a bridge bank could have been established, and all systemically important functions could have been preserved. Instead, the Committee argued that despite claims, Bear was bailed out in ways that benefited several parties, including shareholders, JPMorgan Chase, creditors and debtholders of Bear, and counterparties, all of which were made whole.

The Committee expressed concern about several dimensions of the transaction. The first was the use of government monies to finance a private sector acquisition that resulted in an increase in the market value of JPMorgan Chase. The acquisition involved the Fed accepting a broader range of collateral beyond what was traditionally accepted by central banks at that time. Later, of course, the Fed broadened acceptable collateral in a number of its special facilities. There was also concern that this would encourage political pressure to use Federal Reserve resources

---

[3]Indeed, the system has now instituted backup structures for both the discount window and System Open Market Desk operations.

for other purposes, which subsequently materialized when Congress tapped the Federal Reserve surplus to fund a highway transportation bill in 2015. The Committee suggested that the extension of Federal Reserve support to non-bank entities should also be accompanied by extension of resolution authority for supported entities (2008).

Following the rescue and resolution of Bear Stearns, a series of financial institution failures and financial turmoil occurred in the fall of 2008. In February 2009, the Shadow Committee commented on the range of assistance programs put in place by the Federal Reserve and the government, recognizing not only that such assistance might be required but also suggesting that the options selected should vary according to the circumstances. In structuring programs, not only borrower and lender positions, but also the potential costs to taxpayers, should play a part. Of particular concern were proposals to allow judicial intervention to restructure terms of existing mortgages which would have the unintended consequence of raising the costs of new mortgages. The Committee argued that rather than an *ad hoc* approach, the government should encourage mortgage restructuring negotiations between borrowers and lenders rather than policies promoting foreclosures. Specific options to consider included: encourage loss-sharing between borrower and lender, use of deeds-in-lieu of foreclosure, and explicit consideration of use of taxpayer funds for mitigative rather than destructive legal maneuvers that may give rise to longer-term market inefficiencies and higher costs (2009a).

In May 2009, the Committee issued a statement on Treasury Secretary Geithner's proposals to control systemic risk, which was a precursor to proposals ultimately contained in the Dodd–Frank Act. His plan proposed a macroprudential regulator who would oversee the entire financial system, and be charged with monitoring and identifying areas in the financial system where systemic problems may be developing. The regulator would also be empowered to designate firms as being systemically important, and an agency would be charged with the responsibility of resolving systemically important financial institutions. The Committee focused its attention only on the merits of having an agency charged with monitoring the financial system. It supported the idea of a monitor, and emphasized the need and pointed out a possible structure for a monitoring and data-gathering function focusing on systemic risks. Subsequently, the Financial

Stability Oversight Committee was created and was granted authority to designate financial institutions as systemically important. The Office of Financial Research was created under the Dodd–Frank Act within the Department of the Treasury charged with supporting the monitoring function (2009b).

In April 2010, the Shadow Committee turned its attention to two issues concerning too-big-to-fail banks and systemically important institutions. The recently-held G20 meetings ended up divided over how to deal with the 'too-big-to-fail' problem of systemically important financial institutions. European regulators seemed to accept that some institutions were too big to fail, and they focused on how to share the burden of resolution costs and the institution of special taxes. Others focused on how to eliminate the too-big-to-fail problem itself. The Canadians, in particular, were against burden sharing, and instead, argued for higher capital requirements and reliance upon market discipline. The Committee strongly supported the Canadian position, lamenting the fact that Treasury Secretary Geithner supported international burden-sharing and special taxes on systemically important institutions. At the same time, the Committee also argued that a well-designed contingent capital requirement, combined with effective prompt corrective action and wind-down programs, as envisioned when FDICIA was enacted, would be a much more desirable path to pursue in establishing a more effective regulatory regime. The Committee went on to describe in some detail how such a program might be designed and function (2010b).

At that same April 2010 meeting, the Committee commented on provisions of the Dodd–Frank Act that was under consideration in the U.S. Senate to limit the ability of the government to protect stockholders and other stakeholders in large complex financial institutions that fail. The Committee expressed the view that despite the bill's provisions, regulators, when faced with the choice of enforcing effective market discipline versus orderly resolution, would succumb to the temptation to protect blocks of stakeholders, even if it subsequently undermined market discipline and increased the probabilities of future crises. Despite the bill's attempt to limit bailouts, the Committee noted a recent GAO report discussing regulator use of the systemic risk exemption contained in FDICIA. It concluded that in a crisis, regulators tended to err on the side of protecting creditors, despite the intent to reduce costs of resolution to the FDIC. The Committee urged creation of a modified version of Chapter 11 bankruptcy, which it argued would minimize bailout protections and reduce moral hazard in the future (2010c).

In September 2010, following passage of the Dodd–Frank Act, the Shadow Committee noted that the regulation of non-banking firms that were designated by the FSOC as systemically important institutions, to be assumed by the Federal Reserve, to be what it viewed as a monumental task. The Fed was granted a broad and sweeping authority to mandate risk management policies, capital requirements, and failure resolution plans, just to name a few. Yet, for many of these institutions, like insurance companies, the Fed had no particular expertise or understanding of the business. The Fed, in many cases, lacked the staff and necessary skills to deal with the potential issues it would face. Concern was expressed about the problems of adapting standards to firms with diverse lines of business different from banks and bank holding companies. The Committee's reservations have been born out, as the Fed has attempted to regulate insurance companies like MetLife, AIG, and GE Capital. The FSOC's designation has been successfully challenged in the courts, and the Fed has met resistance as it has attempted to prescribe standards for insurance companies (2010e).

At its May 2011 meeting, the Committee commented on a proposed rulemaking by the FDIC and Fed to implement the "living will" requirements of Dodd–Frank to resolve systemically important institutions, should that prove necessary. The Committee was concerned about the practical problems that institutions and agencies would face because of the sheer scope of having to craft a plan to resolve one of the mega institutions with thousands of subsidiaries, huge size, operations in nearly 200 countries, and involvement with more than 500 clearing and settlement systems. The Committee argued that the estimated 10,000 hours that would be needed to craft a credible plan was unrealistically low. It provided an appendix containing a very long but abbreviated laundry list of issues that would have to be covered in crafting such a plan. It argued that to be credible for a mega institution, a plan would imply a radical corporate restructuring and simplification, and a scaling back of corporate structure. The initial plans were to be submitted in 2012 and annually thereafter. The Committee's skepticism has been proved to be justified. Numerous iterations of plans have occurred and yet, several more years have gone by, and most institutions have yet to construct credible plans acceptable to the regulators (2011b).

In December 2012, consistent with its long-standing position that financial institutions, especially large ones, were substantially undercapitalized, the Shadow commented favorably on proposals under Dodd–Frank and Basel III standards to increase capital requirements on large institutions receiving 'too-big-to-fail' subsidies. However, five weaknesses were identified that have yet to be addressed. First, the standards placed undue reliance upon risk-based capital ratios as opposed to a simple leverage standard. Second, the capital ratios were, in the committee's view, too low. Third, regulators were allocating capital within financial institutions using arbitrary fixed weights, which were arguably inaccurate, not responsive to changes in market risks and distorted incentives and asset allocations. Fourth, the standards created unduly complicated liquidity formulas, which arguably have had unintended consequences of skewing demands for bank reserves and high-quality assets. The standards incorporated a system of haircuts on various assets to count toward meeting the liquidity standards rather than relying upon case assets. The Committee argued that inducing changes in the maturity structure of assets and liabilities via the liquidity standards were not a substitute for more capital. Finally, the standards failed to address regulatory forbearance due to errors in measurement of losses and capital impairment. The Committee argued that the approach reflected fundamental design flaws in the Basel III approach, which were inherent in previous Basel standards as well. The Committee urged U.S. regulators to "walk away" from the Basel III standards, but unfortunately that has not happened (2012e).

In December 2013, the Shadow commented critically on an Office of Financial Research (OFR) report requested by the FSOC to identify systemic risks in investment management firms. The Committee argued that the report's findings were unconvincing. Unlike banks and investment banks that are highly leveraged and whose financial condition can deteriorate, subjecting them to capital losses with potential systemic risk implications, investment management firms do not own the assets they manage and are not highly leveraged. When losses occur, investors bear the losses, not the investment management firms. Fortunately, nothing has come of the proposal and instead, the Department of Labor recently issued rules governing fiduciary responsibility and duty of care for those advising on retirement investments. That ruling has already been subject to litigation on the grounds that the Department of Labor overreached its authority (2013b).

The Dodd–Frank Act was a Congressional attempt to end the perception that some banks were too big to fail. For some, this perception still exists and in response, the Obama Administration in 2010 and more recently Rep. Camp (R-MI) proposed levying a prudential tax on SIFIs as a supplement to existing prudential oversight. In May 2014, the Committee noted three motivations for the proposal: (a) using a tax to induce institutions to shrink in size, (b) using a tax to raise revenues, and (c) using a tax to punish firms that had been bailed out. The Committee argued that the systemic risk concerns were relevant and important; however, it stated that a tax was a blunt instrument and not a good substitute for existing supervisory and prudential tools. The proposal would introduce a wealth tax that made little economic sense and would only unduly complicate an already complex regulatory and supervisory process. Moreover, while a tax might induce firms to reduce their size, it would not necessarily reduce moral hazard (2014b).

In December 2014, the Federal Reserve issued a proposed rulemaking to levy a capital surcharge on institutions that were found to be G-SIFIs, which became the subject of a Shadow statement in February 2015. The Committee applauded the Fed's attempt to raise capital standards. However, it also argued for a less-complex policy that would enable an institution to opt-in to a capital constraint based on the ratio of common equity to total leverage (reflecting both on- and off-balance sheet exposures) that would be double the currently prescribed leverage ratio. In return, the institution would be granted substantial relief, including relief from the proposed capital surcharge. The Committee expressed concern about the fact that construction and degree of opacity of evolving capital and leverage requirements were becoming increasingly complex. The Committee was skeptical about the ability to calibrate the proposed surcharge to the systemic risk exposure of individual institutions with the degree of precision envisioned in the proposal, and argued instead for its simple opt-in that would be more transparent and more resilient to a variety of shocks than the alternatives (2015a).

In its next-to-last meeting in September 2015, the Shadow Committee made several recommendations to strengthen the stress tests mandated by the Dodd–Frank Act. The present approach is principally a top-down approach driven by three successively severe stress scenarios specified by the Federal Reserve. At that time, all the banks successfully passed the most severe tests. These stress tests are also supplemented by the institution's own stress scenarios twice a year. The Committee argued that institution-specific tests should be elevated in importance, since they are geared to the institution's own perceptions as to where it may be the most vulnerable, and could be a valuable source of information for the Fed. If this information is supplemented by market data and traditional examinations, the Committee argued that the whole process would be richer and would reduce the chance that key vulnerabilities are overlooked (2015b).

At its last meeting in December 2015, the Committee took a final stab at a theme common to many of its statements over its long history. It focused on the proposal that systemically important institutions should include measures reflecting Total Loss Absorbing Capacity (TLAC) in their capital structure. The measure would include liabilities, such as subordinated debt and contingent capital, as instruments capable of absorbing losses if a G-SIFI or G-SIB (Globally Systemically Important Bank) experienced financial difficulty. The process by which losses would be apportioned is complex, and was considered by the Committee in its statement. The bottom line was that while the TLAC concept was an advancement, it was not superior to the Committee's previous recommendation to rely heavily on subordinated debt that featured frequent roll over, and to require that firms regularly go to market for a reading on their credit worthiness and market risk (2015c). The current approach to capital regulation is overly complex, burdensome, and too reliant upon deficient risk-based measures of capital. In the end, the Committee states: "Market participants recognized a fundamental truth that apparently eluded the regulators: losses can only be absorbed by common equity, not risk-based capital."

3. Summary and Conclusion

Several consistent themes are evident from this review of the Shadow Committee's views on payment system and systemic risk. First, from the very beginning the Committee has argued against forbearance for failing institutions and has strongly favored prompt corrective action measures, recognition of losses, and recapitalization of troubled institutions, over bailouts and taxpayer support. Bailouts, the Committee argues, have the unintended impact of increasing both moral hazard and the likelihood of future financial crises.

Second, the Committee has consistently voiced the need to protect the interests of taxpayers when bailouts are proposed. Third, the Committee favors simplicity when it comes to imposition of capital constraints and efforts to structure macroprudential policies. Fourth, market mechanisms and pricing are preferable when it comes to determining capital structure. Fifth, reliance upon markets for monitoring and use of prices are preferable tools to discipline management and control risk exposures. This is particularly evident when reviewing the Committee's assessment of how best to reduce risks in the payments system, especially when it comes to the pricing of overdrafts in the large dollar payments systems.

Finally, the Committee has been quick to advocate changes in how the Federal Reserve implements monetary policy and, particularly, its reliance upon the primary dealer system and the tri-party repo markets during and in the wake of the Great Recession. The primary dealer system has proved to be subject to systemic problems. Given current technology and the Fed's electronic bidding process, there is no reason the number of counterparties should not be expanded to include all qualified member banks. In a similar vein, the tri-party repo market is inherently unstable. It is subject to the pyramiding of risks, due to the interconnectedness of the interbank market and the practice of rehypothecation of securities. While reliance upon intraday credit has been substantially reduced, the market is still subject to the risk of fire sales in a crisis, and may be vulnerable should a troubled institution need to be resolved. Consideration should be given to moving the market to a central clearing utility or taken over by the Federal Reserve itself.

References

Benston, G. G., Eisenbeis, R. A., Horvitz, P. M., Kane, E. J. and Kaufman, G. G. (1986). *Perspectives on Safe and Sound Banking: Past Present and Future* (MIT Press, Boston).

Litan, R. (2016). *Financial Crises and Policy Responses: A Market-Based View from the Shadow Financial Regulatory Committee 1986–2015.* American Enterprise Institute, Washington, D.C.

Shadow Financial Regulatory Committee (1986a), The Baker Plan and LDC Lending, Statement No. 2, 14 February.

Shadow Financial Regulatory Committee (1986b), Aid to Failing Banks, Statement No. 2, 14 February.

Shadow Financial Regulatory Committee (1986c), Capital Forbearance Policy for Agricultural and Energy Banks, Statement No. 7, 9 June.

Shadow Financial Regulatory Committee (1989), Federal Reserve Proposal to Modify the Payments System Risk Reduction Programs, Statement No. 45, 18 September.

Shadow Financial Regulatory Committee (1990), Subsidized Federal Reserve Assistance, Statement No. 53, 26 February.

Shadow Financial Regulatory Committee (1992a), Proposed Rule on Interbank Exposure, Statement No. 88, 14 September.

Shadow Financial Regulatory Committee (1992b), Standards for Safety and Soundness, Statement No. 89, 14 September.

Shadow Financial Regulatory Committee (1993), The Policy of Authorizing "Minimal Documentation" Loans, Statement No. 94, 24 May.

Shadow Financial Regulatory Committee (1995), Federal Reserve Proposal for Pricing Daylight Overdrafts, Statement No. 122, 22 May.

Shadow Financial Regulatory Committee (1998), The Issues Posed by the Near-Collapse of Long-Term Capital Management, Statement No. 151, 28 September.

Shadow Financial Regulatory Committee (2006), Open Letter to Federal Reserve Chairman Ben S. Bernanke, Statement No. 229, 13 February.

Shadow Financial Regulatory Committee (2008), If Bear Had Been a Bank, Statement No. 258, 5 May.

Shadow Financial Regulatory Committee (2009a), Bank Bailouts and Borrower Bailouts, Statement No. 270, 9 February.

Shadow Financial Regulatory Committee (2009b), Monitoring Systemic Risk, Statement No. 271, 4 May.

Shadow Financial Regulatory Committee (2009c), Refocusing Financial Rescue Plans, Statement No. 272, 4 May.

Shadow Financial Regulatory Committee (2009d), Reforming the Primary Dealer Structure, Statement No. 280, 14 December.

Shadow Financial Regulatory Committee (2009e), The Resolution of Large, Complex Financial Institutions, Statement No. 281, 14 December.

Shadow Financial Regulatory Committee (2010a), Resolution Regime for Troubled Financial Institutions, Statement No. 286, 22 February.

Shadow Financial Regulatory Committee (2010b), Resolving Systemically Important, International Financial Institutions, Statement No. 289, 26 April.

Shadow Financial Regulatory Committee (2010c), Resolution and Bailout of Large Complex Financial Institutions, Statement No. 292, 26 April.

Shadow Financial Regulatory Committee (2010d), Derivatives, Clearing and Exchange-Trading, Statement No. 293, 26 April.

Shadow Financial Regulatory Committee (2010e), The Monumental Task Assigned to the Fed, Statement No. 298, 13 September.

Shadow Financial Regulatory Committee (2011a), Systemic Risk and Money Market Mutual Funds, Statement No. 309, 14 February.

Shadow Financial Regulatory Committee (2011b), Some Concerns about the FDIC and Federal Reserve System Proposed Rule on Resolution Planning, Statement No. 312, 2 May.

Shadow Financial Regulatory Committee (2011c), MF Global and the Implications for the Primary Dealer Structure, Statement No. 318, 5 December.

Shadow Financial Regulatory Committee (2011d), The Financial Stability Board's Methods for Defining Globally Systemic International Banks, Statement No. 319, 5 December.

Shadow Financial Regulatory Committee (2012a), Some Lessons from the MF Global Debacle, Statement No. 324, 13 February.

Shadow Financial Regulatory Committee (2012b), Regulation of Money Market Funds and Systemic Risk, Statement No. 325, 13 February.

Shadow Financial Regulatory Committee (2012c), Treasury Mismeasurement of the Costs of Federal Financial Stability Programs, Statement No. 327, 7 May.

Shadow Financial Regulatory Committee (2012d), Financial Stability and the Regulation of Money Market Mutual Funds, Statement No. 329, 24 September.

Shadow Financial Regulatory Committee (2012e), Regulation of Bank Capital and Liquidity, Statement No. 332, 10 December.

Shadow Financial Regulatory Committee (2013a), Money Market Funds — A Solution?, Statement No. 342, 13 May.

Shadow Financial Regulatory Committee (2013b), Asset Management and Systemic Risk, Statement No. 347, 9 December.

Shadow Financial Regulatory Committee (2014a), Data Breaches and Payment System Risks, Statement No. 349, 10 February.

Shadow Financial Regulatory Committee (2014b), Limiting Systemic Risk and Too-Big-to-Fail, Statement No. 352, 19 May.

Shadow Financial Regulatory Committee (2014c), The New York Fed and Primary Dealers, Statement No. 355, 8 December.

Shadow Financial Regulatory Committee (2015a), The Fed's SIFI's Surcharge: An Alternative Proposal, Statement No. 357, 9 February.

Shadow Financial Regulatory Committee (2015b), Strengthening Stress Tests, Statement No. 360, 21 September.

Shadow Financial Regulatory Committee (2015c), TLAC: The Last Nail in the Coffin of Too Big to Fail?, Statement No. 361, 7 December.

World Scientific–Now Publishers Series in Business

(Continuation of series card page)

Printed in the United States
By Bookmasters